Transforming Government
Supply Chain Management

IBM Center for
The Business
of Government

THE IBM CENTER FOR THE BUSINESS
OF GOVERNMENT BOOK SERIES

Series Editors: Mark A. Abramson and Paul R. Lawrence

The IBM Center for The Business of Government Book Series explores new approaches to improving the effectiveness of government at the federal, state, and local levels. The Series is aimed at providing cutting-edge knowledge to government leaders, academics, and students about the management of government in the 21st century.

Publications in the series include:

E-Government 2003, *edited by Mark A. Abramson and Therese L. Morin*
E-Government 2001, *edited by Mark A. Abramson and Grady E. Means*
Human Capital 2002, *edited by Mark A. Abramson and Nicole Willenz Gardner*
Innovation, *edited by Mark A. Abramson and Ian D. Littman*
Leaders, *edited by Mark A. Abramson and Kevin M. Bacon*
Managing for Results 2002, *edited by Mark A. Abramson and John M. Kamensky*
Memos to the President: Management Advice from the Nation's Top Public Administrators, *edited by Mark A. Abramson*
New Ways of Doing Business, *edited by Mark A. Abramson and Ann M. Kieffaber*
The Procurement Revolution, *edited by Mark A. Abramson and Roland S. Harris III*
Transforming Organizations, *edited by Mark A. Abramson and Paul R. Lawrence*

Transforming Government Supply Chain Management

EDITED BY

JACQUES S. GANSLER
UNIVERSITY OF MARYLAND
AND
ROBERT E. LUBY JR.
IBM BUSINESS CONSULTING SERVICES

ROWMAN & LITTLEFIELD PUBLISHERS, INC.
Lanham • Boulder • New York • Toronto • Oxford

ROWMAN & LITTLEFIELD PUBLISHERS, INC.

Published in the United States of America
by Rowman & Littlefield Publishers, Inc.
A wholly owned subsidary of The Rowman & Littlefield Publishing Group, Inc.
4501 Forbes Boulevard, Suite 200, Lanham, Maryland 20706
www.rowmanlittlefield.com

PO Box 317
Oxford
OX2 9RU, UK

British Library Cataloguing in Publication Information Available

Library of Congress Cataloging-in-Publication Data Available

ISBN 0-7425-3419-7 (alk. paper)
ISBN 0-7425-3420-0 (pbk. : alk. paper)

Printed in the United States of America

♾™ The paper used in this publication meets the minimum requirements of American National Standard for Information Sciences—Permanence of Paper for Printed Library Materials, ANSI/NISO Z39.48-1992.

TABLE OF CONTENTS

Foreword x

Acknowledgments xiv

Part I: Supply Chain Management 1

Chapter One: What is Supply Chain Management? 3
by Jacques S. Gansler, Robert E. Luby, Jr., and Bonnie Kornberg
The Stakes
Modern Logistics: Supply Chain Management
Evolution of Supply Chain Management
Three Types of Integration: Enterprise, Operational,
and Business Function
Summary
Endnotes

Chapter Two: Supply Chain Management in Government
and Business 19
by Jacques S. Gansler, Robert E. Luby, Jr., and Bonnie Kornberg
Divergent Paths: Business and Government
Why Businesses Have Achieved Results
Government Practices
Barriers to Government Change
Summary
Endnotes

Chapter Three: The Integration Enabler: Information Technology 41
by Jacques S. Gansler, Robert E. Luby, Jr., and Bonnie Kornberg
IT Propels Enterprise Integration
The Impact of IT on Logistics
Integrating Procurement, Finance, and Logistics
Summary
Endnotes

Chapter Four: Supply Chain Tools 57
by Jacques S. Gansler, Robert E. Luby, Jr., and William Lucyshyn
Early Evolution
Integration, Collaboration, and Decision Support
The Next Wave
Summary
Endnotes

**Chapter Five: The Road to Transforming Supply Chain
Management in Government**   77
by Jacques S. Gansler, Robert E. Luby, Jr., and Bonnie Kornberg
A Vision for Modern Government Logistics
How to Achieve Change
Summary
Appendix: Recommendations from the Wye River Forums
Endnotes

Part II: Case Studies   99

Case Studies Introduction   99

**Chapter Six: Caterpillar Logistics Services: Providing "No
Excuses" Logistics Support**   101
by Dzintars Dzilna and William Lucyshyn
Introduction
Company Background
System Description
Implementation of the Current System
Lessons Learned
Future
Conclusion
Endnotes

**Chapter Seven: Defense Logistics Agency's Business Systems
Modernization: Delivering 21st Century Logistics**   117
by William Lucyshyn and Sandra Young
Introduction
Background
The BSM Solution
Endnotes

**Chapter Eight: General Electric Remote Monitoring and
Diagnostics: Leveraging Technology to Automate Logistics**   131
by Brandon Griesel and William Lucyshyn
Introduction
Remote Monitoring and Logistics
Getting the Most from RM&D Technology
What Is Needed to Implement RM&D Technology
Lessons Learned and the Future of RM&D
Endnotes

Chapter Nine: The Boeing Company: Launching an Integrated Financial Management System   141
by Amitabh Brar and William Lucyshyn
Background
Description of Current System
Barriers/Challenges
Lessons Learned
Conclusion
Endnotes

Chapter Ten: Cisco Systems, Inc.: The Building Blocks for a World-Class Financial Management System   153
by Brandon Griesel and William Lucyshyn
Introduction
Background
System Description
Building Blocks
The Future
Conclusion
Endnotes

Chapter Eleven: Defense Finance and Accounting Service: Financial Management of the World's Mightiest Conglomerate   167
by William Lucyshyn and Sandra Young
Introduction
System Description
Implementation
Lessons Learned
Vision for the Future
Conclusion
Endnotes

Chapter Twelve: The National Science Foundation's Centralized Management: Driving Financial Management Successfully   183
by Dzintars Dzilna and William Lucyshyn
Introduction
Background
System Description
Implementation of Current System
Lessons Learned
Future Vision
Conclusion
Endnotes

Chapter Thirteen: Covisint: Driving the Auto Industry   199
by Amitabh Brar and William Lucyshyn
Introduction
Background
Current Situation
Return on Investment/Stakeholder Issues
Future
Conclusion
Endnotes

**Chapter Fourteen: Defense Medical Logistics Standard
Support: The New Department of Defense Medical Logistics
Supply Chain**   211
by Douglas Chin and William Lucyshyn
Introduction
Background
Objective
System Overview
Organizational Issues
E-Commerce
Implementation
E-Commerce Applications
DMMonline
Benefits
Challenges
Conclusion
Endnotes

**Chapter Fifteen: Department of Defense EMALL: Bringing
E-Commerce to DoD**   229
by Wesley Johnson and William Lucyshyn
Introduction
Background
DoD EMALL
Challenges and Benefits
Conclusions
Endnotes

Appendix: Forum Participants   243

Bibliography   249

About the Contributors   255

About the IBM Center for The Business of Government   260

Foreword

World-class, commercial supply chain management standards are now exceptionally high. The best organizations measure order-to-receipt time in two days or less, with near perfect probability. This speed is backed up by nimble systems capable of rapidly responding to unexpected contingencies and surge requirements. Unfortunately, while the commercial sector has been rapidly adopting modern, information-based supply chain systems—in order to remain competitive in the worldwide marketplace—the shift to such systems in the public sector has met with significant resistance and has moved far more slowly.

The intent of this book is to help speed up the needed transformation in the public sector. To do so, over a 10-month period a series of 10 "case studies" of public and private sector "success stories" were written (which form Part II of this book and are continuously referenced throughout Part I) and a set of "Thought Leadership Forums" were held (supported by the IBM Center for The Business of Government and the University of Maryland Center for Public Policy and Private Enterprise). The latter were attended by a select group of senior industry and government leaders (about 30 people at each forum—see the Appendix for a list of attendees). Forum participants reviewed the case studies and, together with the experience they brought to the sessions, identified current barriers to more rapid government implementation and made detailed recommendations for changes to achieve early and effective public sector implementation.

It is the many successful private sector experiences of modern supply chain implementation and the initial efforts in the public sector that represent the "demonstration cases" for future success in the public sector.

First, consider some private sector results. Chapter three describes how Wal-Mart transfers goods between trucks and keeps less than 12 hours of inventory (on average) in its warehouses. Another study found that organizations that had implemented e-procurement procedures increased their delivery performance 15 to 30 percent and cut their inventories by 25 to 60 percent.[1] And, contrary to the historic assumption that you have to pay more to get performance improvements, each of the cases of performance enhancements have led to substantial cost savings. Companies that have used the automotive industry's electronic exchange, Covisint, just for the e-procurement function, for example, have realized from 7 to 16 percent savings. Cisco Systems has saved $560 million per year through efficiencies introduced by usage of an Internet portal.[2] And Cisco also cut its finance administrative costs by 50 percent after implementing a digitally integrated financial management system.

The key to such results has been internal and external digital integration, including new linkages between logistics, procurement, and finance operations. As customers move through the checkout lines, Wal-Mart transmits sales information directly to suppliers, truckers, and warehouse workers so they can make ordering and shipping decisions based on real-time information. Cisco's financial management system is integrated with its supplier information system, allowing Cisco's suppliers to access order demand and its financial managers to see production figures.

On the public sector side, some lawmakers and government managers have recognized the power that information technology, the Internet, and digitally integrated supply chains can have on government administration. The Clinger-Cohen Act, the Federal Acquisition Streamlining Act, and the Government Paperwork Elimination Acts (which are described in chapter two) are among the statutes and regulations that have pushed the government in the direction of automation and greater efficiency. Some government organizations have initiated programs that have sped processes, increased digital integration, saved costs, and generally raised the performance bar.

Chapter twelve describes the National Science Foundation's (NSF) high-performing financial management system, which is integrated with the grants management and human resources systems. The integrated system has cut NSF's cycle time from grant award to funds availability to 48 hours from previous cycle times of as long as two to three months. As chapter fourteen shows, the defense medical logistics community implemented a suite of IT applications including online ordering, product and price comparisons, payment, and business intelligence. These technology improvements reduced days in inventory from 380 to 10 days, cut order-to-receipt time from 20 days to 24 hours, and realized cumulative estimated savings of over $1.2 billion within the first four years.

These and other successful government initiatives, some of which are described in detail in Part II of this book, represent important advances. But to date there has *not* been government-wide implementation, or even strategic planning. Chapter two describes areas to address and barriers to overcome in order to achieve far greater government adoption of supply chain modernization, and chapter five presents recommendations for making the needed government transformation happen.

Within Part I, chapter one serves as a primer on supply chain management; chapters two, three, and four provide overviews of some of the more innovative practices and tools; and chapter five describes a blueprint for government-wide transformation. The case studies in Part II explore the who, what, and how of selected examples of supply chain management excellence. Much of the content of this book focuses on the federal government—and, in particular, the Department of Defense, which, at over $80 billion in yearly logistics expenditures, has by far the largest government supply chain management operation. Nevertheless, the lessons are largely applicable across the federal level and to state and local governments as well.

In one of the Thought Leadership Forums, Paul Joseph, vice president of client services for Cat Logistics, observed that the issues surrounding government supply chain management transformation are like the pieces of a jigsaw puzzle. All the pieces that compose the solution are in a box. What is needed is for leaders to say how to put the pieces together and to provide the incentives to make it happen. He asked what individuals could do to influence change. The ideas, examples, and recommendations presented in these pages provide the seeds to answer this question. *Senior managers will need to embrace supply chain management transformation as one of their highest priorities in order for change to take root.* To further that end, if readers at all levels of government and industry propose cutting-edge projects and persuade government managers that supply chain management needs to be a priority, the inevitable pressure will tip the scales and speed up the pace of change.

Endnotes

1. B. Trebilcock, "Planning for Supply Chain Success," *Modern Materials Handling,* May 1, 2001.

2. S. Boyson and T. Corsi, "The Real-Time Supply Chain," Supply Chain Management Review,. January/February 2001.

Acknowledgments

The authors are deeply indebted to Mark Abramson, executive director of the IBM Center for The Business of Government, who worked closely with us on the planning and implementation of this book. We also wish to thank the IBM Center for The Business of Government for their support of this book, as well as the three Thought Leadership Forums that contributed to the book. We wish to thank Bonnie Kornberg, a research consultant with the University of Maryland's Center for Public Policy and Private Enterprise (CPPPE), and Bill Lucyshyn, senior research scholar with CPPPE, for their extensive research support and excellent writing skills, and without whom this project could not have been completed.

Additionally, we wish to acknowledge Kim Ross, executive director of CPPPE, for her review of the manuscripts and her assistance in coordinating the efforts of all the individuals involved. We greatly appreciate the extraordinary cooperation we received on the case studies from Paul Joseph (Caterpillar Logistics), David J. Falvey (Defense Logistics Agency), Rusty Irving and Anil Varma (General Electric), Richard M. Smoski (The Boeing Company), Andrew Cailes and Susan Keys (Cisco Systems, Inc.), Thomas R. Bloom (Defense Finance and Accounting Service), Thomas N. Cooley (National Science Foundation), Shankar Kiru (Covisint), Colonel George (Dan) Magee (Defense Medical Logistics Standard Support), and Claudia "Scottie" Knott and Don O'Brien (DoD EMALL).

Finally, we want to acknowledge the invaluable contribution of the many industry, government, and university leaders who participated in the three Thought Leadership Forums from which the recommendations in this book evolved. They are listed by name and organization in the Appendix. For the time and effort they contributed to this activity, we will be forever grateful.

Jacques S. Gansler
Robert E. Luby, Jr.

PART I

Supply Chain Management

CHAPTER ONE

What is Supply Chain Management?

Jacques S. Gansler
Robert E. Luby, Jr.
Bonnie Kornberg

The Stakes

What a difference a decade makes. In 2003, the coalition forces were able to deploy, conduct an aggressive military campaign, and oust the Saddam Hussein regime in approximately half the time it took just to pre-position the forces for Desert Storm in 1991. The U.S. military buildup in Southwest Asia for the Gulf War in 1991—which included the deployment of over 500,000 troops, the airlifting of 500,000 tons of material, and the shipping of another 2.3 million tons of equipment—took over five months.[1] This was a significant achievement and remarkable because of its scale. However, retired General William Tuttle, former commander of the Army Materiel Command, characterized the logistics support for Desert Storm as follows: "It was embarrassing.… A lot of it [supplies stockpiled] was just junk. It gave us a chance to turn it over and throw it out."[2]

Since then, the U.S. military has made major investments in information technology and examined the best supply chain practices at private companies from FedEx to Bank of America, in an effort to do it faster and better.[3] For the recent Operation Iraqi Freedom, the Department of Defense (DoD) improved its supply chain significantly by using more integrated supply chain software, barcode labels, and radio frequency identification (RFID) tags. These contributed to reducing the deployment time for Operation Iraqi Freedom to only two months, with significantly improved logistics support for all deployed forces.[4]

The average order-to-receipt time during Desert Storm was *49 days.* This was considered acceptable during the early 1990s, especially for the magnitude of materials moved for the war. Today, DoD has improved that time significantly. The average order-to-receipt time is down to *22 days.* If the benchmark of comparison is government performance during Desert Storm, then this is quite an improvement. However, if the standard is commercial excellence, then much more needs to be done. In the commercial world, those with the best supply chain management practices deliver in *one to two days* domestically and two to four days internationally with 99.9 percent probability. For DoD, although 22 days is now the average order-to-receipt time, the range can extend to two years—introducing huge uncertainties and well behind world-class performance.

Digitally integrating government supply chain management to achieve world-class performance (in response and dependability) is critical and urgent. Adopting modern logistics processes will mean the right equipment and supplies will be available when they are needed at significantly lower cost. Contrast that possibility with today's reality: With high enough priority and enough government financial and labor resources, systems and equipment are available whenever needed. Without mobilizing extra resources, the current government logistics system does not have a high probability of meeting needs quickly. For example, 22 percent of U.S. Air Force aircraft are not fully operational because the required parts are not available. If required, the Air Force can use heroic measures, such as expediting shipments, using the extremely inefficient practice of cannibalizing other aircraft, or flying aircraft that are less than fully operational.

For the government, the stakes are high for achieving a rapid logistics system turnaround. The Department of Defense, Central Intelligence Agency, Federal Bureau of Investigation, Department of Homeland Security—these and other government organizations deal on the front lines, and if information or supplies don't arrive in time, lives may be lost. The historic approach of stockpiling large inventories to react to contingencies often results in the costly practice of maintaining obsolete supplies that must be replaced. Can the government afford to continue these ineffective practices?

The effectiveness of supply chain management drives capability and cost. In fact, it is the single most important factor that drives overall costs.[5] Equally, if not more important, is the government's performance responsibility to the public. The National Science Foundation developed an advanced system for soliciting, awarding, and funding grants. As a result, the agency found that the superior integrity of the new system translated into greater perceived integrity of the organization.

The enhanced effectiveness and lower costs of implementing a world-class supply chain management system will translate into more effective overall government operations. Among the benefits is the potential for greater confidence and public pride in government.

Modern Logistics: Supply Chain Management

How do leading organizations handle challenging logistics situations? The following scenarios illustrate some innovative approaches.

Instant Information. If customers in one Wal-Mart store buy more fleece blankets than the store had forecast, and customers in another store return more blankets than expected, Wal-Mart would be able to respond quickly. The retail information from both stores would be relayed directly from scanners at the cash registers to a satellite network that sends transmissions to suppliers, a fleet of trucks, and distribution centers. At a warehouse, blankets would be removed from a truck destined for the store that has enough blankets and moved onto a truck heading to the store needing more.

Coordination and flexibility. In 1995, Whitbread Beer Company, a brewer, pub, restaurant chain, and hotel company in the United Kingdom, noticed high beer inventories and obsolescence while beer prices were dropping. In response, the company signed a pilot agreement with its supplier Anheuser-Busch to share inventory management. Over the course of several months during which Whitbread also shared forecast and actual sales data with Anheuser-Busch, Whitbread reduced its inventories from eight to four days and saved £300,000—approximately $475,000.[6]

Remote diagnostics. Worried that a locomotive engine needed to be repaired or replaced, a train conductor had visions of waiting for days for repairs or for a new engine to be delivered and installed. In the past, the conductor would have had no choice but to call for help and wait, but this time the conductor called General Electric's Research and Development Center in Schenectady, New York, a group with access to maintenance and troubleshooting information and remotely monitored data specific to this train engine. An expert from Schenectady got on the line and asked the conductor to check whether the electrical panel door was ajar. When the conductor closed the door, the engine started.

Automatic actions. Today, if on return from a mission, a jet plane monitor indicates that an engine part has failed, a message can be automatically relayed to people on the ground. Maintenance personnel are then able to replace the unit when the plane lands. The message from the jet can also trigger a procurement action—the ordering of any spare parts that need to be replaced in inventory.

These are examples of modern supply chain management. Today, the lines that have historically divided organizations, business functions, and operations are blurring, and previously unknown efficiencies are accruing. Separate enterprises, such as Whitbread and Anheuser-Busch, are working together to solve supply problems efficiently. Separate business functions, such as Wal-Mart's sales and distribution divisions, interact. Separate operations, such as jet engine maintenance and parts procurement, cross over. Whereas before, a train conductor might never talk to an R&D representative in the course of a career, this exchange of knowledge is now part of the job.

The new linkages that have emerged enable thinking that takes a broader view of supply chain activities. Using this approach, "all functions or activities need to be understood in terms of how they affect, and are affected by, other elements and activities with which they interact."[7] Where an integrated approach has been adopted, cost savings and higher performance have resulted. In the commercial world, this hits the bottom line. With similar government activities, the public benefits.

What is the difference between "supply chain management" and "logistics"? Not a lot, as you can see by the definitions provided. Some experts use the terms interchangeably. However, the term "supply chain management" connotes integration of all the elements of the supply chain, which includes all of the entities, transactions, and actions that meet a customer's need (for example, those related to finance and procurement, as well as logistics, as shown in Figure 1.1).

Figure 1.1: Integrating E-Procurement and E-Finance with E-Logistics into a Supply Chain: An Enterprise View

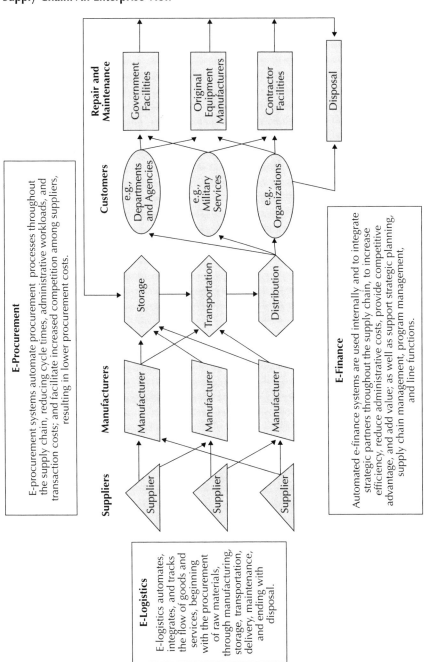

Definitions

Council of Logistics Management Definitions[8]

Logistics is that part of the supply chain process that plans, implements, and controls the efficient, effective forward and reverse flow and storage of goods, services, and related information between the point of origin and the point of consumption in order to meet customers' requirements.

Supply Chain Management (SCM) is the management and control of all materials, funds, and related information in the logistics process from the acquisition of raw materials to the delivery of finished products to the end user.

Department of Defense Definitions[9]

Logistics is, in its most comprehensive sense, those aspects of military operations which deal with: (a) design and development, acquisition, storage, movement, distribution, maintenance, evacuation, and disposition of materiel; (b) movement, evacuation, and hospitalization of personnel; (c) acquisition or construction, maintenance, operation, and disposition of facilities; and (d) acquisition or furnishing of services.

Supply chain management is a cross-functional approach to procuring, producing, and delivering products and services to customers. The broad management scope includes sub-suppliers, suppliers, internal information, and funds flow.

Explaining Terms

The simplest way to think of a supply chain is using a manufactured product, such as a pair of crutches. Say that U.S. forces are deployed in Asia and a medical treatment facility there needs wooden crutches. The supply chain includes every player, transaction, and action involved in getting the crutches to the treatment facility in Asia. Entities include raw materials suppliers for the wood, metal, and rubber parts; manufacturers that turn the raw materials into crutches; transportation companies that deliver them; wholesalers; retailers; and the customer, which is the medical treatment facility. Transactions include every payment and exchange of information that happens to order, produce, and deliver the crutches. Actions include the ordering, movement, and shipment of materials, as well as billing and paying.

Through enterprise integration, players make entity, action, and transaction information accessible to other players within the supply chain. This visibility provides data for enhanced decision making about the supply chain as a whole.

Evolution of Supply Chain Management

Why would traditionally competitive organizations, functions, and opera-tions want to digitally integrate? Ask Ford in the mid-1990s if it would launch a joint venture with its archrival, General Motors (GM), and the answer would have been a resounding "no." Ask Ford in the mid-1990s to consider a venture that would allow GM to not only contact all of Ford's suppliers but to develop collaborative relationships with them, and Ford would have thought you had lost your head. Yet, in February 2000, Ford, GM and automotive rival DaimlerChrysler did exactly that.

Many trends converged to make such a venture not only thinkable but also doable. By the time these automotive companies jointly launched Covisint—a massive information exchange that has procurement, collaboration, and other supply chain management capabilities—they saw value in supply chain integration. This paradigm shift took place in the late 1990s in many indus-tries. Some of the major trends that led to this change include the following:

- **Rise of the Internet and advances in information technology.** The rapid technology changes that occurred during the 1990s allowed collabora-tion across distances, quick transfer of and access to information, and new analysis capability, revolutionizing business practices and processes.
- **More demanding customers.** The advent of faster communications—through fax machines, the Internet, and other factors such as increased product choice—has led to escalated customer expectations. For exam-ple, the Defense Logistics Agency (DLA), the DoD's commodity provider, has had to contend with frustrated end users who want to know why goods such as 2-by-4 lumber are cheaper and delivered more quickly through commercial online than through official DoD channels.[10]
- **Globalization.** The growth of global organizations has led to greater emphasis on logistics because of the increased cost, time, and com-plexity of long-distance shipping.[11]
- **Emphasis on cost cutting.** One of the forces leading companies to invest more in integrating their supply chains is the residual effect of cost-cutting strategies employed in the 1980s. These included just-in-time and total quality management (TQM). By the late 1990s, the pre-vailing thought was that companies could not make any deeper cuts to manufacturing costs. Improving supply chain management was consid-ered the next step to increasing profit. In the public sector, tighter budg-ets have led to pressure for government agencies to do more with less.
- **Industry consolidation.** Because industry players have either merged or shut down as a result of intense competition, the playing field is smaller. The fewer, larger entities have increased buying power and, consequently, greater ability to effect change within the medium and

Understanding Supply Chain Optimization

Picture a very simple system: a traffic light. Perhaps the best time period for the green light to illuminate is 45 seconds. The green light goes on, and 45 seconds later turns off. Now the yellow light is supposed to come on, but there is no light. The allotted time period for the yellow passes, and the red light is supposed to light up, but nothing happens. The green comes back on at its appointed time and functions as planned. This is an example of sub-optimization of a system. Vehicle drivers benefit from the yellow, red, and green lights operating smoothly. The fact that one part of the system—the green light—works well does little for the system's users and may create problems.

Sub-optimization similar to the malfunctioning traffic light is a potential pitfall when one organization or element in a supply chain improves its performance independent of the other elements. Take a baby stroller supply chain, for example. A baby stroller manufacturer is similar to the green light. It has reconfigured all of its workstations and machinery to accelerate the time it takes to produce new strollers. Its internal operations are well coordinated. Costs are down. If the manufacturer interacted directly with expectant parents and other customers, the consumers would receive items quickly and at low prices.

But the manufacturer transfers its finished goods to a distributor, and the distributor transports items to a wholesaler, which provides the products to a retailer. Before the final customer ever sees a baby stroller, it must be transferred to a series of supply chain partners that are, in this example, poorly functioning red and yellow lights. The distributor has fallen behind schedule and takes weeks to pick up new strollers from the manufacturer. The wholesaler doesn't know how many strollers are in its inventory, so is not sure how many to accept from the distributor. The retailer has stocked out and, as a result, consumers have decided to use other retailers.

Through enterprise integration, all members of the supply chain coordinate with each other. With such an approach, the wholesaler not only knows how many strollers are in its own inventory, but also may have access to the distributor's, retailer's, and manufacturer's inventories. Each entity can forecast and plan using information about the entire supply chain, and, in many cases, some of the steps in the prior process can be either reduced or eliminated.

small companies in their supply chain. Two examples that are relevant to this book's case studies are Boeing's mergers with Rockwell and McDonnell Douglas and Daimler-Benz's merger with Chrysler.

- **Enhanced importance of service.** Especially in business-to-business (B2B) markets, delivery lead times and flexibility have taken on greater importance than product features. High product quality has become a minimum expectation, so competitive advantage is more and more a function of high service levels, especially in terms of logistics.
- **Shorter product life cycles.** Many new products, most notably new technology products such as computers, software, cell phones, and digital date books, have short product life cycles. Soon after they arrive on the market, a newer version makes the last one outdated, and this requires shorter logistics lead times. Traditionally, lead times were the time between customer order and delivery. To excel in today's environment, high-performing organizations view lead times from product development, procurement, manufacture, and assembly through to delivery.
- **Deregulation of the transportation industry.** Setting the stage for later supply chain management advances, in the late 1970s and early 1980s the United States government deregulated the airlines and other shipping industries. The new competitive framework made transportation companies more customer-focused and flexible.

As these trends converged, IT supplied the tools to take supply chain thinking to the next level: integration. As opposed to vertical integration, which takes place when companies buy other entities in their supply chain (e.g., Coca-Cola Company buying a bottling plant), this integration is virtual.

Covisint provides a good example. As noted earlier, in the late 1990s each of the three automotive manufacturers—Ford, GM, and Daimler-Chrysler—realized that cost savings and improved efficiency could result from digitally integrating their individual supply chains. Although they each began pursuing independent strategies, they realized that continuing to do so would increase costs and delay deliveries as their suppliers struggled to be interoperable with three different manufacturers' systems. The suppliers' learning curves, response times, and costs would be increased, and after those suppliers who could not support the new cost structure were forced to shut down, the higher cost would be passed on to the manufacturers and the end customers. It was only after the Big Three and other automotive manufacturers recognized the disadvantage of acting individually and the gains that could be achieved by integrating, that they launched Covisint—an unprecedented collaboration.

Supply Chain Integration Practices

Forecasting

One of the biggest challenges companies face is accurate demand forecasting. Manufacturers often have large variances, and cyclical inventory and production patterns due to inefficient information about market demand for their products. Strong forecasting helps companies to reduce inventory levels, plan economical production volumes, and reduce redundant inventories. Many companies have shifted toward a collaborative, planning, forecasting, and replenishment (CPFR) system.[12] This Internet-based software system facilitates collaboration in forecasting efforts between suppliers and retailers.

Coordinated Product Design

Coordinated product design involves careful planning and coordination at the design stage of a product by various departments of an organization and external design partners, with the aim of cost reduction and increase in efficiencies throughout the supply chain.

Modifying product design to incorporate additional aspects of the supply chain leads to reduced inventory holding costs, reduction in transportation costs, and shortening of manufacturing lead times.[13] Product design can often be time-consuming and expensive, especially if the strategy calls for redesigning or changing the existing supply chain. Careful cost-benefit analysis is needed prior to system redesign or product design.

Logistics Network Configuration

An efficient logistics network involves connecting various warehousing locations; determining the optimum number of warehouses that service an area or geographic region; determining production levels for each product at each plant; and establishing efficient transportation systems between plants and warehouses, or from warehouses to retailers, in order to minimize total production, transportation, and inventory costs while simultaneously satisfying customer and service requirements.

Procurement

Procurement management is critical to maintaining cost efficiencies and ensuring timely procurement of the raw materials and supplies integral to the manufacturing of products and quality inputs. Effective procurement involves managing suppliers; identifying resources; requesting bidding contracts, quotations, and tracking orders; and shipping.[14] Factors such as proximity of suppliers to the manufacturing plant, location of warehouses, cross-docking facilities, and a global logistics network need to be considered in decisions involving selection or consolidation of suppliers.

Inventory Management

Through integration, manufacturers, distributors, wholesalers, and retailers all maintain an optimum inventory level, which minimizes inventory ordering and holding costs. Inventory management involves using forecasting tools to predict market demand for products, as well as determining uncertainties in the supply process that could lead to possible stock-outs or inventory buildup.

Financial Management

Financial management involves financial processes, planning and analysis, treasury and revenue management, and electronic customer credit.[15] Organizations use accounting methods such as activity-based costing to capture product costs and analyze the value chain (see chapter two) to determine supply chain costs. Budget and financial forecasting tools are used to help reduce variances in key performance indicators, while credit, cash, and risk management help to reduce financial risk.

Distribution Strategies

Cross-docking, transshipment, and *direct shipment* are some of the strategies to increase distribution efficiencies. *Cross-docking* involves central warehouses, referred to as cross-dock points, which do not stock inventory but serve as *transshipment* locations for outside vendors connecting to the organization's supply chain network.[16] *Direct shipment* from manufacturer to customer reduces the need for intermediate transit or warehouse points.

Customer Service

Customer service involves customers' perceptions of a company's goods and services, timely deliveries, pricing, and value-added services, to name a few. Build-to-order assembly plants used by Dell[17] to lower product costs, and FedEx overnight deliveries[18] to reduce transit time, are some of the supply chain innovations introduced and practiced by many companies today with the aim of increasing customer service.

Information Technology

Information technology has been progressively integrated in every core function of enterprises. Companies automate their internal resources with Enterprise Resource Planning (ERP) systems, which integrate the various operations of the company. Extended supply chain IT initiatives—encompassing partners, suppliers, and customers to enhance profitability and market leadership—involve data warehousing, Decision Support Systems (DSS) tools, networking, e-commerce, and Internet solutions.

Three Types of Integration:
Enterprise, Operational, and Business Function

Integration such as this earns its power from the way it bridges formerly segregated organizations, activities, and groups. Operations that never interacted before, such as product development and manufacturing, become interconnected. Business functions such as finance and information technology make decisions together. Organizations such as Ford and GM collaborate.

Enterprise integration enables performance improvement by digitally connecting distinct organizations. Two other types of integration—operational and business function—are internally focused. The following paragraphs demonstrate how, together, operational, business function, and enterprise integration have stimulated new levels of innovation in supply chain management.

Enterprise Integration

Although examples of business function and operational integration represent internal collaboration, some of the most successful examples of supply chain management involve integration across enterprises. Cisco Systems, for instance, developed an information system that provides its suppliers with daily information on product backlogs and lead times. This enables suppliers to make rapid choices about manufacturing levels. Cisco also has what it terms a "networked ecosystem" with several trusted suppliers. In these symbiotic relationships, demand and supply information is transparent to each involved company. Cisco's partnerships with its key suppliers are at such a high level of interdependency that each company relies on the other's information to succeed.

Operational Integration

At the Defense Logistics Agency, the organization responsible for DoD commodity purchases, a new information technology system links various activities and organizations. The DLA vision for their Business Systems Modernization (BSM) is to integrate procurement activities with repair and overhaul operations. This operational integration will give the people performing repairs and overhauls access to ordering information and will give the procurement staff knowledge of the repair group's material needs. As a result, both groups make better decisions.

Business Functions

The Defense Logistics Agency's Business Systems Modernization also provides a good example of business function integration. To establish the BSM program, DLA solicited input from logistics and IT departments. An internal management structure for the program included equal participation from each department.

The DoD medical logistics community also created a cross-functional management team to develop, implement, and manage a new logistics IT system called the Defense Medical Logistics Standard Support (DMLSS) system. Senior executives, the Military Health System (MHS) chief information officer, and senior IT and logistics managers collaborated. As Figure 1.2 shows, even though the logistics, IT, and medical managers came from different organizations within DoD, they worked together as one management team.

This blending of business functions creates a more capable organization. As departments become more interdependent, what's best for the organization as a whole rather than what's best for individual departments becomes more apparent.

Figure 1.2: DMLSS Management Organization[19]

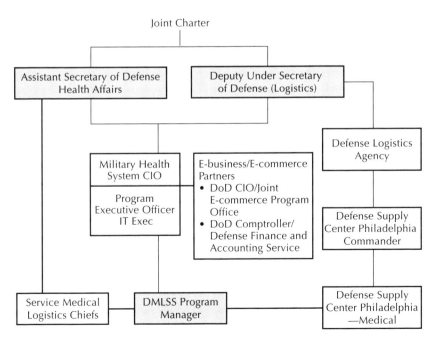

Summary

This chapter describes the importance of transforming government supply chain management practices and explains key terms and concepts. Central points include:

- The need for change in government supply chain management is urgent. Supply chain management has a direct impact on government performance in general, and in the case of organizations dealing with national and local security, it affects their readiness to respond to threats. In many cases today, when pressing needs arise, the modus operandi for logistics support involves diverting and increasing people and financial resources. A better alternative is establishing systems that can use information to respond rapidly and smartly, with associated cost savings.

- Organizations with leading-edge logistics practices have digitally integrated operations, business functions, and enterprises. The results of this network thinking include overall reductions in delivery times and costs, improvements in customer service, and the ability to respond in extremely short notice to changes in requirements.

- When one part of the supply chain, such as a procurement department, improves independently of other elements, such as the finance and IT departments, sub-optimization can occur. In those cases, the end customer may not experience the desired—or potential—service levels.

- Various trends converged in the 1990s to lead some organizations to adopt enterprise integration. Foremost among these trends were the rapid advances in information technology that enabled virtual connectivity.

In the next chapter, barriers that have prevented widespread supply chain management change in government are presented. The chapter also delves into specific cases where commercial and government organizations have employed logistics innovations, and examines the characteristics that have helped those initiatives succeed.

Endnotes

1. Martin Christopher, *Logistics and Supply Chain Management—Strategies for Reducing Cost and Improving Service*. London: Financial Times, Prentice Hall, 1998.

2. David Phinney, "Technology Helps DoD Better Track Equipment for Troops," *Federal Times Online*, March 31, 2003. Viewed at http://federaltimes.com/index.php?S=1718107, April 4, 2003.

3. Daivid Kiley, "Military Uses Private Sector Supply Tactics," *USA Today*, April 18, 2003, p. 5B.

4. Phinney.

5. Kate Vitasek, "Logistics Terms and Glossary," The Council of Logistics Management, August 1, 2002. Viewed at http://www.clm1.org/resource/downloads/glossary.pdf, April 18, 2003.

6. Christopher.

7. Douglas Lambert, J. Stock, and L. Ellram, *Fundamentals of Logistics Management*. Boston: Irwin McGraw-Hill, 1998.

8. Mike Green, *Starting a Supply Chain Revolution*. New York: Cap Gemini Ernst & Young, February 2001. Viewed at http://www.infoworld.com/article/02/11/01/021104ctcpg_1.html.

9. Department of Defense Dictionary of Military and Associated Terms, April 12, 2001 (as amended through August 14, 2002).

10. The Center for Public Policy and Private Enterprise, University of Maryland. *Moving Toward an Effective Public-Private Partnership for the DoD Supply Chain,* June 2002.

11. Lambert, Stock, and Ellram, p. 6.

12. Green.

13. David Simchi-Levi, Philip Kaminsky, and Edith Simchi-Levi, *Designing and Managing the Supply Chain*. Boston: Irwin McGraw-Hill, 2000.

14. Ibid.

15. Cisco Systems, "Cisco Internet Business Roadmap: Financial Management," Solution Guide, 2001, p. 1.

16. Simchi-Levi.

17. Ibid.

18. www.fedex.com

19. See chapter fourteen, the DMLSS case study.

CHAPTER TWO

Supply Chain Management in Government and Business

Jacques S. Gansler
Robert E. Luby; Jr.
Bonnie Kornberg

Divergent Paths: Business and Government

The enormous size of the U.S. government translates into unparalleled purchasing power and a potential for large (i.e., multibillion dollar) annual savings and efficiencies. The Department of Defense alone, with an FY 2002 budget of $334 billion, topped sales at Exxon-Mobil, the world's largest company, by over $100 billion that same year (see chapter eleven, the DFAS case study). Eighty billion of that total is logistics; DoD has a $60 billion inventory, of which the General Accounting Office found 50 percent to be obsolete.[1] The total 2002 federal budget was approximately $1.7 trillion. Almost half the assets of most government organizations are operating materials, supplies, and equipment,[2] which could be reduced significantly through modern supply chain management practices. Even a small percentage reduction in costs would have a startling impact. If DoD alone could introduce new processes that reduced logistics costs by 10 percent, the result would be an extraordinary $8 billion dollars in annual savings.

Although DoD pioneered many logistics concepts in the past, the latest innovations in supply chain management have come from the commercial side. World-class companies have formed supply chain networks that digitally share sales, inventory, forecasting, delivery, procurement, financial management, and other logistics data. Some government agencies have recently begun to implement model initiatives as well; however, the inertia of large bureaucracies and other barriers to change have prevented widescale government transformation. As chapter five will detail, these barriers can be dismantled or worked around, and the steps that leading companies have taken can provide ideas for achieving government change. This chapter explores the factors that have contributed to divergent approaches in the private and public sectors—thus indicating where the government should focus its attention—and highlights some successful government examples.

Why Businesses Have Achieved Results

In cases where private companies have succeeded in digitally integrating supply chain elements, certain common themes emerge. Leading enterprises took similar actions and learned some of the same lessons, including the following:

- **Having Committed, High-Level Leadership.** To capitalize on supply chain efficiencies and change the way companies had been doing business, leaders at the very top levels have gotten involved. It took the chief executive officers (CEOs) of Ford, GM, and DaimlerChrysler to decide to form Covisint, and CEOs at numerous companies to decide

Figure 2.1: Cisco's Value Chain

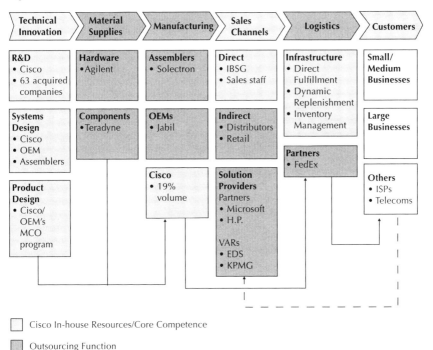

☐ Cisco In-house Resources/Core Competence

▨ Outsourcing Function

to outsource their logistics services. The chief financial officer of Cisco Systems led development of a new, fully integrated financial system. He challenged the development team to implement a system that reduced costs and improved decision making, and he ensured that sufficient tools and resources were available to achieve those goals. This direction and commitment from senior leaders produced results. In one example, Cisco answered the CFO's call by cutting the finance cost as a percentage of revenue by half and increasing the finance department's productivity by more than 90 percent (see chapter ten, the Cisco Systems case study).

- **Focusing on Core Competencies.** One of the business analysis techniques fundamental to supply chain integration has been value chain analysis. The value chain, which is illustrated by Cisco's Value Chain in Figure 2.1, breaks the entire chain of supply activities—from concept development to disposal—into individual components. Using value chain analysis, companies review the cost of each activity and consider where their core competencies lie. Business units that do not leverage core competencies are sold or shut down.

- **Outsourcing Logistics Services.** As an outgrowth of value chain analysis, companies have begun to outsource their logistics support. Third parties with core competencies in logistics have focused solely on this expertise and made new advances in the field. These companies provide many logistics services, including ordering, distribution, electronic system integration, data review and analysis, and new system implementation. By outsourcing, clients benefit by saving costs and time, thus improving their bottom lines and their customer satisfaction.
- **Developing a Customer Focus.** One of the major trends of the last few years has been more demanding customers, and many companies have revamped their processes and services to consider customer needs first. In these organizations, a customer orientation has replaced a process focus as the main driver of operational improvement. For example, Cat Logistics aims to provide "maximum end-user value" (see chapter six, the Cat Logistics case study). Cat Logistics did this in the cellular phone industry by developing a distribution strategy to allow retail stores to keep phones on hand rather than mailing phones after the sale. Leaving the store with a phone improves customer satisfaction. For other customers with expensive industrial equipment, Cat Logistics aims to anticipate part failure and to order parts as they are available, on time. Through Cat Logistics' systems, its customers can maintain low inventories but still have parts on hand when equipment breaks.
- **Minimizing Distrust and Stressing Security/Confidentiality.** The cost-cutting and performance pressures that led the Big Three automobile manufacturers to initiate Covisint did not simultaneously remove the threat of competition and historic distrust among players in the automotive industry. Covisint and those in other industries involved in supply chain integration have had to strategize to increase trust. Covisint cites its independence as a key to remaining unbiased and gaining acceptance. It also sought to ease concerns of potential customers by identifying what those concerns were and developing marketing strategies based on them. Its information security measures have eased fears over confidentiality. IT firewalls keep automakers from accessing each others' proprietary information, including electronic bids.

Cat Logistics has used strict protocols surrounding confidentiality, a robust IT infrastructure, and its strong reputation in logistics to build trust between members of the same supply chain. Remarkably, Cat Logistics has developed such a good name as an honest broker and third party logistics provider that one of its parent company's main competitors, CNH (the maker of Case construction equipment), trusts it to digitally integrate its supply chain and manage its logistics functions.

Another way industry players have built confidence is to establish long-running relationships. General Electric enters into long-term contracts, some of which last as long as 10 years, with some customers. These contracts develop relationships and also have built-in incentives for performance. Within the context of these long contracts, rewarding the right results enhances trust by demonstrating that all players are working toward the same outcomes. In its airline contracts with Southwest and US Airways, GE is responsible for the capital costs of engines. This arrangement rewards GE for long-lasting, reliable engines, which helps the airlines better achieve their goals.

- **Using the Right Metrics.** The vice president of worldwide field operations finance at Cisco Systems summed up the need for metrics when he said, "A company can't improve what it can't measure" (see the Cisco Systems case study). One common approach, which Cisco uses, is the Balanced Scorecard, which is illustrated in Figure 2.2. This technique divides corporate performance into categories including financial

Figure 2.2: Balanced Scorecard

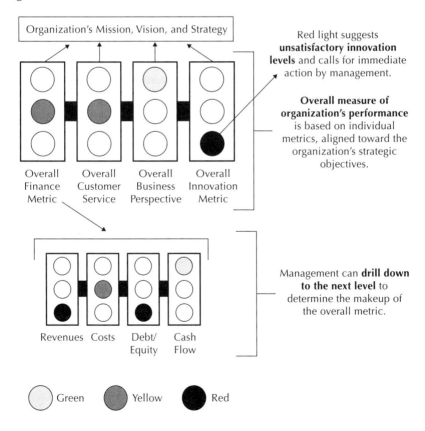

Definition of "Balanced Scorecard"

This is an organizational tool that translates an organization's mission strategy into objectives and measures organized into multiple different perspectives: for example, financial, customer, internal business process, and learning and growth. It provides all employees with information they can use to affect the multiple results the organization is achieving.

This definition is based on a 1992 article in the *Harvard Business Review* by Robert Kaplan and David Norton entitled "The Balanced Scorecard—Measures That Drive Performance."

---

performance, customer service, employee learning and innovation, and internal operations. Within this framework, each level of an organization uses goals that were formed one level up to determine more detailed mid-level goals. This process translates the organization's mission into a working context. It also enables high-level managers to dig deeply into the sources of top-tier metric results. At Cisco, review teams study metrics related to the company's financial management system and use the metrics to enhance the system and solve problems. Table 2.1 presents metrics used at IBM to assess their supply chain transformation.

Companies with world-class practices have also been careful to establish contracts that are based on the right metrics. Some contracts for General Electric's maintenance services are structured so that the company is paid based on the speed of parts installment. The incentive is to install parts quickly, reducing the customer's overall costs and increasing system uptime. GE uses Radio Frequency Indicator (RFID) tags to keep track of where parts are during transit and accelerate its part replacement process. Contrast this with the practice, which many private and public organizations still use, of paying based on how many parts are installed. The incentive on those contracts is for contractors to install more parts, increasing overall costs and increasing system downtime.

- **Adopting New Supply Chain Technology.** Just as Covisint developed an electronic exchange and Cisco Systems developed an integrated financial management system, numerous companies have implemented new technology to drive supply chain efficiencies. Cat Logistics uses software applications to increase visibility into the entire supply chain. With data including inventory levels, ordering plans, and warehouse distances, Cat Logistics can make predictions about supply and demand and find places to cut costs.

  In implementing technology solutions, the private sector has leaned toward commercial-off-the-shelf (COTS) products. In developing

Table 2.1: IBM Metrics on Supply Chain Effectiveness

Metric	Early 1990s	Current
Sourcing expertise in place	<10%	100%
Cost savings	?	$5.4 billion
Supplier quality	85%	99%
Escapes (maverick buying)	>35%	<0.2%
Acceptable business controls	55%	92%
Client satisfaction	40%	80%
Electronic catalogs	0	280
E-enabled suppliers	<500	35,000
Electronic purchases	<20%	95%
PO process time	30 days	<1 day

a new integrated financial management system, Boeing considered and rejected a customized solution built from the ground up. The company feared customization would lead to expensive "scope creep" and implemented a COTS solution instead.

- **Aggressively Incorporating Information Security Measures.** With the degree of competition and proprietary information in the commercial world, supply chain integration would not work without strong information security. Covisint and Cat Logistics both have clients that compete with each other. Ford would not want GM to know its production plans or any other confidential information. To ensure that there are no leaks to unauthorized sources, Covisint uses a robust security approach that involves an information security division, audits (including semiannual sanctioned hacking), and close coordination with manufacturers' information security departments.

  Similar to some government departments, Cat Logistics furthers its security precautions through a "need to know" company culture. Employees keep client information private, sharing it only with those who have a "need to know." Information domains, which are separated by firewalls and passwords, are only accessible to people with the proper clearance. A security team monitors firewalls and makes any needed changes to configurations.

Government Practices

Within the government, incremental changes at the sub-system level have occurred to date. Some of these changes are exceptional and should be replicated. As "Driving Change: Federal Policies" shows, policy makers realize the importance of electronic tools and diminished bureaucracy. Many of these laws, their associated directives, and regulations have been catalysts for government programs that incorporate business practices and electronic commerce. In many organizations, various factors pose challenges that, if confronted, could yield results. To reach a new level, the key will be addressing those challenges, refining or changing policies, and dealing with barriers.

Government Advances

Various government agencies have pursued transformative initiatives. The Defense Finance and Accounting Service implemented a new electronic financial system that reduced the number of individual DoD financial management systems from 324 to 65 (see the DFAS case study). Consequently, the amount of manual reconciliation needed dropped dramatically. As a result of the National Science Foundation's new financial management system, the agency was able to divert funds from operations toward its mission of promoting research and education. The NSF was able to make a greater impact with the same number of staff people.

The Defense Logistics Agency's Business Systems Modernization, the Defense Medical Logistics Standard Support system, and the Joint Strike Fighter program also offer models for government change. In particular these initiatives illustrate how to approach the following key elements of supply chain management.

Leadership

Some government leaders have recognized that one strategic means to integrate supply chain processes is to first integrate leadership teams. The DoD Joint Strike Fighter (JSF) office is a prime example. The aircraft is being developed for the Air Force, Navy, Marines, and the United Kingdom's military (as well as other participating nations), so it follows that U.S. program leadership would represent each of the participating organizations. The way to accomplish that representation is not as obvious. The JSF program has developed a rotating top leadership post, where direct reports may come from different services (for example, a Navy captain may report to an Air Force general). This unusual structure has been working well, aided by support from each of the participating services. To motivate cooperation, the incentives for each of the program leaders are aligned with the goals of the program.

Driving Change: Federal Policies

The Federal Acquisition Streamlining Act of 1994 (FASA) made a number of changes in the way goods and services, at or below $100,000, are acquired. The act replaces the $25,000 threshold with a new "Simplified Acquisition Threshold" (SAT) of $100,000 once an agency (or procuring activity within the agency) has achieved certain electronic commerce (FACNET) capabilities, is using them, and certifies that it has met the criteria. Until that time, the threshold is only increased to $50,000.

The Government Performance and Results Act of 1993 (GPRA) requires multi-year strategic and annual goals, performance measurement, and continual reporting on progress.

The Government Paperwork Elimination Acts of 1995 and 1998 directed efforts to streamline government processes and reduce the associated paperwork.

The Information Technology Management Reform Act of 1996 (Clinger-Cohen Act) designates a chief information officer within each executive federal agency and puts forward best practices to be used in linking IT planning and investment decisions to agencies' missions and goals.

The Federal Financial Management Improvement Act (FFMIA) (1996) requires federal agency compliance with Federal Financial Management System requirements, Federal Accounting Standards, and the U.S. Government Standard General Ledger. This act also prescribes continual auditing and control practices.

Joint Vision 2020, issued by the chairman of the Joint Chiefs of Staff, called for the adoption of *"Focused Logistics"*—the fusion of information, logistics, and transportation technologies in order to provide a more rapid response, one providing support in hours or days versus weeks.

President's Management Council's Electronic Processes Initiatives Committee, March 1998, "Electronic Commerce for Buyers and Sellers: A Strategic Plan for Electronic Federal Purchasing and Payment" outlines strategies for government e-commerce applications—"customer-friendly electronic purchasing tools integrated with end-to-end commercial processing of payment, accounting, and performance reporting information."

The 1999 DoD Authorization Act directed that the DoD create a one-stop electronic marketplace where suppliers and their goods could be consolidated.

The Electronic Signatures in Global and National Commerce Act ("E-SIGN") was enacted on June 30, 2000. E-SIGN eliminates legal barriers to the use of electronic technology to form and sign contracts, collect and store documents, and send and receive notices and disclosures.

The Defense Medical Logistics Standard Support (DMLSS) program also assembled a representative leadership team to helm its project implementation. The cross-functional software implementation team included medical logistics heads, chief information officers, and the DoD comptroller.

A factor that contributed to the success of the DMLSS program was having the right level of leadership. Two of the highest DoD officials for health and for logistics ran the implementation jointly. Having the assistant secretary of defense for health affairs and the deputy under secretary of defense (logistics) in charge meant that the program had the authority to get things done.

Metrics

Using the right metrics makes the difference between a new program and a new successful program. The DMLSS program set numeric goals to motivate change, focusing on customer needs and lowering inventories. Program goals include customer receipt of 80 percent of items in less than 24 hours and the other 20 percent within 48 to 72 hours, as well as near elimination of inventories of supplies and drugs. The virtue of putting in place the right metric goals such as these is evident from the results. The new system led to a reduction in average order-to-receipt times from 20 days to 24 hours, a 65 percent decrease in medical inventory at DoD depots, and an 81 percent decrease in medical inventory at DoD hospitals (see chapter fourteen, the DMLSS case study).

The DMLSS program exemplifies another key to developing the right metrics: a focus on performance, not just costs. DoD's performance is determined by its readiness. DMLSS's key metrics include getting the right items into the customers' hands quickly and holding minimal inventory. As an outcome, medics have what they need to handle peacetime health problems and wartime casualties. Reducing inventories and buying directly from vendors decreases the likelihood of storing and shipping expired medical products. For critical functions, such as those performed by DMLSS, performance improvements and metrics form the basis of measuring program progress. And, even though true logistics costs are difficult to assess with the current accounting systems, the realized savings are clearly significant.

Supply Chain Technology

In the summer of 2002, Army General Tommy Franks, then commander in chief of the U.S. Central Command, ordered the use of radio frequency identification (RFID) tags on certain military shipments. Army General Paul Kern, commander of the Army Materiel Command, subsequently issued a similar, Army-wide order in January 2003. The use of these tags has allowed DoD to use scanners (such as those used with smart tags to electronically "collect" car tolls) to identify package contents and divert shipments, if necessary. These technology improvements, which support a just-in-time logistics capability, enabled the 2002–2003 buildup in the Persian Gulf to be accomplished in half the time as in 1991.[3]

Other technology tools used by DoD include the medical logistics community's use of an Internet portal, a web-based electronic trading exchange, and business intelligence software. (Chapters three and four provide details on how these technologies enable superior supply chain management.) Without these electronic tools, DMLSS's goals could not have been achieved.

The National Science Foundation exists to further scientific research, so its incorporation of information technology into its supply chain management processes is somewhat predictable. Its new financial management system incorporates web-based payment functionality and internally developed financial accounting software. Unexpected, however, is the extent to which the NSF has developed an organizational culture of change. Innovation and new system implementation have pervaded the NSF's business processes in the same way these practices characterize private high-technology companies. Also similar to Cisco Systems, the NSF has developed a financial management system that fosters interdependency among various departments. Any change to the Financial Accounting System requires input and coordination between all departments.

Information Security

Not only does the NSF rival high-technology companies in its culture of innovation; it also stands out with its information security procedures. The financial management system employs a user profile system that prevents unauthorized access, and the inspector general reviews security planning and management practices annually, with risk assessments of mission-critical systems.

Areas for Government Improvement

Even though the examples of leadership, metrics, technology, and information security just described provide government models worth replicating, these and other areas are still fertile for supply chain management improvements. While some government organizations and programs have leveraged systems thinking and new technology to develop initiatives, many practices still reflect a dated reality. In addition, not enough is happening to facilitate imitation of successes. While the size and complexity of the government make widespread change challenging, the following areas for improvement, based on leading-edge practices, offer some insight into where to begin.

Outsource Logistics

Having decided that logistics was not a core competency, many private companies have contracted with logistics experts for some or all of their logistics operations. The public sector is moving more slowly. Many agencies are reluctant to tinker with a system that works, even if inefficiently. There have, however, been successful pilot programs—one approach that has been particularly successful is contracting with a prime vendor, which is a private company that consolidates government purchases and ships directly to end users. With the DoD EMALL (see chapter fifteen, the DoD EMALL case study), the government has adopted online direct procurement. However, outsourcing logistics services remains the exception. DoD still has many warehouses filled with government inventories and managed by government personnel, and agencies such as the Federal Emergency Management Agency and the Department of State still manage their own logistics processes.

Raise the Level of Leadership and Sustain High-Level Commitment

Lacking authority over all parties, the Defense Finance and Accounting Service was able to integrate only 259 of the 324 DoD financial management systems (see the DFAS case study). The remaining 65 may finally be integrated in the next few years because the level of leadership has been raised to the under secretary of defense (comptroller), who has commissioned a study on developing a DoD enterprise-wide system architecture.

Even when leaders at the appropriate level have driven supply chain innovation, projects can sputter to a halt as a result of the political process. Projects need enough momentum and high enough profiles to be sustained over changes in administrations and political appointees.

Establish Longer-Term Contracts

A culture of distrust of contractors has led to the proliferation of short, often one-year supply contracts. One of the keys to enterprise integration has been developing trust through long-running relationships between entities. The federal acquisition regulation allows for contracts up to five years, with the ability to exercise extension options up to five additional years. The options create the ability to continue to use a contractor that is performing well, but to maintain the pressure of competition, which has been found to result in better performance at lower costs. While not every case requires contracts of these lengths, one-year agreements are limiting. Prior to establishing long-term contracts, organizations should undertake a thorough spend analysis, initiate a strategic sourcing program, and implement commodity councils as necessary.

Focus on the Right Metrics

Government contracts contain incentives for contractor performance, but too many times contracts encourage inefficiencies by rewarding the wrong actions (see Table 2.2). Payments based on parts replaced or repaired encourage higher numbers of replacements and repairs. Instead, the government should encourage system availability and reduced assets by rewarding such factors as system uptime (i.e., higher readiness levels) with lowered costs.

Digitally Integrate

Some dramatic improvements in the use of IT have occurred within government agencies, including, as noted in the previous section, the tracking of DoD shipments using RFID technology. Nevertheless, government organizations have yet to realize the world-class level of digital operational, business function, and enterprise integration that organizations such as Cat Logistics and Wal-Mart have achieved.

Sub-optimization has been a problem with new technology implementations. Organizations have focused on improving their internal IT systems without considering external interoperability. As a result, the multiplier

Table 2.2: Focusing on Metrics

Metric		Outcome
Wrong Metrics	**Orders Placed:** Incentive tied to placing more orders—i.e., parts ordered per month per division	Large accumulation of inventories, higher storage costs, increased inventory costs
	Number of Repairs: Program incentive tied to total number of repairs carried out	Increased number of repairs leads to increase in costs and inefficiencies
Correct Metrics	**System Availability:** Availability of systems and ability to be deployed at short notice—i.e., deployment of cargo planes or aircraft carrier systems	Increased efficiency, preparedness, lower lead times, and lower costs
	Customer Service: Collaboration with customers and suppliers, providing value-based solutions, and training and experience for employees to serve the customer better	Improved timeliness and accuracy of data for better decision making, and full integration of customer and supplier information critical for success as well as building strong alliances with suppliers and customers
	Order-to-Receipt Time: Metric tracked based on total completed orders to receipt time of orders	Reduction in lead times for procurement results in overall reduction in inventory holding costs and stock-outs

effect of digital integration is still out of reach. When digital integration occurs, organizational buying power increases and access to knowledge expands. Data has to be entered only once and is automatically disseminated to appropriate finance, procurement, and logistics areas. The ability to respond to surge requirements is based on information flow rather than on stockpiles.

In addition, digital integration would enable government auditors and managers to review accurate and complete top-level reporting based on data automatically rolled up from lower levels. Delving into detailed financial data now embedded in organizational layers would become much simpler. This ability is badly needed, particularly in DoD. As it stands, besides not being able to account for over $2.3 trillion in historic transactions,[4] DoD cannot correctly report its net cost of operations or account for all of its assets (see the DFAS case study). Consequently, DoD and federal decision makers are handicapped by incomplete knowledge.

Reengineer Processes Before Changing Systems

Implementing electronic systems without first evaluating processes and making needed changes leads to the automation of outdated processes. Although DFAS recognized that it could have achieved much more with process reengineering, the organization did not review or change processes prior to implementing its new system. With the DoD medical logistics system implementation, process change was an original goal. Now that the system is in place, however, no clear incentives exist for further process change before making system changes. As a result, program managers are motivated by short-term requirements and may make changes to the electronic system with minimal or no business process reevaluation.

Even when process change has taken place internally, relationships with other organizations are often overlooked. In larger agencies, offices do not generally share logistics information with other offices, not to mention other departments and agencies. Even within offices, managers often view business functions such as procurement, financial management, and logistics as unrelated.

Barriers to Government Change

Although innovative public and private sector initiatives offer compelling examples, various barriers have prevented a government-wide transformation in supply chain management. The previous section described general areas for government attention. This section covers obstacles that, unless removed or worked around, will hinder modernization. These are cultural, legal, administrative, and resource, as opposed to technological hurdles. In chapter five, we will discuss how to move past these barriers.

Cultural Barriers

Widely held perceptions about poor outcomes and about the lack of necessity for new supply chain management practices still need to be overcome. Both organizational negativity and indifference obstruct progress.

Lack of Perceived Urgency at the Top

To change a business-as-usual organizational mind-set requires strong leadership from the very top levels. To create Covisint, the CEOs of the Big Three auto companies led the effort. To overhaul Cisco Systems' financial management practices, the company's chief financial officer directed change. In government departments and agencies, many Secretaries and other agency leaders have not yet recognized the urgency of transforming supply chain management. High-level government leaders can focus only on three to four priorities during their tenure. Without supply chain management making that short list, stovepipes, turf stand-offs, risk avoidance, and other derailing forces will maintain the status quo. Change will not happen. In addition, even if supply chain management does make a leader's list, the priority needs to carry over to the next leader's agenda until enough momentum makes change sustainable.

Distrust of the System

Because medics have experience receiving expired medications and Navy ship supply officers know that they will have to wait an average of 22 days to receive items, these end users have developed work-arounds. They need to get the right supplies and don't trust the system to get them what they need when they need it, so they order more than they need. Without the trust of end users, system costs and inefficiencies will remain.

Fear of Change

When the Defense Finance and Accounting Service started to consolidate its distinct financial systems, people who were used to the old processes resisted. To make the system changes, DFAS needed coding data from field experts within the military services, who did not want to help. The field personnel were worried about being held accountable for discrepancies between the old and new systems.

The National Science Foundation recognizes that its staff members may fear new processes and systems because of concerns that their jobs will become less important or that they will be forced to do something they won't like. In general, government employees fear partnerships with the private sector because of concerns that they will lose their jobs to contractors. When not acknowledged and confronted by managers, these fears can halt change.

Distrust of the Private Sector

Demand can be unpredictable in the government, especially in organizations that need to respond to wars, natural disasters, and other crises. Some government leaders and personnel fear that the private sector won't meet emergency needs. While this concern is valid and must be addressed, it can be used as an excuse not to change. In fact, examples within the private sector show flexibility and rapid response are achieved successfully.

One example of a commercial company's quick reaction in confronting a crisis with surge requirements was Caterpillar's response to the 1980 Mount St. Helens eruption. Disaster response teams brought in Caterpillar heavy industrial equipment for rescue operations, but because of the extreme conditions, some equipment broke down. Ash and dust jammed many of the catalytic converters. Caterpillar used its logistics system to track down catalytic converters from sites around the world to keep the operation on track.

Despite this and numerous other private sector examples of fast response to unexpected demand, distrust persists. Government offices often resist sharing demand information with suppliers, who therefore must forecast and plan based on best guesses of government need.

Legal Barriers

Federal laws and agency rules enacted to spur economic development, to promote disadvantaged business segments, or—in some cases—to help constituent causes occasionally create unintended hurdles to supply chain management change. These statutes and regulations may keep government departments and agencies from acting as quickly or with as much flexibility as commercial actors.

Statutory and Regulatory Compliance

Earlier in this chapter, "Driving Change: Federal Policies" described regulations that are designed to spur government transformation. On the flip side, however, some legislation is hindering reform. For its Business Systems Modernization implementation, the Defense Logistics Agency had to develop ways to deal with 17 such policy issues. The agency either got the policies changed or spent time developing extra systems to meet the requirements.

The DoD EMALL also hit regulatory speed bumps. Well-intentioned regulations such as small business protection acts, the Javits-Wagner-O'Day

Act, and the Buy American Act require government offices to give preference to certain types of companies (see "Statutory and Regulatory Hoops" on page 36 for details on these acts.) As the DLA example shows, this type of regulatory compliance puts the government on a different playing field than private industry. For the DoD EMALL to publish entire catalogs, the program must either establish that all catalog items meet regulatory requirements (including the difficult task of ascertaining that every item in a catalog was made in America) or must obtain exemptions. Either way, because of the regulations, the timeline for online publishing is considerably longer than what a commercial business would experience.

Time-consuming and meaningless paperwork has also been a burdensome outcome of some legislation. The Government Performance and Results Act of 1993 (GPRA) and the Information Technology Management Reform Act of 1996 (Clinger-Cohen) aim to achieve changes consistent with supply chain management reform. However, the heavy reporting requirements for GPRA and the out-of-date business case parameters outlined in Clinger-Cohen present unnecessary obstacles.

OMB Circular A-76 is another example of a policy that is helpful to promoting supply chain management reform but at the same time requires cumbersome and lengthy justifications. Although studies and subsequent competitions have taken as long as four years to complete, the revised circular A-76 has attempted to improve the process and restricts the competitions to 12 months (with one six-month extension permitted).[5]

OMB Circular A-76

OMB Circular A-76 Performance of Commercial Activities was issued in 1966 by the Office of Management and Budget (OMB), which established the policy for acquiring commercial activities. In 1979, OMB issued procedures for A-76 cost comparison studies to determine whether commercial activities should be performed by government, by another federal agency, or by the private sector. The objective of A-76 is to provide a "fair" public-private competitive sourcing process, seeking to determine the most cost-effective method of obtaining services that are available from the commercial market. In an effort to improve the process, OMB revised the circular in May 2003. The changes include setting up two types of competitions: streamlined (which now eliminates the direct conversion process) and standard competition (a modified version of the more traditional A-76 approach of writing a statement of work and competing it against the private sector); the provision for using "best value" criteria in selected competitions; and imposing a 12-month requirement (with provision for one six-month extension) for completing standard competitions.

Statutory and Regulatory Hoops

While none of the following federal laws were intended to impede supply chain management reform, they nonetheless present hurdles to change.

- **Small business protection acts.** These laws were created to open opportunities for small and disadvantaged businesses, including minority and women-owned enterprises. Such laws hamper supply chain management transformation because they place restrictions on supplier selection—thus often limiting the use of commercial off-the-shelf (COTS) systems (see DoD EMALL case study).

- **Javits-Wagner-O'Day Act.** This law also limits supplier selection for certain office products. It directs federal offices to purchase these supplies through nonprofit agencies that employ people who are blind or have other severe disabilities (see the DoD EMALL case study).

- **Buy American Act, 41 U.S.C. 10a et seq.** This act, which has been on the books since 1933, permits federal agencies to buy only goods that have been "mined, produced, or manufactured in the United States except in cases where (1) U.S. goods are not available in sufficient quantity and satisfactory quality; (2) the cost is unreasonable; or (3) it is inconsistent with the public interest to purchase U.S. articles, materials, or supplies" (see the DoD EMALL case study). The global nature of sourcing today makes compliance with this law difficult, and to circumvent it, extra paperwork builds extra time into the contracting process.

- **Berry Amendment (DoD Appropriations Act, 1993).** This act, which applies to DoD only (for purchases over $100,000 in most circumstances) supplements the Buy American Act. This law requires that all materials used to produce finished goods come from U.S. sources. This is difficult to verify since suppliers do not necessarily know where the materials their vendors use to produce their goods originated, and in some cases the place of origin can change from lot to lot.

- **United States Code, Section 2464, Title 10.** This act specifies that "core" work needs to be performed by government employees in government facilities. (The meaning of core is, of course, subject to interpretation.)

- **United States Code, Section 2466, Title 10.** (*Limitations on the performance of depot-level maintenance of materiel,* commonly known as the "50/50 rule.") This law limits the amount of outsourcing possible in DoD repair and maintenance facilities, called depots. These depots, which employ over 64,000 government personnel, repair, maintain, and produce military equipment, spare parts, and weapon systems. According to the 50/50 rule, no more than 50 percent of depot-level maintenance and repair work may be contracted out. The resultant monopoly situation raises program costs and diminishes performance, compared to commercial situations, where free competition occurs.

One way the public sector has sped up buying and reduced paperwork and bureaucracy is through micro-purchases. Initiated by the Federal Acquisition Streamlining Act of 1994 (FASA), micro-purchases permit authorized personnel to buy goods directly from commercial suppliers, often using government-issued purchase cards. Purchase cards saved over $120 per purchase according to a 1999 study.[6] However, currently the low $2,500 threshold keeps this program from realizing more sweeping improvements.

Another major regulatory impediment is the 50/50 rule (United States Code, Section 2466, Title 10, which is described in "Statutory and Regulatory Hoops"). This rule, which affects only the Defense Department, covers approximately $16 billion[7] in annual repair and maintenance depot[8] spending. The law's proponents claim that by requiring that at least 50 percent of the funding for depot repair and maintenance work remain in-house, government-controlled sources of repair will be available to meet wartime surge requirements. The law serves as a precaution should the private sector be unable to react to unexpected, urgent needs.

As a consequence of the law's restrictions, those attempting to improve military repair and maintenance performance have limited options. In the case of the Army's Apache helicopter, for example, leaders tried to pursue an opportunity to outsource logistics services to improve performance and cost savings but faced a catch-22 situation. To outsource Apache work, Army leaders would have had to simultaneously increase in-house spending on depot operations to make up the difference, because of the way the depots are funded. The net result would be wasteful spending. As discussed earlier, under the cultural barriers section (distrust of the private sector), concerns about the ability of contractors to react to surge requirements may be based more on cultural biases than actual examples.

Regulatory Interpretation

In the spirit of carrying out contracting rules, contracting officers often establish short contract performance periods, thereby requiring frequent competition. This practice is perceived as promoting fairness and enabling the government to keep quality high and prices low. However, when competition occurs too frequently, this can interfere with one of the facilitators of supply chain integration: partnerships developed over time. Without the opportunity to develop strong relationships between private and public enterprises, the potential for change is impaired. As already discussed in this chapter, under the areas for government improvement section (establish longer-term contracts), as long as performance continues to improve and costs continue to fall, there should be no need for frequent competitions. However, it is necessary to maintain the option for competition, should performance fall off or costs rise.

Administrative Barriers

Business-as-usual can present problems for modernizing supply chain management. The following management issues need to change to lay the foundations for digital supply chain integration.

Inability to Make a Business Case Based on Financial Data

In a typical investment scenario, project cost is a key factor in deciding whether to proceed. In a government setting, one of the questions is how much will be saved. This question is a barrier to change, especially in DoD. Two issues that arise are poor government accounting records in general and the lack of activity-based costing (ABC).[9] Even where historical cost data is accurate, it does not adequately delineate which costs apply to logistics the way ABC would. Consequently, baseline cost data often do not exist to make a business case or to compare government and contractor costs. If starting an innovative supply chain project hinges on supplying precise cost savings projections to a comptroller or a manager, the project will most likely stall due to the lack of full-cost baseline data for the current government approach.

Noncompliance with Information Security Requirements

Several government policies provide direction for implementing strong information security. The Government Information Security Reform Act of 2000, OMB Circular A-130, and the GAO Audit Guide on how to conduct security reviews stress the importance of proper steps, including risk assessments and training. However, many agencies and departments are not in compliance with these and other rules. In those organizations, the information security infrastructure is not in place to support digitally integrated supply chains. Information security procedures need to be integral to new information system implementations.

Resource Barriers

As with any change initiative, leaders must back up the desire to transform practices with sufficient resources to make it happen. In this case, digitally integrating elements of government supply chains will require the acknowledgment that many legacy IT systems need to be replaced. This and other supply chain management transformation activities will require dedicated funding.

Legacy Systems

Many government IT systems are outdated and ill equipped to interface with other systems to handle modern problems in a timely way. One unfortunate result was a slower than necessary response as operations in Afghanistan began in 2001. The DoD procurement process could not keep up with the military needs.[10] Regardless of how much funding was provided at the time, the legacy systems could not respond quickly.

Insufficient Funding

Some of the barriers discussed above, including the difficulty of initiating new projects because of unrealistic business case requirements and the low priority given to supply chain management change, have made it difficult for new projects to obtain needed funding. Upgrading old or implementing new IT systems, training personnel, ensuring adequate information security, establishing new supply chain management-focused contracts, and other logistics transformation activities need adequate and sustained funding levels to achieve change.

Summary

This chapter summarized private and public sector best practices in supply chain integration, specified areas for government attention, and detailed obstacles to remove or circumvent in order to achieve world-class supply chain management. Key points include:

- Digital integration requires leadership—at the highest government levels—willing to invest the needed resources and put in place structures that last beyond the initiators' tenures. For projects that integrate enterprises, business functions, or operations, successful organizational structures have been cross-functional and inter-departmental. Currently, needed government investments include replacements for and improvement to IT legacy systems, enhanced information security, and training in new competencies.
- One of the primary success factors for leading companies has been analyzing operations and deciding whether to outsource all or part of their supply chain services. In many cases, moving to companies with core competencies in logistics has resulted in increased supply chain integration, improvement in customer orientation, and reduced costs.
- When aligned to match organizational goals, metrics used for contract and employee incentives produce new efficiencies. Misaligned metrics that reward counterproductive results lead to waste as well as distrust.
- As in any large and complex organization, change in government is difficult. Cultural biases rather than fact-based arguments often become the basis for defending the status quo.

The next chapter describes the role of IT as a driver in modern supply chain management practices, and illustrates some of the results of digital integration.

Endnotes

1. Jacques S. Gansler, William Lucyshyn, and Kimberly Ross, "Digitally Integrating the Government Supply Chain: E-Procurement, E-Finance, and E-Logistics," IBM Center for The Business of Government, February 2003.

2. GAO/AIMD Report: *Financial Management: Federal Aviation Administration Lacks Accountability for Major Assets*. AIMD-98-62, February 18, 1998.

3. Dan Caterinicchia, "DoD Builds High-Tech Supply Chain," *Federal Computer Week*, February 24, 2003.

4. Steve Horn, Agency Financial Management, Congressional testimony, May 8, 2001.

5. Gansler, Lucyshyn, and Ross.

6. The 1999 DoD study found that at the Defense Logistics Agency, it cost $146 to process manual transactions and $25.62 for purchase card transactions (from Gansler, Lucyshyn, and Ross).

7. Gansler, Lucyshyn, and Ross.

8. Military services maintain in-house depots that repair and produce spare parts or weapons systems ranging from F-16 fighter planes to M1A1 tanks to Nimitz class aircraft carriers.

9. ABC is a management accounting method that breaks costs into lines that show production, delivery, and resource (e.g., labor and materials) amounts.

10. Gansler, Lucyshyn, and Ross.

CHAPTER THREE

The Integration Enabler: Information Technology

Jacques S. Gansler
Robert E. Luby, Jr.
Bonnie Kornberg

IT Propels Enterprise Integration

As the microcomputer business evolved in the 1980s and 1990s, the big players distributed computers the same general way the automotive, hardware, and packaged-goods industries distributed cars, screwdrivers, and canned food. For the most part, each link of the supply chain—manufacturers, distributors, wholesalers, and retailers—concentrated on their own business processes. In other words, no supply-chain-wide collaboration or analysis took place. In addition, communication occurred sequentially, with each supply chain echelon interacting with the next.

Dell Computer did things differently. Dell used information technology to make supply chain management its competitive advantage. As the Internet grew, so did Dell's reliance on it as a means to take orders and collaborate with suppliers. Instead of using retailers, Dell sold directly to consumers. While Hewlett-Packard, IBM, and others were forecasting demand for various product configurations and manufacturing computers accordingly, Dell was waiting to assemble computers until after customers placed orders. Using IT to gain visibility into its supply chain, Dell started steering buying decisions by letting customers know which components were available. In 1998, most computer companies were trying to achieve inventory turns every four weeks. Dell, on the other hand, had lowered its inventory levels to eight days while personalizing computers in response to customer demands.[1]

Dell has treated its suppliers as part of its organization. Suppliers receive electronic notice of customer web orders at the same time as Dell and respond by sending components either to Dell's assembly plants or, with major components such as monitors, directly to customers. Dell also uses virtual collaboration with partners to design new products.

At Dell and other leading enterprises, IT has driven change, causing new thinking about how to handle logistics. Sharing expected demand with supply chain partners, planning and designing products jointly, setting systemwide goals and priorities, and basing decisions on end customers' needs are some of the advances catalyzed by IT.

The speed of information transfer, visibility across organizational and geographical boundaries, and the capability to model systems have predictably produced results. Constraints related to geographic separation and enterprise divisions previously limited the cooperation now possible through digital infrastructures such as Covisint's e-procurement portal. As a result of Covisint's services, companies have reported savings between 4 and 17 percent (see chapter thirteen, the Covisint case study). By electronically integrating Caterpillar's supply chain, Cat Logistics now ships 99.8 percent of Caterpillar's replacement parts in less than one day (see chapter six, the Cat Logistics case study).

These changes have been possible only within the last several years. As Figure 3.1 demonstrates, the realm of possibility in supply chain evolution continues to grow along with advances in IT capabilities.

Supply chain solutions have evolved dramatically over the last 15 years from rigid, inflexible systems to integrated collaborative systems hosted on the Internet. An organization is best prepared to leverage the full value of collaborative systems if it has:

- Undertaken internal business process reengineering, improving and standardizing processes; process integration and optimization; and legacy system transformation and adopting an Enterprise Resource Planning system
- Established a vision and adopted an enterprise point of view that includes suppliers, other business partners, and customers
- Embraced and practiced change management

Figure 3.1: Supply Chain Evolution

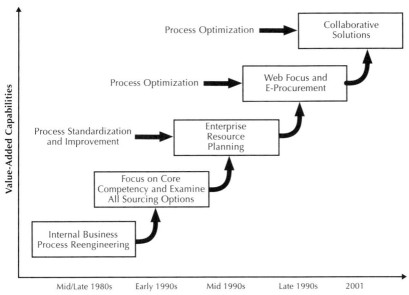

Previous Norms

The old way of thinking, which is still the way many organizations operate, involves optimizing individual organization and business functions, or operational processes and systems. Without collaboration or cooperation across the supply chain, individual organizations try to protect against uncertainty. In inventory-intensive industries, this leads to problems, including a situation called the bullwhip effect. This means that the further upstream (i.e., closer to the point of the goods' origin) an entity is in the value chain, the more inaccurate forecasts become (see Figure 3.2). This makes sense on an intuitive level because manufacturers and other upstream entities are more removed from the customer or end user. Similar to the children's game of "telephone," where an initiator whispers a phrase to one person, who then whispers it to the next person and on down the line, the people at the end of the chain receive less reliable information and receive it more slowly.

Several factors lead to this variability in conventional, non-integrated supply chains where phone calls, faxes, and letters are used to spread demand information.

- **Attempts to balance preparedness with cost-consciousness.** Organizations protect against unforeseen demand requirements by maintaining safety stock, which is inventory that is on hand and in the order pipeline. Organizations plan to meet expected demand by establishing order-up-to levels. As actual demand changes over time, safety stock and order-up-to levels fluctuate. Additionally, when prices vary substantially or shortages exist, firms buy extra inventory to take advantage of low prices and availability. These reactions to market forces also lead to variability in inventory levels.
- **Magnifying effects of small changes in lead times.** Small changes in lead times can result in large changes in order quantities. If organizations

Figure 3.2: The Bullwhip Effect

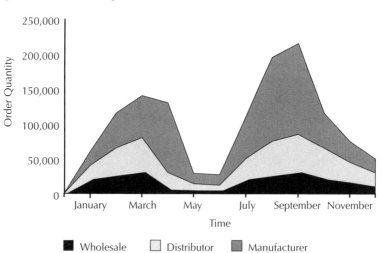

learn that it will take slightly longer to receive certain shipments, they try to maintain adequate inventories to meet demand by increasing order quantities. If shipments can be delivered slightly more quickly, firms will want to capitalize on the cost savings by ordering less. As a result, small lead-time changes can intensify order and inventory variability. This effect can be shown mathematically.[2]

- **Economic pressures to order in batches.** Economy-of-scale discounts, bulk transportation discounts, and seasonal demand swings can lead firms to buy in batches, which contributes to uncertainty up the supply chain. Imagine that a retailer makes batch buys. The wholesaler will experience long periods of inactivity and then bursts of high-volume sales. To plan for demand requirements, the wholesaler, who does not know when the retailer will choose to make a large buy, needs to carry sufficient inventory at all times and will change its inventory levels to respond to changes in retailer orders.

Taking into account the factors discussed above, a wholesaler's inventory variations will be more exaggerated than a retailer's when supply chain collaboration does not occur. By extension, a manufacturer's inventory variability will be even greater than a wholesaler's, and this inventory and ordering inflation will continue up each echelon of a supply chain. See "The Bullwhip Effect—A Scenario" on page 46 for an example illustrating how this effect can impact the supply chain at various levels.

The Impact of IT on Logistics

In the 1960s, business management authority Peter Drucker described logistics as one of the last fields where significant new efficiencies could be realized.[3] That was before the Internet and vast improvements in computing capabilities had been developed. Today, IT enables changes no one imagined in the 1960s. Among the most significant outcomes when IT is applied to logistics processes are greater flexibility, speed, decision making, accuracy, and productivity, along with reduced costs. However, in many parts of the government, Drucker's statement is still true today, though it need not be.

- **Flexibility.** The large inventories that characterize the bullwhip effect are intended to hedge against uncertainty. With coordinated information systems, much of that uncertainty is removed, and organizations can respond quickly to emerging requirements. Information, to some extent, replaces inventories. Wal-Mart's techniques have become famous for their flexibility in responding to changing information. Using a satellite communications network and bar-code scanners at retail stores, Wal-

---

The Bullwhip Effect—A Scenario

To make the bullwhip effect concept more concrete, take three echelons of an office supplies supply chain—a retailer, wholesaler, and manufacturer—in a fictitious scenario. To simplify this example, assume that a manufacturer supplies only one wholesaler, who in turn supplies only one retailer.

- In January, the retailer orders 15,000 staplers from the wholesaler.
- The wholesaler, which has based its inventory levels on previous orders, has a safety stock of 5,000 and a total inventory level, including safety stock, of 20,000. Thus, after filling the order, it retains 5,000 staplers in inventory and must order more to prepare for future orders.
- The wholesaler learns that the manufacturer has excess inventory and is offering a price break for large quantity buys.
- The wholesaler also learns that some of the trucks in its fleet are being repaired, so lead times for delivery are slightly longer than usual.
- To prepare for the retailer's next order and to build in precautions in case the retailer's next orders occur more rapidly than in the past, the wholesaler decides to order 40,000 staplers.
- The manufacturer fills the order and then bases its order decisions on the wholesaler's orders. To provide a buffer in case the wholesaler's next order is even higher, the manufacturer increases its production quantities to 50,000 for the next month.

These decisions are made based on incomplete information. As you can see, even if the retailer orders exactly the same number of staplers the next month, the wholesaler and the manufacturer will have excess inventories and unnecessary costs.

Mart transmits current retail needs directly to its suppliers. Armed with up-to-date information, suppliers ship the right quantities. When goods arrive at warehouses, they usually spend less than 12 hours in storage.[4] Warehouses, which receive satellite updates as well, have become cross-docking points where goods are redistributed among trucks based on the latest store needs. Wal-Mart's extensive use of IT in this way has led to its direct costs being 3 percent lower than the industry average and has made it an industry leader.

- **Speed.** By sharing demand and other information simultaneously throughout the supply chain, IT tools foster quicker deliveries. To accomplish next-day delivery of 2.5 million packages every day, FedEx workers use portable bar-code scanners to upload package information into a single database for monitoring and management. To put this task in perspective, in a little more than a week, FedEx handles more deliveries than the number of requisitions the Department of Defense handles in one year.[5]

FedEx's partnership with Proflowers.com shows how a single event triggers multiple actions. When a customer orders flowers through the Proflowers website, both FedEx and Proflowers receive the information instantaneously. FedEx responds by sending the Proflowers server a request for pickup and a shipping label, which is provided to a grower. By the time a FedEx truck arrives at the grower's site, a bouquet has been arranged, and the grower has affixed the shipping label to the package.[6]

- **Empowered decision making.** An outgrowth of advances in IT and use of the Internet is the development of an "Internet culture." Both Cisco Systems and the National Science Foundation have developed such a culture where employees throughout the organization are empowered to try out new ideas and welcome, rather than resist, change. The Internet provides easy access to senior managers. With better information received more quickly, everyone can make good decisions, and a flattened organizational structure supports informed risk taking.
- **Higher accuracy, increased productivity, and lower costs.** Cisco Systems' digitally integrated financial management system reduced the cost of finance as a percentage of revenue by 50 percent, increased productivity of the finance department by 90 percent, and improved the accuracy of financial data. These improvements have been driven by applications that provide different resources to different types of employees, including rapid employee expense reimbursement, sales commission reports, notices of problems with customer orders, and high-level performance metrics for executives.

Building on these characteristics of IT usage, *a new sense and respond concept of logistics* has emerged. This demand-focused idea centers on the people closest to the action. These are the people who have the most detailed understanding of need, whether they are in a hospital, at the scene of a disaster, or on the front lines of a battlefield. The sense and respond concept focuses on *flexibility* rather than planning, and *demand* rather than supply. The evolving theory includes using IT to enable small, individualized shipments to field personnel and final transshipments of goods between end users (e.g., military units). Some technologies—such as Internet portals (to be described in the next section) and Radio Frequency Identification (RFID)—that are needed to make this possible already exist. However, for this concept to play out (for example, taking individual packages that are assembled based on recently received messages and delivering them directly to soldiers and units dispersed on the ground in or near enemy territory), new approaches will need to be developed.[7]

How Integration Occurs

Enterprise integration occurs through electronic hubs that serve as either entryways to information or messaging systems that relay information. Portals, which reside on the Internet and allow users access to remotely managed information, are one tool for integration. Covisint, the U.S. Air Force, the defense medical logistics community, and the DoD EMALL all use portals to integrate segments of their respective supply chains.

Figure 3.3 shows how combining customer-focused portals with supplier portals can create enterprise integration. Such electronic system integration, which spreads customer demand information evenly throughout the supply chain, enables all firms, including those that are the farthest upstream, to make decisions based on end-customer input. This removes the bullwhip effect, opening the potential for huge savings. Cisco Systems, for example, has saved $560 million per year by using an Internet portal for more than half of its orders.[8] It ties its customer interface into an integrated electronic supplier network that receives automatic notices when orders differ from forecasts.

The 1999 Defense Authorization Act directed the development of a single electronic window for defense purchases and suppliers' inventories. The Air Force is developing such a pilot portal that provides end-to-end visibility of supply chain activities. The initial Air Force demonstration of the B-1 bomber's F-101 gas turbine engine includes data on spare parts, maintenance, repair, and use. The Air Force portal's designers intend to simplify decision-making tools through user-friendly interfaces and enhance supply chain performance through real-time data and collaboration.[9]

Cat Logistics accomplishes the integration effects of a portal through its Enterprise Application Integration (EAI) gateway. This electronic architecture translates between systems that use different languages. The EAI gateway makes external and internal applications visible to each other and integrates with commercial off-the-shelf software. Still, some legacy systems need to be replaced before organizations can achieve full interoperability with the Cat Logistics EAI and other members of their supply chains.

The EAI is an application of middleware. This type of programming serves to integrate separate IT systems that would not otherwise be able to communicate. This benefit is essential for many supply chain integration efforts. Separate enterprises, and even different departments within a single organization, will often use different software packages. Figure 3.4 shows how middleware can facilitate linkages between diverse enterprises and a portal.

Figure 3.3: Real-Time Supply Chain[10]

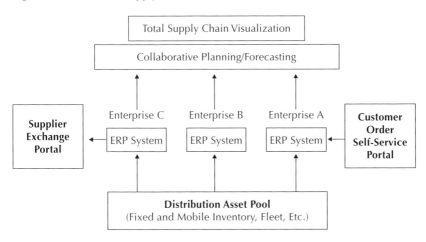

An order placed through the Customer Order Portal activates a series of order fulfillment activities. Real-time inventory fluctuations across the Supply Chain are recorded in the collaborative planning layer, and reorders of necessary supplies, parts, and components are automatically submitted to multiple suppliers through the Supplier Exchange.

Figure 3.4: Portal-Based Architecture[11]

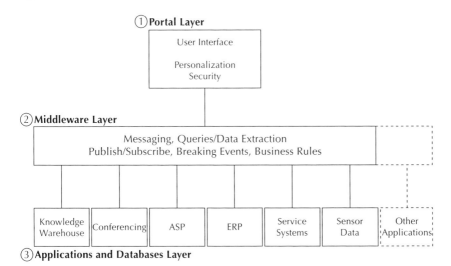

Integrating Procurement, Finance, and Logistics

Despite overlapping objectives and synergistic processes, procurement, finance, and logistics have often been managed as unrelated functions. When digitally integrated, however, these areas lead to much higher performance levels as well as lower costs. Digital integration provides quick and accurate data that managers can use for routine and strategic decision making. Integrating online purchases with delivery tracking and invoices creates a thorough and easily accessed audit trail. Purchase information that is automatically provided to logistics managers enables better inventory planning. Connected financial management and procurement systems allow procurement managers to review timely available balance and payment information and make ordering decisions accordingly. Resulting performance increases include higher system availability, lower inventory levels, faster deliveries, and lower administrative burdens. Simultaneously, inventory holding, administrative, and transaction costs decrease.

Some innovative organizations that have automated their logistics, procurement, and finance functions illustrate these outcomes. Figure 3.5 depicts how these different areas affect each other.

Figure 3.5: Effects of Financial Management, Procurement, and Supply Chain Management Issues on Each Other[12]

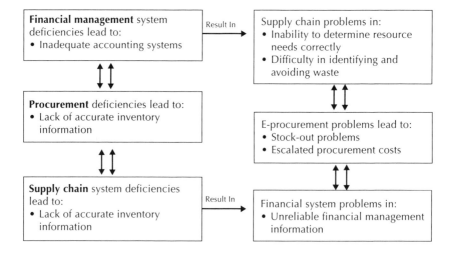

Using IT for Better Procurement

The case for e-procurement lies in its impact. Although it may be intuitive that automating paper-based processes would improve performance, results back up that assumption. After implementing e-procurement practices, organizations have reduced inventories 25 to 60 percent, raised delivery performance 15 to 30 percent, and increased productivity 10 to 16 percent.[13] In terms of cost, federal and state governments together spend approximately $550 billion annually on procurement from private companies.[14] Consequently, procurement is an area where efficiencies could result in tremendous savings. General Electric, for example, saved more than $400 million in the first six months of its "e-Buy" initiative.[15]

Procurement tools proliferate. Covisint uses electronic request for quotes, online auctions, and online catalogs. The defense medical logistics community uses some of these tools as well as web-based billing and payments and business intelligence software. The DoD EMALL portal is set up to give the user the impression of viewing one consolidated product source. However, suppliers maintain their own product information for individual catalogs.

As with the DoD EMALL, the Defense Medical Logistics Standard Support, or DMLSS, provides online catalogs and the capability for end-user ordering and credit card payments. With DMLSS, buyers receive additional savings beyond the immediate benefits of shifting from manual to electronic processes. The IT tools track activity, and cumulative purchases result in discounts. An online trading exchange that provides suppliers and federal customers with product and price information cuts the request-for-quote (RFQ)-to-procurement cycle time from days to minutes. Savings from DMLSS web functionality alone have surpassed $8 million.[16]

Automating medical logistics through DMLSS cut order and delivery times and inventory levels. Procurement times dropped from up to 45 days to two days or less, medical inventory levels were slashed by up to 85 percent, and the fill rate increased to 95 percent within 24 hours. With its advanced system, the defense medical logistics community saved more than $1.253 billion from 1996 to 2000 (see chapter fourteen, the DMLSS case study).

The use of IT speeds up processes and lowers costs for all purchases but can be particularly helpful for out-of-the-ordinary buys. One-third of corporate purchases deviate from normal contracting practices. On average, these purchases cost 18 to 27 percent more than volume buys.[17] Consequently, advances in this area could return large savings.

The benefits of these savings go beyond good business practices. The defense medical logistics reforms demonstrate in a poignant way how e-procurement can deliver outcomes. As a direct consequence of process automation, medical workers now spend less time on logistics and have more time to care for the 8 million personnel and retirees who rely on the military health care system. It would be difficult to quantify the savings in lives and improved health.

Importance of Integrating the Finance Function

Just as implementing e-procurement processes causes agencies to be more effective in their mission areas, so does implementing e-finance initiatives. The National Science Foundation was motivated to implement an integrated, electronic financial management system by the desire to improve its core function: grant making. Its new financial accounting system communicates with a customer-focused website and helps the agency award, issue, and monitor its grants electronically. Grantees can log in to an agency website and use a personal identification number (PIN) to access their accounts and request electronic funds transfers. As a result of the automated systems, grants are available within 48 hours of awards. Prior to the integrated electronic system, grantees might have been forced to wait two to three months for authorization to spend funds (see chapter twelve, the NSF case study).

When automated financial accounting systems are integrated into logistics and procurement systems, they provide decision makers with daily financial, procurement, operations, and logistics information. With this degree of integration, placing an order online, for example, creates a financial obligation that is automatically uploaded to the financial management system. Payment on the procurement side and recording of an expenditure on the financial management side happen seamlessly without paperwork and other manual processes. In addition to ordering, billing, and payment processes, electronic applications can also tie together cost, inventory levels, cash levels, and production plans.

The NSF system saves time and money by eliminating multiple data-entry repetition. Data entry occurs once, and relevant information populates throughout the finance, grants management, and human resources systems. Even end users are incorporated into the system. Grantees use an electronic template to prepare expense reports, and these are automatically uploaded to the financial accounting system to record expenses. The greater the degree of IT integration, the less data reconciliation is needed. NSF's strategy is to have complete integration, where no reconciliation is needed.

By maintaining one IT system with data that is useful throughout an organization, logistics, procurement, finance, operations, and line personnel, as well as senior managers, make decisions based on the same information. With some firewalls and security protections in place, external members of the same supply chain also use the data. Cost and time savings result. Through its financial management system and a high level of internal and external integration, Cisco achieved its goals of closing its books in one day and decreasing finance administrative costs by 50 percent (see chapter ten, the Cisco Systems case study).

While the cost, time, and decision-making benefits of integrating finance functions into an overall IT system seem evident, finance can be an after-thought when organizations implement logistics systems. At one of GE's jet engine maintenance facilities, critical parts are tagged for tracking to monitor their location and progress through the facility. The parts are scanned and their status is recorded in an automated system. Even with this high-technology logistics system, GE still has a separate financial system. So, factory employees maintain a paper log with data that is later entered into an automated accounting system. The delays that this manual process causes hit the corporate bottom line.

In implementing integrated financial management systems, the degree of customization for each user group must be balanced against the benefits of standardization. With its financial management system, Cisco initially erred on the side of customization and began to have trouble implementing system upgrades. It now aims to maintain one back-end system that accommodates some personalization without hindering the ability to upgrade software. Some language compromises also needed to be reached. The sales, manufacturing, and accounting groups defined certain terms differently. For the integrated financial system to be useful company-wide, senior management determined common meanings for terms, including "bookings" and "backlogs."

Cisco was small enough to insist on implementing standardization. By contrast, Boeing (especially after a series of major corporate acquisitions) found it far more effective to allow large operating entities to utilize whatever financial system they found most effective. Headquarters simply stated what corporate financial data they required and in what format. As long as the operating entities could generate that data, they did not have to go back and make major changes to their individual systems just for the sake of standardization. Thus, the important issue is interoperability—not standardization.

In addition to enhancing usefulness and facilitating upgrades, IT integration standards provide the means for internal and external linkages. IT software standards throughout NSF enabled the financial management system to span functional areas, including grant making and human resources. In instances where several agencies want to integrate their IT systems, it is not necessary for each enterprise to use common software. Again, each organization must develop the ability to interface with others using a linking mechanism such as middleware or a portal connection. Interoperability is the critical issue.

Summary

IT has played a pivotal role in enterprise integration and new supply chain management practices. The following lessons summarize the logistics advances IT has made possible.

- In paper-based, non-cooperative supply chains, demand forecasting tends to be more accurate the closer entities are to the consumer. Using digital integration to share information with supply chain partners benefits the supply chain as a whole and negates this "bullwhip effect."
- Common IT systems are not necessary for digital integration; interoperable systems are. Middleware and portals make different IT programs interoperable and enable integration across geographic and organizational boundaries. COTS applications are often needed to interface with middleware and portals.
- Digitally integrating procurement, finance, and logistics functions—often considered unrelated areas—results in significant performance improvements and cost reductions.

Chapter four describes the latest technologies to modernize logistics, further exploring many of the concepts introduced in this chapter, and discusses additional tools for executing supply chain management at world-class levels.

Endnotes

1. David Simchi-Levi, Philip Kaminsky, and Edith Simchi-Levi, *Designing and Managing the Supply Chain*. Boston: Irwin McGraw-Hill, 2000.

2. To determine the order-up-to point, supply planners use the average (AVG) and standard deviation (STD) of daily or weekly customer demand, lead times (L), and a constant (k). Planners select the constant k from statistical tables to equate the probability of stock-outs during lead time with a desired level of service. The formula for calculating order-up-to points is: $L * AVG + k * STD * \sqrt{L}$. [* = multiplication sign] For a more detailed explanation of why small changes in lead times can have significant effects on order levels, see Simchi-Levi, pp. 86-88.

3. Douglas Lambert, J. Stock, and L. Ellram *Fundamentals of Logistics Management*. Boston: Irwin McGraw-Hill, 1998.

4. Simchi-Levi, Kaminsky, and Simchi-Levi.

5. DoD processes approximately 18 million requisitions per year: from Jacques S. Gansler, "Diffusing Netcentricity in DoD: The Supply Chain (An Example Case)," a presentation, April 23, 2002.

6. Sandor Boyson and Thomas Corsi, "The Real-Time Supply Chain," *Supply Chain Management Review,* January/February 2001.

7. Captain Linda Lewandowski and Jeffrey Cares, Department of Defense Office of Force Transformation, *Sense and Respond Logistics: Turning Supply Chains into Demand Networks*, December 20, 2002. (unpublished).

8. Boyson and Corsi.

9. The Center for Public Policy and Private Enterprise, University of Maryland. *Moving Toward an Effective Public-Private Partnership for the DoD Supply Chain,* June 2002.

10. Sandor Boyson and Thomas Corsi, "Managing the Real-Time Supply Chain," Proceedings of the 35th Annual Hawaii International Conference on System Science (HICSS-35'02), 2002.

11. The Center for Public Policy and Private Enterprise, University of Maryland. *Moving Toward an Effective Public-Private Partnership for the DoD Supply Chain.*

12. Jacques S. Gansler, William Lucyshyn, and Kimberly Ross, "Digitally Integrating the Government Supply Chain: E-Procurement, E-Finance, and E-Logistics," IBM Center for The Business of Government, February 2003.

13. B. Trebilcock, "Planning for Supply Chain Success," *Modern Materials Handling,* May 1, 2001.

14. M. Symonds "The Next Revolution," *The Economist,* June 24, 2000.

15. Mark Stonich, "GE Brings E-Procurement to Life," *PRTM Insight,* Summer/Fall 2001, Vol. 13, No. 2, 37.

16. From chapter fourteen, the DMLSS case study.

17. Gansler, Lucyshyn, and Ross.

CHAPTER FOUR

Supply Chain Tools

Jacques S. Gansler
Robert E. Luby, Jr.
William Lucyshyn

Early Evolution

Introduction

The revolution in information and communications technologies has enabled organizations to automate and integrate their supply chains—resulting in improved performance and reduced costs. While this transformation really took off during the last decade, one of the earliest applications of computers was to automate simple business applications in the federal government in the mid-1950s—systems that were being used for supply, logistics, and financial management operations. Even these early uses were efforts to integrate the supply transaction reporting system with the financial accounting systems. The adoption of these first supply chain tools enabled a degree of automation, higher accuracy in reporting, improvements in management control, and a limited consolidation of data. The increased accuracy of data, albeit in separate reports, saved managers' (as well as auditors') time by not having to check the data repeatedly—resulting in more time to devote to other strategic tasks. Even the adoption of these rudimentary "tools" and early efforts at automating logistics processes resulted in millions of dollars in savings.[1]

During the 1980s, the increased capabilities of information systems coupled with the pressures of global competition forced organizations to examine their supply chain performance. In this new environment, companies became more specialized and fewer companies were vertically integrated; companies searched for suppliers that could reliably provide low-cost, quality materials and then formed strategic partnerships and alliances with them. The market responded by developing increasingly complex systems to plan for and manage these multifaceted relationships.

The true automation of supply chains began in the 1960s with the development of Electronic Data Interchange (EDI). EDI created standard formats and processes so that companies could trade and track business documents, such as purchase orders, invoices, payments, shipping manifests, and delivery schedules. These documents were translated into a universally understood language and then transmitted on dedicated communication links to the trading partners. As these processes matured, standards were developed to formalize EDI, emphasizing security and reliability. There was also a move away from the limiting proprietary communications protocols to a ubiquitous standard called ANSI X-12. This combination of standard formats and communications protocols produced the EDI system still in use today.[2]

There were many benefits to be gained from streamlining an organization's interactions with its trading partners. First, firms benefited from significant cost savings that resulted from automating their records-intensive processes. This increased flow of information resulted in decreased inventories, improved forecasting, and decreased shipping costs. By eliminating much of the paper from their transactions, transaction costs and errors were reduced by orders of magnitude. Organizations also benefited from the increased security that was gained from transmitting proprietary company data on dedicated communications links. These benefits resulted in improved performance and increased customer satisfaction, as well as reduced costs.[3]

Model the Processes

When an organization decides it wants to implement or upgrade its supply chain management, it must first select a disciplined, methodical framework to analyze its supply chain. The SCOR (Supply-Chain Operations Reference) model, developed in 1996 by the not-for-profit Supply Chain Council to improve communications among supply chain partners, provides one such approach. This model provides a detailed step-by-step method to identify, evaluate, and optimize supply chains by helping organizations to identify and map the "as-is" state of a process in order to achieve the desired "to-be" future state. Additionally, it allows organizations to establish goals based on "best-in-class" results in similar companies.[4] Organizations implementing this model are able to better understand how the processes of one organization affect the processes of the next organization. The model can also be used to understand how information supports or does not support existing or planned logistics processes. It is capable of handling a wide range of size and complexity, and in addition to being used by some of the best-known and best-run companies in the world, this model was also adopted for use by the Department of Defense.[5]

The SCOR model is based on five distinct management processes: plan, source, make, deliver, and return. The objective is to integrate horizontal processes to balance the multiple links of a supply chain—when balanced, manufacturers produce at the same rate that customers consume. Although not a new concept, this model allows companies to effectively use common terminology, identified process categories, and performance metrics to decompose processes so they can be integrated vertically as well. This ability to "drill down" enables organizations to identify supply chain problems that obstruct information and material flow.[6]

The model contains three levels of process detail. Level 1 provides the definition of the scope and content for the SCOR model. Here organizations set their targets for competitive performance. At Level 2, an organization can select from 30 core "process categories" that are possible components of a supply chain to implement their operations strategy. Organizations can

Figure 4.1: The SCOR Model

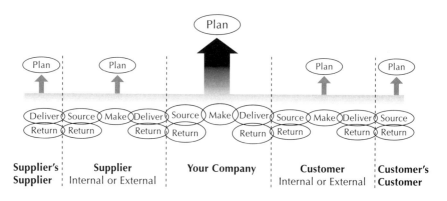

fine-tune their operations strategy at Level 3 by defining process elements as well as their inputs and outputs and identifying the appropriate performance metrics, best practices, and required system capabilities. At Level 4, organizations focus on specific implementation performance metrics, which would be specific for each company and therefore not in the scope of the model.[7]

Integration, Collaboration, and Decision Support

Supply chain automation and integration really took off with advances in information technology, the key enabler to supply chain management strategy. The explosive growth of the Internet accelerated the move of these strategies to reality. Although computers and the Internet did not directly cause supply chain innovation, they have accelerated the process by enabling rapid communications, especially the transfer of large amounts of digital data between organizations. According to IBM Research, advances in information technologies and the Internet have had a huge impact on the design of supply chains including:[8]

- Customers becoming more informed and demanding
- Business processes shifting toward greater collaboration between companies and their partners, customers, and employees
- Communications speeding orders through the supply chain at incredible rates, in addition to improving business performance based on real-time business and market intelligence

- The drive for a rapid turnover of products; increased flexibility in choosing suppliers and customers
- The opportunity to optimize globally across geographies, plant shipping costs, labor, tariffs, processes, and customers

The following tools, now reasonably mature, were developed and implemented to take advantage of the new technologies and capabilities, with often dramatic results.

Enterprise Resource Planning

Enterprise Resource Planning (ERP) software has its heritage in Europe, where the German company SAP released its mainframe program that integrated financial and operational data into a single database in the early 1990s. This initial program was soon upgraded and modified to run on a client-server application; the rest is history. By the first year of the new millennium, 15,000 companies in 120 countries were operating 36,000 installations of SAP's ERP software, and many other companies were supplying ERP software.[9]

The goal of ERP software is to integrate business processes across an enterprise. Instead of sales, operations, finance, and human resources all operating their own stand-alone computer systems, they would all use one common system with integrated modules to perform their required functions. Many benefits accrue from implementing an ERP system. The first is the elimination of redundant tasks—in many cases, data now have to be entered only once, with the expected benefit of reducing errors. The availability of current data across the enterprise increases effectiveness and efficiency, eventually producing considerable cost savings. Finally, the enterprise should improve its performance, resulting in increased customer satisfaction. These ERP systems have become very popular, due in large measure to the trends in globalization, short product life cycles, and uncertain markets. Seventy percent of the Fortune 1000 have or soon will have an ERP system, and vendors are expected to market these more aggressively to smaller companies.[10]

When an order is taken with an ERP implementation, it is typed directly into the enterprise system. The sales representative can view the customer's credit rating, manufacturing immediately gets the order, and finance is able to track the order and see when it is shipped. There are no more delays generated by orders sitting in in-boxes, waiting to be typed and/or faxed. Now, instead of the situation that frequently occurred—a customer inquires about an order and no one has the current status—the ERP system allows everyone involved to have access to current information and to be able to provide accurate responses to customer queries.

The decision to transition to an ERP system is not without costs. The systems are expensive and can be time-consuming to implement (see Table 4.1). There are also many hidden costs involved in transitioning to an ERP system, which often takes longer and costs more than planned.[11]

- The cost of training is almost always underestimated. Although enterprise employees are experienced, many of the internal processes will have been changed and will have to be learned along with the new software interfaces.

- Integration and testing of the ERP software with any of the legacy systems that need to be interfaced or with custom modules that have been added takes more effort than usually anticipated.

- Customization of the "core" ERP software is not only costly the first time, but also is an issue with every software upgrade.

- Data conversion of legacy databases—such as customer and supplier records and product design data—which must be combined with the ERP application, is always a double effort. The enterprise must first "clean up" the data and then convert it.

- Human resource impacts extend, in many cases, to replacing the talented team responsible for ERP development and implementation. Once they are experienced with the system, they are often recruited for higher-paying jobs in other organizations.

- The return on investment is generally not immediate and, in most cases, takes longer than planned.

In spite of the challenges to implementing ERP, the prospects for the continued growth in its use, although at a lower rate than previously believed, are still high. ERP developers will continue to increase its functionality to include capabilities of other niche software, such as customer relationship management and advance demand planning.[13]

Table 4.1: ERP Implementation[12]

Business Size (Revenue)	Average Project Cost	Average Project Duration
Less than $100 million	$3.1 million	15.9 months
$100 million to $499 million	$3.6 million	20.6 months
$500 million to $999 million	$13.1 million	27.1 months
$1 billion to $4.9 billion	$16.8 million	30.2 months

Enterprise Application Integration

If one were designing a large enterprise from scratch, the goal would be to have all the data reside on a single database. There would be no duplication, and there would be no need for integration or system interfaces. The reality for most organizations is very different; they generally have legacy applications and databases. Additionally, different departments such as finance, human resources, and manufacturing, as well as their partners and customers, may have implemented various enterprise applications that need information from other parts of the enterprise. These various applications may have dedicated modules and interfaces to go and grab the data they need, but this can hardly be referred to as an integrated system.

Enterprise Application Integration (EAI) software (sometimes referred to as "middleware") enables an organization to link different applications and databases—these can be both commercial off-the-shelf software and internally developed—into a cohesive system. Introduced in the mid-1990s, EAI allows the sharing of both data and processes across the enterprise and could be expanded to include business partners and customers.

EAI can be implemented in place of an ERP system or can incorporate ERP, serving to connect multiple, different ERP systems. By using existing applications, this can be achieved with lower costs and less programming than in the past, where this was accomplished by rewriting the software on both systems. EAI middleware serves as an integration layer that can act as a bridge between the various applications rather than through point-to-

Figure 4.2: EAI Middleware

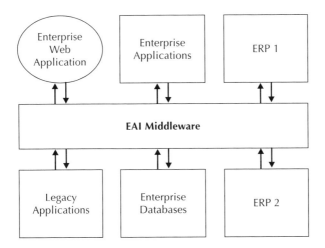

point[14] integration.[15] EAI integration is still not a trivial task; it involves systems that operate on different platforms, with different operating systems, and often with a broad range of incompatibilities.

EAI can provide an organization with permanent middleware that can manage the flow of data between an ERP system (or multiple ERP systems) and legacy and other systems. It also reduces the cost of future software upgrades. This cost reduction is possible because the developer needs to change only the interface to the EAI; the organization does not have to worry about modifying its other applications or databases.[16] When undertaken independently of an ERP implementation, an EAI generally can be completed in less time. Moreover, introducing an ERP will force the adoption of standard business processes and a centralized business strategy and will lock the company into a single (monopoly) supplier. EAI, on the other hand, can accommodate a variety of processes and a decentralized business strategy.

Web-Based Portals

Most readers are familiar with portals, even if they don't know them as such. Yahoo!, Excite, and Google are public Internet portals that address the entire Internet. In general terms, web-based portals serve as centralized points of entry to a large variety of content and applications from a variety of internal or external sources. Those relevant to supply chain management are normally organized around a specific business (corporate or enterprise portals) or industry. The corporate or enterprise intranet portals are designed for use by employees to improve access to and the sharing of information internally across the enterprise. Extended enterprise portals widen the reach of the enterprise to its customers via the Internet for a variety of purposes such as ordering, billing, customer service, and self-service.[17] A familiar example is the United Parcel Service's (UPS) portal that enables customers to view the internal tracking status of their packages using UPS tracking numbers. Another type of portal is an e-marketplace portal designed to conduct business-to-business (B2B) transactions of supplies and materials.

Web-based portals are altering the way employees work and business is conducted. They allow an organization to present a single, consistent view of its business to its employees, customers, suppliers, partners, and visitors. Users can personalize their interface, filtering out unneeded information and applications and reducing information overload. Portals can also provide an inexpensive way to integrate across an enterprise, enhancing collaboration and improving interoperability and, as a result, increasing productivity. Finally, they can significantly reduce the cost of disseminating and sharing content and applications across the enterprise.[18]

Organizations that have deployed portals are seeing significant benefits. The insurance giant CIGNA, for example, has deployed its customer-facing portal, called myCIGNA, and views it as an unqualified success. The portal now handles 6,000 users a day, and more than 2,000 new users register each day. Customers can access many services—from managing their insurance plans to reviewing medical claims, ordering medications, and receiving personalized health news. As a result, 83 percent of CIGNA customers believe the portal is a valuable benefit. Moreover, the portal also adds significantly to the bottom line: Costs of a typical call-center transaction run between $3 and $7, while online transactions run between $0.05 and $0.15, and the company saves $9 million from publishing directories and handbooks online instead of in print—significant gains not previously thought possible.[19] Such results and benefits are bolstering the trend toward portal deployment. The Department of Defense is incrementally implementing a similar capability with its Tricare Online portal, which targets 8.7 million beneficiaries and 140,000 health care providers in 50 states and 80 countries.[20]

EDI for the Internet

Since EDI requires a significant investment, not only for the software but also for the communication links and the time and expertise to implement it, its use has generally been restricted to larger companies with established trading partners. Even though the potential savings are significant (in 1999 Gartner estimated the cost to process an EDI purchase order was $2.50, as opposed to $50 for a paper-based purchase order[21]), many small and medium size companies have continued to use more traditional means such as phones, fax, and mail to communicate with their trading partners. The cost of maintaining the EDI-required value-added-networks (VAN) is not insignificant even for large companies, as VANs charge by the byte for each EDI message.

The ubiquitous Internet, on the other hand, offers an attractive alternative. Organizations can connect to the Internet for a modest fee, without additional per message charges. And, the Internet offers global connectivity where partners can dynamically link, even though there was no prior business relationship. In September 2002, Wal-Mart decided to transition its EDI transactions from VANs to the Internet. Although this has been technically possible for years, in the past it meant that both the company and its partners would have to load the same software. Two developments have increased the utility. First, the adoption of an EDI Internet Integration Applicability Statement 2 (AS2) protocol provides a data compression standard for better performance, coupled with certificate-based encryption for security. The second development is the interoperability testing of AS2 products by the

Uniform Code Council Inc. This means organizations can buy a certified software package and be confident that it will work with its partners' systems—as long as they also buy certified products.[22]

The Next Wave

In today's competitive environment with global corporations and distributed operations, a single enterprise alone cannot provide the best value to its customers; rather, the whole supply chain, with all of the extended partners, must be considered. The goal then becomes to optimize the entire supply chain, not just individual elements, because optimizing single elements may sub-optimize the whole. And, for these enterprises to remain world class, this process must be one of continual evaluation and improvement. For that reason, although there has been much progress, there are continued efforts to develop technologies and processes to further these improvements. The following are a summary of the most promising that are now being developed and tested in pilot studies and should be widely implemented in the near future.

Extensible Markup Language (XML)

Extensible Markup Language (XML) is a non-proprietary data interchange standard developed in 1996. XML complements rather than replaces Hypertext Markup Language (HTML) used extensively on the World Wide Web. It can be used to create or transform documents containing data in a structured format, so that they can be exchanged on the web. Although technically not a language but a meta-language, it can be used to define these formats. When these "metadata tags" are defined and agreed to, anyone can read a message that contains the tags and data sent using the accepted standard.[23]

XML can provide another alternative to EDI, one that will allow many supply chain interactions to take place on the Internet. Some of the standards, such as specifications for tagging and displaying, have been largely developed and agreed to. Other standards, such as identifying potential business partners, exchanging precise information about the nature of proposed transactions, and executing agreed-upon transactions in a legally binding manner, are still being developed.[24] As a consequence, acceptance is still guarded—44 percent of respondents to a recent survey plan to remain on the sidelines for now, and 54 percent believed the transition to this new technology was still too expensive.[25]

Remote Tracking

A critical element of any supply chain is knowing what you have and where it is. This appears to be a fairly straightforward problem; but when you consider that large organizations can have millions of items in hundreds of different locations, the complexity can increase quickly. Remote tracking technologies can help to address this problem. Familiar applications of this technology (for example, e-payment) are making human toll collectors a thing of the past, as more and more people attach "smart passes" to their windshields, allowing them to quickly pass through electronic tollbooths. ExxonMobil's Speedpass, used to buy gas, is another similar application.

The basic Radio Frequency Identification (RFID) technology consists of three components: an antenna or coil, a transceiver with a decoder, and a transponder (commonly called an RF tag). The transponder can be electronically programmed with unique information. RFID transponders have a significant advantage over bar codes, which must be optically scanned to be read, and the RFID transponder can contain more information (such as individual item serial numbers, date codes, manufacturing location, and other supply chain information).

Although the concept has been around for decades, the use of RFID technology was restricted because of the cost of the tags, which ranged from $1 to $20. As a result, RFID technology traditionally has been used to help track high-value parts through a facility or to track parts that are being distributed to customers. General Electric, for example, uses these tags on their service contracts to better track replacement parts and to determine what parts they have available. Improved tracking results in lower inventory and lower distribution costs for GE. RFID technology has also been used in the supply chain to track parts flow during maintenance procedures, providing a mechanism to monitor progress and the process (see chapter eight, the GE case study). However, the real potential of RFID technology extends beyond the immediate benefits afforded by examples like the payment or simple tracking function, and has the capability to instantaneously provide key information to multiple downstream business systems within the enterprise.

Based on research at the Massachusetts Institute of Technology, RFID tags are now approaching a price that could expand their use throughout the supply chain. Tag costs are projected to drop to as low as 5 cents for large-volume production. A big company such as Procter and Gamble could use over 2 billion chips a year if it fully implemented this concept. These tags could be used on virtually any item, including low-cost consumer goods. Home Depot says it could eventually put these tags on all 50,000 products it sells—providing real-time inventory.

As previously noted, Desert Storm was a great victory, but in preparation, mountains of equipment were shipped to Kuwait. Countless unopened shipping containers and 90 percent of the ammunition were returned. Tracking what was shipped and where it was located was still primarily a manual process. In contrast, for the recent conflict with Iraq, the Department of Defense insisted that all shipping containers moving to deploy and resupply U.S. forces be equipped with an RFID tag. The tags are coded with the contents, and as a consequence, cargo does not sit around as long as it once did, since users have faster access to the information they need to move it.[26]

The National Aeronautics and Space Administration is advancing this technology by developing a "sprayable" RFID tag, which should be commercially available in three to five years. It could, for example, be sprayed on components to monitor them during assembly, and then later to help service those parts in the field.[27] RFID tags provide a tracking solution that works at short ranges; for longer ranges (transportation and distribution), other technologies are available.

Global Positioning System (GPS) technology used in conjunction with a communication network (such as a dedicated UHF/VHF radio, a satellite network, or wireless) can be used to track trucks, trailers, ships, or shipping containers, with an accuracy of 10 to 20 meters as they travel worldwide. The GPS receiver, which calculates the position, heading, and speed of the object, is installed in the vehicle and then communicates that information to the base station. This level of tracking information is critical in today's "just-in-time" supply chain world.

Recent improvements, based on technology developed by the Defense Advanced Research Projects Agency (DARPA), have improved on the GPS tracking systems. Known as Global Locating Systems (GLS), this technology performs the positioning calculation centrally and eliminates the need to have a GPS receiver on the vehicle, significantly reducing costs and power requirements. This service, launched by the private company SkyBitz, is initially available only in North America.[28]

These technologies will allow organizations to have greater visibility into their supply chains all the way down to individual products. Greater visibility provides the ability to simultaneously know when a product was manufactured, where it was received, and where it is currently located. Organizations will then be able to manipulate this data and share it, as appropriate, across the enterprise.

Collaborative Planning, Forecasting, and Replenishment (CPFR)

Imagine the difficulty of coordinating a promotional sale at a retail store. Projecting and coordinating sales between product manufacturers, company sales reps, and store managers is a difficult task. This was a real problem for Ace Hardware, where shoppers anticipating a great bargain were often greeted by an empty shelf. To resolve the problem, Ace implemented a model already in use by other large retailers, known as Collaborative Planning, Forecasting, and Replenishment (CPFR).[29]

Effective collaboration between both internal and external organizations is crucial to the successful implementation of an integrated supply chain. Without effective collaboration, the flow of information can be distorted (the bullwhip effect), resulting in surpluses for the supplier or shortages at the retail level. A recent survey indicated that there are more than $1 trillion worth of finished goods in inventory in stores, distribution centers, and manufacturing plants in the United States alone. Increased visibility and collaboration could obviate the need for much of this inventory.[30]

A recent development, CPFR software builds on the ideas behind EDI and ERP, and is being adopted as a way to integrate all members of the supply chain to optimize information sharing, including distribution and retail activities. The objective of CPFR is to determine retail-level demand forecasts, share that information with enterprise partners, and synchronize replenishment and production plans throughout the supply chain— getting everyone, from internal departments to external partners, on the same page. Although this collaboration can be done with EDI and e-mail, CPFR systems are Internet-based and require extensive process and technology reengineering. Effectively, CPFR is viewed as a replacement for EDI.[31]

There has been continuing evolution since Wal-Mart conducted its initial pilot study of the collaborative forecasting model in 1996, known at that time as collaboration, forecasting, and replenishment (CFAR). During this limited study, done with supply chain partner Warner Lambert, Wal-Mart was able to cut weeks of inventory out of the Listerine supply chain.[32] The current CPFR model emphasizes collaboration of production and purchase planning, demand forecasting, and inventory replenishment from Tier 3 vendors through fabrication and assembly, distribution, and finally the retailer. Although only data from pilot projects is available, the benefits are anticipated to be significant. From the retailer's perspective, it is anticipated that there will be higher in-stock levels, faster order response times, and lower product inventories, with the added benefit of less obsolescence and deterioration. The manufacturer is anticipated to have higher fill rates for orders, lower product inventories, faster cycle times, and reduced capacity requirements. And, finally, from a supply chain perspective, there is expected to be a reduced number of stocking points, improved forecast accuracy, and a lower system expense.[33]

Remote Monitoring and Diagnosis

Using available information technology, sophisticated algorithms, and the Internet, high-value equipment and machinery can be monitored around the clock from virtually anywhere. Plant owners are using this concept to decrease downtime and lower their operating costs. Software exists to monitor production lines at the machine level, and the data collected on individual machines will alert on-site engineers and operators when control limits are exceeded.[34] Manufacturers and service providers are using this concept to monitor high-value equipment, perform trend analysis, and then attempt to predict problems. They can improve customer satisfaction by minimizing equipment downtime, the subject of the GE case study in chapter eight.

Supply Chain Event Management[35]

Hiccups in the supply chain can escalate and cause serious repercussions that lead to unforeseen costs and ultimately to unsatisfied customers. In 2000, for example, there was a fire at a chip plant owned by a supplier for the mobile phone company Ericsson. The disruption in the supply of chips caused Ericsson to lose three market share points to its rival, Nokia. As a result, Ericsson was forced to leave the handset market. A set of recent technologies, dubbed supply chain event management by AMR research, have been developed to assist in managing these types of hiccups by simulating, monitoring, measuring, and controlling supply chain activities, and notifying management with real-time alert messages when there are problems or exceptions.[36]

Currently, most organizations do not manage the events in their supply chain—they react to them. These reactions are often ad hoc, and the results are often less than satisfactory. Organizations with, and those that aspire to have, world-class supply chains are always looking for ways to improve them. Two ways to make these improvements are to reduce the number of variables and to reduce the number of surprises that occur in the supply chain. That is the goal of Supply Chain Event Management (SCEM).

Information technology can provide a wealth of data, but the effect, in fact, may be to overload decision makers. A recent Teradata survey confirmed this trend.[37] One hundred and thirteen executives at U.S. companies with annual revenues exceeding $500 million were queried. A key finding was that decision makers are increasingly faced with greater amounts of data, more decisions to make, and less time to make them. The top three areas identified as being most at risk because of poor decision making were profits, revenue impact, and employee morale. Over two-thirds of the respondents also identified productivity, long-term growth, and customer loyalty as being at risk.

SCEM can help to bridge the gap between supply chain planning and execution. SCEM software will permit managers to not only see specific events in the supply chain in real time, but also alert them to the time-critical exceptions that cause havoc in the supply chain. Users will also be able to customize the SCEM software to monitor specific events such as purchase orders, demand forecasts, and advanced shipping notices, and then provide an alert anytime a predefined exception occurs.

The Adaptive Supply Chain: Sense-and-Respond

An adaptive supply chain will dynamically integrate demand and supply management with logistics and fulfillment, improving service and reducing cost across an extended enterprise. It can be thought of as a control system for large logistics problems where the objects in the system can automatically change their behaviors and characteristics if the object encounters conditions that warrant a change of behavior. These changes might include source, destination, route, and priority.

Supply chain event management software will become even more powerful when alerts for critical exceptions can be programmed to trigger a resolution response such as generating a request for quote (RFQ), initiating a competitive bidding event, or suggesting a solution to the individual alerted. In 2002, Gartner generalized this SCEM concept to cover event monitoring of most any business activity, coining the term Business Activity Management (BAM).[38]

Some industries, such as energy, telecommunications, and aerospace, already have some capability to monitor and react to changes in their environments. Their frequently occurring hiccups, such as a telecommunications network node or a power-generating plant dropping offline, are detected and resolved in real time. Recent technological advances in SCEM software, computational capability, adaptive agent technology, and RFID technology have made the extension of these capabilities to physical goods supply chains possible as well.[39]

As information can be sensed or shared when and where it is needed, it can be reacted to across the enterprise. To describe this concept, business strategists have borrowed a phrase from biologists, who describe organisms as having the capability to "sense-and-respond" to events that present a threat or an opportunity in their environment.[40] The concept of operating with a "sense-and-respond" (pull) philosophy, as opposed to the traditional "make-and-sell" (push) business management philosophy, will fundamentally change the way businesses operate and interact. Organizations will strive to transform their value chain[41] planning and execution into a sense-and-respond adaptive system—continually adapting and optimizing in real time based on customer needs and the competitive environment.[42]

Businesspeople will expect this optimization technology to produce fast, frequent, and accurate decisions. Information must be sensed, processed, and filtered quickly to provide the key parameters required by sense-and-respond optimization programs. The decisions produced by these programs must be quickly communicated to flexible and adaptive business processes. These decisions will often involve the allocation of scarce resources. In addition to improving overall performance, costs will be reduced when these resources can be better utilized. The challenge is to develop a system that can quickly detect and react to changes in inherently variable environmental factors, such as supply, demand, usage, and timing.

Let's examine how a sense-and-respond value chain may work. An alert is received from an order-tracking sensor at 9:43 a.m. indicating that orders for a company's products in a certain region have been significantly lower than planned in the last two weeks. At 9:45 a.m. the system generates an automatic inquiry and confirms an unexpected reduction in demand. An analysis of other regions is triggered. Soon the trend in decreasing demand is identified and quantified. The sense-and-respond system triggers alerts at

Table 4.2: Traditional Supply Chains vs. Adaptive Supply Chains[43]

	Traditional Supply Chains	Adaptive Supply Chains
Self-perception	• Deterministic "machines" with predictable inputs and outputs	• Complex adaptive systems with nonlinear behavior
Operational guidance provided by	• Long-term plans based on expected conditions	• Decisions made on-the-fly based on actual conditions
Organizational design supported	• Command and control • Centralized decision rights	• Risk-taking, entrepreneurial • Distributed decisions rights
Response time to unforeseen events	• Hours	• Seconds
Input for decision making	• Historical data	• Real-time data from execution systems and physical assets
Most of supply chain managers' time spent on	• Planning and anticipating • Fulfilling preset targets	• Experimenting and learning • Revising assumptions

9:55 a.m. to the sales manager and the supply chain manager. At that time, the action is taken to identify all excess inventory. The sense-and-respond system then automatically generates new proposed schedules for procurement, production, and promotional sales. Managers can review, modify, and approve the plan. The affected suppliers are notified and, finally, at 10:30 a.m. the excess inventory is sold through special promotions at the company's marketplaces.[44]

Although the full sense-and-respond capability is still a few years away, the vision is clear. As the emerging technologies are developed, the full potential of this strategy can be achieved.

Summary

In today's competitive environment, a single organization alone cannot provide the best value to its customers; rather, the whole supply chain, with all of the extended partners, must be considered. The goal then becomes to optimize the entire supply chain, not just individual elements. Although there have been many tools developed to achieve that goal, the effort to develop better tools and processes continues. This chapter summarizes the background and status of the most important supply chain tools, and then examines emerging supply chain tools and technologies and their impact on the supply chain. Key points include:

- The true automation of supply chains began in the 1960s with the development of Electronic Data Interchange, allowing companies to trade purchase orders, invoices, and other business documents. During the 1980s, increased global competition coupled with advancements in information technologies forced companies to examine and look for ways to improve their supply chain performance. When an organization decides to upgrade its supply chain management, the first step is to analyze its supply chain using a methodical framework such as the SCOR model.
- Organizations implement ERP software to integrate business processes across an enterprise. Instead of sales, operations, finance, and human resources all operating their own stand-alone computer systems, they would all use one common system—eliminating redundant tasks, increasing effectiveness, improving performance, and eventually producing considerable cost savings.
- Enterprise Application Integration software enables an organization to link different applications and databases into a cohesive system.
- A web-based portal allows an organization to present a single, consistent view of its business to its employees, customers, suppliers, partners, and visitors. Users can personalize their interface, filtering out unneeded information and applications and reducing information overload.

- EDI for the Internet offers an attractive alternative to EDI transactions, which must be conducted exclusively over expensive VANs.
- Extensible Markup Language is a non-proprietary data interchange standard developed to create or transform documents containing data in a structured format so that they can be exchanged on the web. It provides another alternative to EDI.
- Radio Frequency Identification technologies can help organizations track what they have and where it is. As this technology becomes less expensive to implement, enterprises will be able to use it throughout the supply chain to improve information flow and reduce inventory and distribution costs.
- CPFR software builds on the ideas behind EDI and ERP and increases the collaboration between an enterprise's internal and external organizations. Effective collaboration can reduce inventories and minimize the bullwhip effect.
- Information technology can provide a wealth of data, but can easily overload decision makers. SCEM can help managers to not only see specific events in the supply chain in real time, but also alert them to the time-critical exceptions that cause havoc in the supply chain. SCEM can be customized to monitor specific events such as purchase orders, demand forecasts, and advanced shipping notices, and then provide an alert anytime a predefined exception occurs.
- The ultimate vision is to create an adaptive supply network capability to monitor an enterprise's supply chain and automatically trigger a resolution response, in an effort to continually optimize the supply chain.

The next chapter complements chapter two, which presented barriers to change in government supply chain management and areas for improvement. It explains how to overcome the barriers described and how to move in a strategic way toward government-wide transformation.

Endnotes

1. "Survey of Progress and Trend of Development and Use of Automatic Data Processing in Business and Management Control Systems of the Federal Government, as of December 1957—III", *Communications of the ACM*, September 1959, Vol. 2, Issue 9, 34.

2. Howard Millman, "A Brief History of EDI," *InfoWorld*, April 6, 1998, Vol. 20, Issue 14, 83.

3. Ibid.

4. "SCOR Model Is Key Link to Stronger Supply Chain," *Automatic I.D. News*, Sept. 1998, Vol. 14, Issue 10.

5. Ibid.

6. William Frank Quiett, "Embracing Supply Chain Management," *Supply Chain Management Review*, September 1, 2002.

7. SCOR Model 5.0.

8. Grace Lin, et al., "The Sense and Respond Enterprise," *Operations Research and Management Science*, April 2002. Viewed at http://www.lionhrtpub.com/orms/orms-4-02/valuechain.html, April 2003.

9. Robert D. Austin, et al., "Enterprise Resource Planning," A Technology Note, 9-699-020, The Harvard Business School, March 14, 2003.

10. Prasad Bingi, et al., "Critical Issues Affecting an ERP Implementation," *Information and Systems Management*, Summer 1999, Vol. 16, Issue 3, 7.

11. Christopher Koch, "The ABCs of ERP," *CIO.com*. Viewed at http://www.cio.com/research/erp/edit/erpbasics.html, April 16, 2003.

12. "Making the ERP Commitment: What Controllers Say about Implementation Time and Cost," *The Controller's Report*, May 2001.

13. Austin, et al., op. cit.

14. Point-to-point refers to a traditional type of integration where one node connects and communicates to just one other node at a time.

15. Jinyoul Lee, et al., "Enterprise Integration with ERP and EAI," *Communications of the ACM*, February 2003, Vol. 46, No. 2, 54.

16. Antone Gosalves, "Value of EAI Grows as Integration Needs Expand," *InformationWeek*, May 28, 2001, 60.

17. Portals Community, *Fundamentals of Portals*. Viewed at http://www.portalscommunity.com/ library/fundamentals.cfm 18 April 2003.

18. Jeff Phillips et al., "Portal Products vs. Vendors," *Transform Magazine*, October 1, 2002, 35.

19. Samuel Greengard, "Portals Shape the Promise of the Internet," *Internet World*, April 2003, Vol. 9, Issue 4, 26.

20. Dibya Sarkar, "People Key to Portal Process," *Federal Computer Week,* April 23, 2003. Viewed at http://www.fcw.com/fcw/articles/2003/0421/web-afcea-04-23-03.asp, April 2003.

21. Morris Edwards, "An EDI Whose Time Has Come," *Communications News*, Sept. 1999, Vol. 36, Issue 9, 104.

22. Robert L. Scheier, "Internet EDI Grows Up," *Computerworld*, January 20, 2003, Vol. 37, Issue 3, 38.

23. Dale Neef, *e-Procurement*. Upper Saddle River, NJ: Prentice–Hall, Inc., 2001, 102.

24. GAO Report, "Challenges to Effective Adoption of Extensible Markup Language," GAO-02-327, April 2002.

25. James A. Cooke, "Is XML the Next Big Thing," *Logistics Management*, May 1, 2002, 53.

26. David Phinney, "Technology Helps DoD Better Track Equipment for Troops," *Federal Times Online*, March 31, 2003. Viewed at http://federaltimes.com/index.php?S=1718107, April 4, 2003.

27. David M. Ewalt, "Pinpoint Control: Tiny Chips May Revolutionize All Areas of Supply Chain Management," *InformationWeek*, Sept. 30, 2002. Viewed at http://www.informationweek.com/ story/showArticle.jhtml?articleID=6503191.

28. New Satellite-Based Tracking Service To Revolutionize Global Transportation; Proven Technology Breakthrough Sets New Standard For Transportation, Logistics Industries, Internet Wire, October 28, 2002.

29. Bridget McCrea, "CPFR Comes of Age," *Supply Chain Management Review*, March/April 2003, Vol. 7, Issue 2, 65.

30. Lin et al., op. cit.

31. Gene Fliender, "CPFR: An Emerging Supply Chain Tool," *Industrial and Management Data Systems*, Vol. 103, Issue 1, 14–21.

32. Jean Schenck, "CPFR: A Glimpse into Retail's Future?" *Automatic I.D. News*, Nov. 1998, Vol. 14, Issue 12, 51.

33. Fliender, op. cit.

34. Larry Adams, "Diagnostics from Afar," *Quality*, November 2001, Vol. 40, Issue 11, 26.

35. The authors are grateful to Steve Buckley, from the IBM TJ Watson Research Center, Yorktown Heights, N.Y., for his valuable contributions for the SCEM sense-and-respond sections.

36. Victoria Furness, "Preparing for the Unexpected," *Computer Business Review*, July 2002, Vol. 10, Issue 7, 10.

37. Teradata, "The 2002 Teradata Report on Enterprise Decision-Making," NCR Corporation, Dayton, Ohio, 2002.

38. Carolyn April, "BAM To Speed App Reports—Industry Heavyweights Target Business Process Performance," *InfoWorld*, Vol. 24, No., 44, 4 Nov. 2002, 27.

39. Navi Radjou, "Adaptive Supply Networks," *TechStrategy Brief*, Forrester Research, February 22, 2002.

40. Stephan Haeckel of IBM had predicted this business trend in 1999 in his seminal book *Adaptive Enterprise: Creating and Leading Sense-and-Respond Organizations*.

41. A group of companies/organizations working together to develop a product or provide a service to satisfy a demand. The goal of value chain management is to maximize the total performance and added value across an entire process by reviewing each internal and external operation, and the links between these operations.

42. Grace Lin, "Sense and Respond Value Chain Optimization," Presentation at 3rd Annual NetCentricity Conference, R. H. Smith Business School, University of Maryland, April 4, 2003, viewed at http://www.rhsmith.umd.edu/netconference/presentations.html, April 2003.

43. Navi Radjou, "Executive Overview: Adaptive Supply Networks," *Forrester TechStrategy Brief*, February 22, 2002.

44. Lin et al., op. cit.

CHAPTER FIVE

The Road to Transforming Supply Chain Management in Government

Jacques S. Gansler
Robert E. Luby, Jr.
Bonnie Kornberg

A Vision for Modern Government Logistics

Today, Wal-Mart's satellite network—which instantly communicates retail needs and prompts suppliers, truck drivers, and warehouse workers to originate, change, and reroute shipments—could be applied to government logistics. So could General Electric's remote diagnostics system, which detects and solves system problems from a central location, lowering maintenance time and costs. Such systems could be established government-wide, as could one- to two-day order-to-delivery times and greatly reduced government inventories. A fully integrated, digitized, world-class supply chain management system could make the government quick, flexible, and highly efficient. This is how the system would operate:

- **Rapid delivery.** At the center of a new logistics system would be delivery speed. Today, Cat Logistics uses a suite of IT and wireless systems as well as high-performance management processes to ship 99.8 percent of all orders within 24 hours. Cat Logistics meets this standard for approximately 28 million Caterpillar orders each year.[1] The Department of Defense, by comparison, averages 22 days for order-to-receipt times on 18 million orders per year—10 million fewer orders than Cat Logistics handles for its parent company, Caterpillar. The government of the future would meet or exceed the Cat Logistics standard.

- **Light government inventories.** As the medical logistics community learned during Desert Storm (see chapter fourteen), storing supplies in case of a surge requirement can backfire. As shelf life and expiration dates pass, the government loses millions on worthless inventory. Obsolescence, especially today with the quick pace of new product development, also leads to losses. On top of these costs are holding and warehouse handling costs that apply across the board for all items in government inventories.

    The government of the future would empty out its warehouses and shift holding and handling costs to the private sector. It would hedge against the risk of uncertain requirements through information instead of inventory, and manage orders, deliveries, and billings through real-time information systems.

- **Operational integration.** Just as Cisco Systems and its major suppliers have created a "networked ecosystem" where demand and supply information are visible to those performing manufacture, distribution, and wholesaling, this vision of government includes linked contractors, end users, and government managers who would share demand, supply, and transit data.

- **Functional integration.** The National Science Foundation has already realized the functional integration part of the future vision. As a model for how the rest of government could function, the NSF has used its financial accounting system to create interdependencies and electronic information sharing between the finance, procurement, and operational parts of the organization.

- **Enterprise integration.** Every item procured by the National Aeronautics and Space Administration, the Department of Agriculture, or any other government organization belongs to the public. In a future government logistics environment with total visibility of assets, all items could be handled as national assets. If there were a disaster and the Federal Emergency Management Agency needed parts in the Defense Department's inventories, the transfer could happen effortlessly. Visibility into parts buying and contract pricing across offices and agencies would lead to more effective contract negotiations. Imagine a procurement specialist at NASA being able to negotiate down a price based on what the Department of Defense paid for the same item. Or NASA and DoD could pool their purchases and receive economy-of-scale discounts.

- **Predictive intervention.** Where appropriate, equipment monitors, as opposed to pre-determined timetables, would indicate when to replace parts. Commercially, for example, some companies now use jet engine temperature gauges to alert maintenance personnel that parts need attention. Since each unique part experiences different environmental and usage conditions, using timetables instead of actual data to determine when to replace parts introduces waste and risk. A part may last much longer than the timetable indicates or could fail earlier. By using actual data to predict failure, individual parts can be replaced before they fail, but not too soon.

   In some cases, an even more advanced maintenance process can minimize the need for human intervention. Autonomic systems, which are being developed for DoD's Joint Strike Fighter program, automatically monitor, regulate, optimize, and indicate repair of equipment.

- **Robust information security.** All necessary precautions would be implemented up front with new IT systems and would be retrofitted to legacy systems to ensure vigorous privacy and national security protections are in place. Public key infrastructure (PKI), data encryption, data ownership rules and rights, and regular security audits would be features of information security controls.

- **Customer-driven processes.** Demand rather than supply would become the focus of logistics. A "sense-and-respond"[2] environment would enable end users to place small orders as the need arose. Similar to Dell's ability to ship single computers to customers at reasonable prices, virtual supply chain integration would make this highly personalized scenario possible.

- **Continuous review and improvement.** Analysis of distribution times and modes, inventory levels, customer satisfaction, cost, and other key logistics variables would be intrinsic to the new logistics system. Analysts would use statistical techniques to work toward optimizing supply chain functioning. Based on feedback from data analysts, managers would continuously improve processes and systems.

How to Achieve Change

For the above vision of the future to become reality, certain barriers need to be dismantled or avoided.

Each barrier that was covered in chapter two can be overcome. If removing the barrier is too difficult, workarounds or alternative approaches can be used. Demonstrating success by focusing on the "80/20" rule (the maxim that 20 percent of a set of items causes 80 percent of the impact) can help sway decision makers to remove barriers that are too hard to break down at first. Early successes will further acceptance, but leaders must be realistic about the time frame and cost of large-scale change. New digital systems may take three to five years to implement. Costs for change may appear high, but with inaccurate (and low) baseline cost data, savings often won't be understood until much later.

Overcoming the cultural, legal, administrative, and resource barriers will take coordination, strategic planning, commitment, and creativity. Most of all, it will require determined leadership.

Removing Cultural Barriers

Make Supply Chain Management Transformation a Top Priority
To make logistics transformation one of the goals on senior leaders' short lists, advocates from all sides—including industry, the Office of Management and Budget, and internal agency champions—should articulate the impact of logistics on overall agency performance. Table 5.1 offers supporting data and specific examples.

Engender Trust in the System
One simple way to gain trust is to give end users direct access to commercial sources. By expanding applications such as the DoD EMALL, which provides online ordering capability, end users would experience the same responsiveness at work as they do when they order online at home. Changing end-user opinions and behaviors will require consistent delivery, over time, of the right parts—quickly.

Table 5.1: Objectives and Results

Objective	Example	Results
Increase Availability	**Defense Logistics Agency**—Hamilton Standard, as prime vendor, contract to supply replacement parts from its existing stock and production to Warner Robbins Air Force Depot.	Availability of parts increased by 30%, with 84% delivery on time within 4 days of ordering.
Improve Financial Management	**Defense Finance and Accounting Service (DFAS)**—Fully integrated system implementation program for an integrated financial system with a centralized data system to translate data from unique systems into standard data accessible by users from different systems.	93% reduction in cost, with annual savings amounting to $120 million in FY98.
Increase Procurement Efficiency	**Defense Medical Logistics Standard Support (DMLSS) Prime Vendor Electronic Commerce/Electronic Data Interchange initiatives** to convert from a proprietary vendor order-entry system to an e-commerce environment, supporting electronic purchases, reducing communication bottlenecks, and reengineering and standardizing purchase ordering across all military medical facilities.	Reduction in procurement time from 45 days to 2 days or less; 95% of orders placed on the system are confirmed within 45 minutes.
Reduce Inventory	**Auxiliary Power Unit Total Logistics Support (APU-TLS) program,** a public-private venture between companies (Honeywell and Caterpillar Logistics) and the Navy to provide data management, inventory management, engineering support, and parts delivery.	Reduction in days of inventory from 380 to 10 days in APUs. Similarly, for DMLSS, reduction of medical inventory in DoD depots by 65% and DoD hospitals by 81%.
Increase Customer Satisfaction	**Business Systems Modernization (BSM) program at the Defense Logistics Agency (DLA)** to reengineer logistics processes to reflect best commercial practices	Collaboration with customers and suppliers and full integration of information.
Increase Performance	**Defense Logistics Agency Industrial Vendor Program** to transfer management of maintenance of depot bins from depot employees to outside companies. Prime Vendor companies are charged with monitoring and refilling bins.	Fill rates increased from 85% to 98%, and refills achieved in less than 24 hours.

Motivate Employees to Accept Change

Employee concerns that they will lose their jobs or be forced to do something they don't like need to be addressed directly by leaders and managers. Change will not lead to many lost jobs but will require new types of skills. While the vision for change will be formulated by senior leaders, middle- and program-level managers will communicate and implement that vision. Managers should be trained in new logistics concepts and in how to motivate employees to accept new roles. The system should reward employees for implementing changes that lead to performance improvements. Fear of change is natural and unavoidable, and managers should be coached to understand this, be empathetic, and realize that during the transition to new norms they will encounter employee resistance. However, with adherence to the new vision and alignment of performance appraisal and reward systems with organizational priorities, most employees will accept change over time.

Develop Trust between the Public and Private Sectors

Concerns about the private sector's dependability persist in the government. This distrust, despite proof to the contrary—such as contractors working in battlefields, responding to disasters, and working side-by-side with government maintenance specialists—is used as a reason to maintain the status quo. This distrustful thinking bolsters arguments for retaining government maintenance depots and for limiting data sharing.

The private sector offers some examples for how to address this obstacle. Covisint and Cat Logistics have dealt successfully with mistrust between companies. As outsiders, both companies have served as honest brokers. They work directly with competitors and establish rules and firewalls to keep proprietary information safe. By outsourcing to companies that do not have the vested interests of original equipment managers (OEMs), the government could ease fears about contractor motives.

Contract requirements also affect contractor performance and contribute to distrust. When contractors are paid based on how many parts are replaced or delivered, a perverse incentive is created to replace or provide more parts—not to improve reliability or performance. Some of GE's contracts are structured to focus on the customers' performance requirements. GE is rewarded for keeping systems running rather than for fixing systems that fail.[3] Structuring government contracts that way could help to enhance trust.

Overcoming Legal Barriers

Two options exist for dealing with regulatory barriers. Logistics transformation champions could confront the regulatory challenges directly by seeking change or elimination, or they could change how the rules are interpreted. The following are some approaches to handling certain regulatory and statutory obstacles.

Address the "50/50" Rule

One major impediment to logistics modernization within DoD is the "50/50" rule, which requires 50 percent of all government depot work to be performed by government personnel in government depots. This rule affects a large part of the DoD budget, with depot expenditures topping $16 billion. OMB and the Secretary of Defense should work together to eliminate the 50/50 rule and competitively source DoD's depot work.

Barring this more complete solution, the 50/50 rule could be reinterpreted to allow greater flexibility. Interpretations that would permit additional outsourcing include looking only at touch labor (maintenance personnel) funds or working with the DoD comptroller to redefine the base used in the calculation.

Reduce Paperwork Requirements

OMB should focus on streamlining the reporting requirements associated with the Government Performance and Results Act and simplify the business case requirements for IT projects. More appropriate requirements for IT projects would involve risk assessments and projected outcomes, rather than the outdated requirements demanded by the Clinger-Cohen Act. OMB recently revised the Circular A-76 with expanded authority to conduct streamlined competitions for 65 or fewer positions. The full impact has yet to be assessed. OMB should also encourage the adoption of activity-based costing (ABC) throughout the government. This would provide the data for better analysis and for comparing alternative approaches.

Change Micro-Purchase Restrictions

Micro-purchases have saved the government money and time. OMB should push to increase the micro-purchase threshold to encourage greater use of online purchasing and purchase cards. Another way to increase the use of purchase cards would be to permit rebates that currently go to the Treasury to be returned to the buyers' organizations.

Address Preferential Contracting Rules

Legislation that gives advantages to small-business contracts do good but also hinder reform. One persuasive argument for obtaining exceptions or changing these laws would be to show proof that these organizations would benefit from reform. The small-business laws are in place to help businesses compete against bigger players. If logistics modernization enhanced the ability of small businesses to compete, the regulations would not be as necessary. In fact, where acquisition reforms have been implemented, small-business awards have increased significantly. Using multiple award contracts allowed under the Federal Acquisition Streamlining Act, or FASA, the value of small-business awards increased from 1994 to 1999 from $500 million to $2 billion, or from 8 percent to 16 percent of all FASA awards. In the same period, using another acquisition streamlining vehicle—General Services Administration (GSA) schedules—small-business shares increased from $500 million to $3 billion, or from 26 percent to 36 percent of GSA schedule work.[4] This evidence shows that using the Internet and other simplified acquisition processes to make comparative cost and product information more available to government buyers makes it easier for small companies to compete. This data could be used to convince lawmakers to change regulations or at least make logistics reform efforts exempt from regulations.

Additionally, for recent large IT outsourcing efforts, such as the National Security Agency and the Navy-Marine intranet, a significant share of the subcontracts (e.g., 35 percent) had to go to small businesses. Such a requirement could be considered by agencies working to achieve small-business goals.

Change False Perceptions about Regulatory Restrictions

Senior agency officials should take steps, including directives and training if necessary, to change the mind-set of contracting officers who think that frequent competition is preferred. In fact, longer-term contracts with options are allowed by some current regulations (as long as contracts don't exceed five years plus five option years) and should be used to foster public-private partnerships. This type of contracting, with built-in incentives for performance improvement and the option for competition if performance falls or costs rise, promotes productivity and efficiency.

Senior agency officials must also change rules or perceptions that hamper data sharing with contractors. To increase efficiencies across supply chains, contractors need demand information. Any fears that demand information would give individual contractors a competitive advantage could be addressed through training and the proliferation of examples that demonstrate the contrary.

Tackling Administrative Hurdles

Simplify Business Case Requirements

In departments such as DoD, where accurate current and historical full-cost data are hard to obtain, making a business case based on expected cost savings is difficult. The best way to solve the dilemma, where financial justifications are required for new projects but cannot be accurately developed, is to involve government comptrollers in the solution. The senior comptroller of each department and agency must make the problem a top priority. As part of the solution, activity-based costing should be implemented throughout government to enable comparisons between different activities. Additionally, the degree of detail and analysis needed to make a business case is a high hurdle. The bar should be lowered for approval of pilot projects, which can be iteratively expanded or cancelled. Additionally, analogy to cost savings on comparable commercial programs should be allowable to establish the initial basis for going ahead (in the absence of good government baseline cost data).

Aggressively Implement Information Security

Stringent information security policies exist, but some government organizations are out of compliance. Concerns over the vulnerability of IT to viruses, hacker attacks, and other security breaches and information integrity threats have been factors in keeping government systems from becoming digitized. Senior agency officials should make sure that personnel feel confident conducting sensitive business electronically. They should also require security and privacy measures to be integral to new system development and penalize offices that don't comply. Once systems are being used, active user training programs and regular security audits should be mandated and audit findings enforced.

Addressing Resource Obstacles

Upgrade IT Systems

While up-front investments in new IT systems may be high, the payoff will be exponentially greater performance improvements. Unless replaced, legacy systems, especially those that cannot interface with other IT systems, will pose an additional barrier to supply chain integration.

Provide Sufficient Funding

OMB must fund agencies and departments, or, when necessary, require them to invest adequately in supply chain management projects. To facilitate a smart, coordinated government-wide change, OMB should be involved in prioritizing project funding. OMB should help departments and agencies strategize and determine how to make progress quickly through the "B" or "80 percent" solution, if appropriate.

Transforming Government Logistics

Concurrent with efforts to remove barriers, the following measures will help inaugurate modern logistics.

Catalyze Leaders

Logistics leadership needs to be at the right level: the very top.

As the Defense Finance and Accounting Service initiative demonstrates, delegating authority down the chain of command will not suffice. Without authority over all DoD organizations, DFAS could not accomplish total consolidation of DoD financial systems. As a result, 11 years after DFAS began its consolidation efforts, the level of leadership has now been moved to the highest finance official in DoD, the under secretary of defense (comptroller). Even at that level, however, integration with other functional areas such as procurement and logistics may not be considered. It may require the Secretary of Defense to make this integration effort a top priority before the umbrella becomes wide enough to contain all functions.

Since Secretaries will not manage day-to-day implementation activities, major government departments may need to establish a senior-level change leader for this effort. The senior leader should have the following: (1) authority to integrate finance, procurement, and logistics functions; (2) accountability to the organization's top official; and (3) adequate resources to implement change.

Legacy Systems

When organizations begin to transform their supply chains, they are often forced to face the questions of how to handle their legacy systems. The very qualities that make legacy systems so valuable—their ability to support unique business functions, their large reservoirs of priceless data, and their general reliability—can stand in the way of supply chain transformation. Additionally, legacy system users know how to use these systems, feel comfortable with their performance, and will often resist efforts to replace them.

Legacy systems were often developed independently, in a piecemeal fashion, rather than with an integrated enterprise approach. These systems are often unable to talk to one another, and may be proprietary as well. As a consequence, they can pose a significant barrier as organizations attempt to leverage these legacy systems to evolve their business and operational requirements.

Starting over—that is, replacing them with new applications—is often not feasible, affordable, or practical. At the same time, however, adapting legacy systems and integrating them with enterprise systems, in a way that accommodates change and enables business improvements, has never been more critical. As organizations struggle to decide how to adapt and leverage these systems, they must consider business, financial, functional, operational, and technological factors.

As the agency that promotes prudent government management practices and sets federal funding priorities, OMB should work with department and agency leaders to develop the vision and strategy for change. This should include the establishment of a cross-government logistics council with senior logistics, finance, procurement, IT, and management representatives from a variety of agencies. This council should set needed standards and cross-pollinate successes and lessons.

Well-represented leadership teams such as these have succeeded at micro-levels within government and have worked in commercial settings. To overcome the problem of the transience of senior leaders, the Defense Logistics Agency created a cross-functional executive board to oversee its Business Systems Modernization program. This board, with senior representatives from finance, IT, and logistics departments, was required to approve any changes in the BSM program goals. Because the board members became invested in the program and retained ownership and significant control over the goals, the BSM program weathered top leadership changes. The group became more powerful than individual agendas and ensured that the momentum of the program was not slowed.

Institute Change Management Strategies

Lone government initiatives, such as the National Science Foundation's integrated financial management system and the DoD EMALL, fail to expand or to be replicated because there is no consistent top-level strategy for implementing change. Cultural change will require incentives for employees, managers, and contractors that are aligned with organizational priorities. Rewards for innovation and logistics system improvements should be instituted for employees. Managers need incentives to continue to improve processes. Contracts must be structured to reward contractors for improving performance and making government equipment more available at lower costs. Performance guarantees, which provide incentives to improve performance each period, and multiyear contracts (based on improved performance at lowered costs) are useful tools.

Crucial to the promotion of pilot programs is the message that business processes must be changed prior to—or as part of—implementing digital systems. As part of a forum on e-logistics, a participant said, "Digitizing a bad process just results in doing something bad faster."[5] This was a key lesson learned by DFAS during its financial system upgrade. Because of its peer relationship to other agencies involved in the system change, DFAS could not dictate process change prior to changing automated systems but recognized that the gains would have been significantly greater if that had occurred. Process change was one of the fundamental tenets of Cisco Systems' highly successful financial management system implementation.

Start Small and Build on Successes

The top-level logistics transformation vision should be carried out through small, low-level pilot programs that are subsequently proven and scaled up. Leaders should cultivate an environment for quickly launching, evaluating, and improving many low-cost pilots. These pilots can help prove new logistics practices and advance their acceptance. In business, this is a form of "learning by doing." When applied to IT systems or engineering capabilities, a similar pattern of low-cost development, rapid fielding, and continual evaluation and upgrade should occur. Called "spiral development," this process for incremental technology releases (see Figure 5.1) should happen within an "evolutionary acquisition" environment (i.e., ratcheting up capability until reaching an end state)—and always within an overall interoperable master architecture.[6]

Rapidly implemented pilots will help demonstrate the value of supply chain integration to players who are resistant to change. Starting at the ground level will help foster buy-in from employees since people tend to support what they help create. Department and agency leaders should support the expansion and replication of pilots that work.

Empower Program Personnel

Besides communicating the importance of an innovative culture, leaders must provide sufficient resources for program managers to focus on "best value" rather than lowest cost options. This may cost more in the short run, but should result in optimized cost and performance over time.

Direct Interoperability

While decentralized management makes sense, process and electronic system interoperability is essential. One of the most important strategic decisions for the cross-government logistics council would be how to achieve interoperability between and within departments and agencies. *Interoperability* means the ability to work together as opposed to commonality, which requires exactly the same systems and processes. To encourage interoperability, some commonality will be required. For example, differences in nomenclature, numbering, and processes hinder collaboration. The board should decide standards for certain items including data descriptions, IT standards, inventory/asset tracking systems, and higher-level cost accounting systems. Additionally, to enable government material handling and transportation equipment to interface with commercial air and ground transportation vehicles, the board should develop standards for this type of government equipment.

Boeing's post-merger handling of its financial accounting system exemplifies how to develop interoperability and still maintain decentralized systems and practices. After Boeing merged with Rockwell and McDonnell

Figure 5.1: Integrated Spiral Development Approach

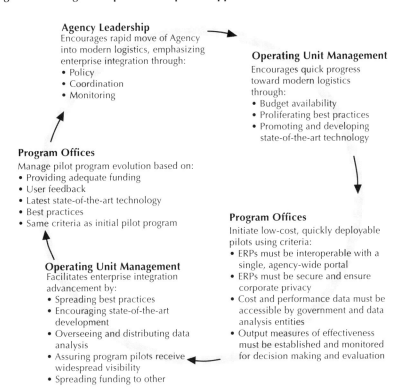

Agency Leadership
Encourages rapid move of Agency
into modern logistics, emphasizing
enterprise integration through:
• Policy
• Coordination
• Monitoring

Operating Unit Management
Encourages quick progress
toward modern logistics
through:
• Budget availability
• Proliferating best practices
• Promoting and developing
  state-of-the-art technology

Program Offices
Manage pilot program evolution based on:
• Providing adequate funding
• User feedback
• Latest state-of-the-art technology
• Best practices
• Same criteria as initial pilot program

Program Offices
Initiate low-cost, quickly deployable
pilots using criteria:
• ERPs must be interoperable with a
  single, agency-wide portal
• ERPs must be secure and ensure
  corporate privacy
• Cost and performance data must be
  accessible by government and data
  analysis entities
• Output measures of effectiveness
  must be established and monitored
  for decision making and evaluation

Operating Unit Management
Facilitates enterprise integration
advancement by:
• Spreading best practices
• Encouraging state-of-the-art
  development
• Overseeing and distributing data
  analysis
• Assuring program pilots receive
  widespread visibility
• Spreading funding to other

Douglas, legacy systems made it difficult to consolidate financial reporting. Boeing's solution was to allow business units to manage their financial accounts in their own way as long as data required by headquarters could be electronically merged into the headquarters' system. The business units became responsible for mapping their unique financial accounts to a standard corporate chart of accounts.

Boeing's model should be adopted in the public sector. The degree of business practice and electronic system diversity in the government (there are over 1,000 different IT systems in DoD logistics alone) make it well suited to decentralized management. However, requiring individual offices to be interoperable with a central system, such as a portal, would stimulate unprecedented opportunities. Exponentially higher levels of functioning could be realized if all departments and agencies of the federal government were connected. This could be accomplished with the use of middleware and several portals that are interoperable with each other. This type of policy is much more cost-effective and feasible in large organizations than promoting one common information system for the entire agency.

Promote Coordination and Collaboration

Many government legacy systems were not developed to share data within a single organization, much less with other government agencies or contractors. Since information sharing is critical to logistics modernization, agency leaders should endorse a proliferation of new information systems as long as they are interoperable with each other through central portals or other means (and fully tested to assure this interoperability).

Implement the Right Metrics

As discussed, cost does not work well as an initial metric in government settings where accurate historical cost data are not available. With the right metrics focused on performance improvements and aligned with top-level goals, managers can motivate employees, assess the progress of change, and evaluate contractors. Effective performance metrics focus on speed of delivery, system availability, and customer satisfaction. Management systems focused on metrics, such as the balanced scorecard and Six Sigma, have been highly effective in commercial settings, and agencies and departments may want to adopt similar systems. Of course, as the government begins to get full-cost visibility (via activity-based costing or some equivalent method), then cost will become one of the critical metrics being monitored. However, it should never be the sole measure; performance measures will always be equally critical.

Use Commercial Software, Items, and Services

Besides being cheaper and faster, commercial off-the-shelf (COTS) products help with interoperability, as supplies move to "open systems." When investigating alternatives for its new financial management system, Boeing found that COTS software would be more efficient than in-house development. The company also liked the fact that a COTS software package would incorporate financial management best practices, whereas Boeing would be somewhat limited by its biases toward current corporate practices if it developed software internally.

While using COTS sounds simple on the surface, sometimes it requires difficult decisions. One reason that offices sometimes prefer customized IT solutions is that the applications conform to existing processes. When using COTS—although some customization is possible—processes need to be revised to conform to best-practice electronic systems. Top agency officials should continue to actively promote the use of COTS. Government agencies should not devote resources to product development when private companies have already developed suitable cutting-edge applications.

Focus on Core Competencies

Corporations such as Cat Logistics and Cisco Systems have developed expertise in their core competencies. Cat Logistics performs logistics services only and Cisco Systems focuses on design and fulfillment processes. Likewise, each government organization has its own core competency. For example, the Federal Emergency Management Agency's is disaster response and DoD's is war fighting. Logistics enables the missions of these and many other government departments, but in most cases logistics is not the mission itself. Government agencies should concentrate on their core competencies and should hire specialist companies to help perform supply chain management.

In most cases, the appropriate roles for government personnel are managing overall services, providing system configuration control, overseeing contracts, and assuring interoperability (via middleware and portals). Original equipment managers, or OEMs, should be accountable for their systems' performance and management of their supply chains. Third-party logistics providers should be involved in their areas of expertise: warehousing, distribution, transportation, and information systems.

Develop a New Type of Government Logistics Professional

While employee fears are a real issue that needs to be addressed, an opportunity currently exists to change the makeup of the government logistics workforce. Over the next five years, more than 25 percent of government employees will be eligible to retire. While motivating the remaining workers to adopt different, more challenging logistics roles will not be easy, mass retirements could open the opportunity for hiring new people experienced in or interested in modern, technology-driven logistics practices.

New job descriptions and career paths for logistics personnel must evolve. New supply chain management practices require different skill sets. Future logisticians will be managers of doers, instead of doers themselves, and will need more IT and management skills. A complete career development and management program should be institutionalized to ensure that people are trained with the right skills and that they stay in government and advance through the ranks. This program should include rotations between government agencies.

Additionally, rotations from the private sector into government posts should be expanded, and vice versa. As a new venture requiring expertise in the automotive field, Covisint attributes some of its success to its hiring of automotive industry veterans. Bringing experienced commercial sector supply chain management professionals into government could help the government transition into modern logistics operations. Similarly, government people spending a few years in a world-class logistics operation will bring back invaluable experience.

Considering the magnitude of skills training that needs to happen (with the 75 percent of the government workforce that is not eligible for retirement in the next five years), a thorough education program should be implemented. To reach as many people as possible and keep training costs down, web-based training should be used heavily. Agencies should develop executive training that includes case studies on the latest logistics advances. This training should emphasize new technology adoption, selection of appropriate metrics, and methods for continuously improving practices.

Analyze Data and Implement Continuous Improvements

The primary benefit of increased supply chain visibility is the ability to capture data, model processes, and find previously untapped efficiencies in the overall system. Cat Logistics does this for its clients and has reduced costs, sped delivery time, minimized system downtimes, and increased customer satisfaction. To fully realize the potential of supply chain integration, the government should make data sharing and analysis a priority. Once this data is provided, program managers should be evaluated based on their use of the data to make improvements.

Besides analysis of operational data, OMB should study and record pilot projects that succeed. The organization can use hard data from model programs to spread methods that work, analyze other initiatives, and develop improved models and simulations of government logistics processes.

Summary

Chapter five complements chapter two, which presented barriers to government supply chain management change and areas for improvement. This chapter shows how to overcome the barriers described in chapter two and how to move in a strategic way toward government-wide transformation. The key points are:

- Supply chain management transformation requires the commitment of top leaders. Unless these reforms become one of the three to five major priorities selected by agency heads, the vision of government-wide, digitally integrated supply chains will remain out of reach. Concurrently, OMB will need to work with leaders to develop strategies and structures to maintain the momentum for change beyond the tenure of the initiators.

- Interoperability rather than common software should be promoted. Much more feasible and cost-effective than requiring the implementation of one agency-wide software system, interoperability can be accomplished through portals and middleware. To achieve government-wide integration, one or more portals should be developed, and interoperability with these portals should be mandated.

- Certain legislative and regulatory barriers need to be overcome before world-class supply chain management practices can be implemented throughout the government.
- The need to address human resource issues, including hiring new professionals, developing new career paths, training, and overcoming fears of change, cannot be overstated. These areas will require substantial energies and investments.
- Incentives to motivate change should align with organizational goals. Employees and contractors should be rewarded for improving equipment performance as well as overall supply chain management system performance.
- To demonstrate quick successes and inspire expansion and replication, small pilot programs should be encouraged. To facilitate these, business case requirements should focus on performance rather than cost, and the amount of required detail should be reduced.

Part II presents case studies on innovative public and private sector supply chain management initiatives. These cover e-logistics, e-finance, and e-procurement projects and practices. Many of these cases provide an expanded context for the examples used in Part I, supporting the conclusions and recommendations described here.

Appendix:
Recommendations from
the Wye River Forums

To engage government and business leaders in addressing these issues, the Center for Public Policy and Private Enterprise at the University of Maryland's School of Public Affairs hosted three three-day Thought Leadership Forums:

- "Delivering on the Promise of E-Commerce: Greater Government Effectiveness through e-Procurement," December 2–4, 2001
- "Incorporating Financial Management into a Digitally Integrated Supply Chain," April 28–30, 2002
- "Achieving a Modern Government Logistics System: The Critical Element in a Digitally Integrated Supply Chain," October 27–29, 2002[7]

These forums were supported by the IBM Center for The Business of Government. Forum participants from senior government, industry, and academia examined business and government case studies, identified key issues, and analyzed lessons learned from successful public and private sector efforts. They then made recommendations for the implementation and integration of electronic procurement, electronic financial management systems, and automated logistics systems into an overall, digitally integrated supply chain. These recommendations are presented in the tables on pages 95, 96, and 97.

The participants at all three of the forums identified committed senior leadership as the most critical element to achieve a transformation and integration of the government's supply chain, and to overcome existing legislative, regulatory, and organizational barriers. These leaders must develop incentives and metrics to change the culture and monitor progress—they need to empower employees and then hold them accountable for progress. As new systems are developed, they must link the procurement and finance functions with logistics into an integrated, digital supply chain with an architecture that creates interoperability within the government and with the private sector. The participants also recognized the government's existing interaction with the private sector and the benefits derived; and recommended increasing public-private interaction to create the "best value" for the government. Finally, they also acknowledged that, as the government moves to an automated and integrated supply chain, the nature of many government jobs will change. To facilitate the transition to this new environment, they concluded that government agencies and departments must aggressively develop and provide training to reshape and sustain the workforce.

With the current nexus of the advances in information technology (from communication to computing), the motivation for change, and the clear need and opportunity for government process improvements, forum recommendations will be useful for leaders in the Bush Administration to realize the potential of electronic procurement, electronic financial management, and logistics systems improvements in an overall, digitally integrated supply chain.

E-Procurement Recommendations from Wye River Forum I

Recommendation Area	Implementor	Recommendations
Leadership	Department and agency heads	1. Identify and strongly support an agency "Leader of Change." 2. Set the vision and strategy for implementing e-procurement, and achieve some early successes. 3. Transform procurement processes while investing in technology.
Architecture	Office of Management and Budget in conjunction with department and agency heads	4. Develop a government-wide architecture. 5. Ensure interoperability within the government and with the private sector. 6. Integrate the supply chain; don't just focus on procurement. 7. Adopt commercial "best of breed." 8. Implement appropriate security controls.
Integration/ Coordination	Office of Management and Budget in conjunction with department and agency heads	9. Improve public/private interaction and cooperation. 10. Improve interagency coordination.
Human Capital	Office of Management and Budget in conjunction with department and agency heads	11. Develop the required human capital.
Overcoming Barriers	Office of Management and Budget	12. Increase the micro-purchase threshold. 13. Remove regulatory barriers. 14. Provide the required resources.

E-Finance Recommendations from Wye River Forum II

Recommendation Area	Implementor	Recommendations
Leadership	The President	1. Create the vision.
	Office of Management and Budget	2. Identify a financial management "Leader of Change."
	Department and agency heads	3. Identify and strongly support an agency "Leader of Change." 4. Assume change and manage it.
	Office of Management and Budget in conjunction with department and agency heads	5. Develop a strategic plan to add value. 6. Use a balanced scorecard to measure progress.
Integration/ Interoperability	Office of Management and Budget	7. Standardize interfaces, not systems.
	Department and agency heads	8. Reengineer financial management processes while automating. 9. Make finance a key part of operations. 10. Define essential requirements— and stick to them. 11. Focus on security and privacy.
Public-Private Interaction	Department and agency heads	12. Buy or outsource; don't build. 13. Partner with the private sector.
	Office of Management and Budget	14. Develop a Center of Excellence for public-private lessons learned.
Overcoming Barriers	Office of Management and Budget	15. Streamline the oversight process—reduce paperwork. 16. Adopt activity-based costing.
	Office of Management and Budget in conjunction with department and agency heads	17. Provide the required resources.
Human Resources	Department and agency heads	18. Transition to a knowledge worker environment. 19. Link appraisals to performance.

E-Logistics Recommendations from Wye River Forum III

Recommendation Area	Implementor	Recommendations
Leadership	Office of Management and Budget in conjunction with department and agency heads	1. Make logistics a top management priority.
	Department and agency heads	2. Develop transformation momentum. 3. Create incentives to change the culture. 4. Measure the right things. 5. Get the facts and make them widely available.
Coordination and Collaboration	Office of Management and Budget in conjunction with department and agency heads	6. Develop a strategic plan. 7. Develop standards to improve interoperability. 8. Improve interagency coordination.
Public-Private Interaction	Office of Management and Budget in conjunction with department and agency heads	9. Use pilot programs to build trust and demonstrate value. 10. Use COTS and the web. 11. Ensure information security and privacy.
Overcoming Barriers	Office of Management and Budget in conjunction with department and agency heads	12. Review and modify acquisition guidance. 13. Implement activity-based costing (ABC). 14. Provide the required resources.
	Office of Management and Budget in conjunction with the secretary of defense	15. Address the "50/50" rule.
Human Resources	Department and agency heads	16. Redesign logistics jobs. 17. Greatly expand education and training.

Endnotes

1. Jacques S. Gansler, "Diffusing Netcentricity in DoD: The Supply Chain (An Example Case)," a presentation, April 23, 2002.

2. This concept is taken from Captain Linda Lewandowski and Jeffrey Cares, Department of Defense Office of Force Transformation, *Sense and Respond Logistics: Turning Supply Chains into Demand Networks*, December 20, 2002. (unpublished).

3. "Remote Monitoring and Diagnostics and Its Effect on the Supply Chain—A Case Study on General Electric," a presentation, October 28, 2002.

4. Jacques S. Gansler, "A Vision of the Government as a World-Class Buyer: Major Procurement Issues for the Coming Decade," IBM Center for The Business of Government, January 2002.

5. Jacques S. Gansler, William Lucyshyn, and Kimberly Ross, "Digitally Integrating the Government Supply Chain: E-Procurement, E-Finance, and E-Logistics," IBM Center for The Business of Government, February 2003.

6. E. C. Aldridge, Jr., Under Secretary of Defense, Acquisition, Technology, and Logistics, to staff, interoffice memo, *Evolutionary Acquisition and Spiral Development,* April 12, 2002.

7. For additional findings from the three Wye River Forums, see Gansler, Lucyshyn, and Ross.

PART II

Case Studies

Introduction

As noted, much of the material in Part I is based on the detailed case studies of successful supply chain modernizations contained in Part II. There are five examples drawn from the private sector and five from the public sector. (The first three focus on logistics, the next four on finance, and the final three on procurement.)

The case studies were conducted at different times over the course of this project and represent a useful snapshot of the programs at the time. In each case, the organization involved played a major role in putting together the case and then presenting it to one of three "Thought Leadership Forums" (on logistics, finance, and procurement). At these sessions, the selected audience of senior government and industry leaders (see the Appendix for their names and affiliations) critiqued the cases and then drew from them the findings and recommendations that are contained in Part I.

It is important to point out that while the forums were each focused on a major element of the overall supply chain (logistics, finance, and procurement), the most critical finding of the overall effort was the essentiality of fully integrating these three elements in an end-to-end, digitally integrated supply chain. Only in this way can the full performance and cost benefits of modern, world-class supply chains be realized by the government in the future.

CHAPTER SIX

Caterpillar Logistics Services: Providing "No Excuses" Logistics Support

Dzintars Dzilna
and
William Lucyshyn

Introduction[1]

Caterpillar Logistics Services, Inc. ("Cat Logistics") has developed a digitally integrated logistics system that has demonstrated the ability to ship an incredible 99.8 percent of Caterpillar replacement parts orders—from a selection of more than 550,000 parts worldwide—on the same day the order is received from the customer. This case study provides an overview of this digitally integrated logistics system that Cat Logistics uses as the internal logistics manager for Caterpillar Inc., and for its external clients as a third-party logistics provider. This chapter first reviews the company's mission and organization to provide background information about Cat Logistics' development and values. Second, the system's architecture and applications are examined, providing an overview of the major technologies that enable the system to deliver operationally. The system's capabilities are then tied to the company's strategic objectives of providing both high-quality logistics service and reductions in client costs. The chapter also examines aspects such as security, standards and metrics, and challenges that clients face in developing a digitally integrated logistics system. The conclusion provides lessons learned from Caterpillar's experience and a look at trends that will affect logistics system development in the future.

Company Background

Mission

Cat Logistics had its genesis in managing the logistics for Caterpillar Inc.'s manufactured construction equipment. Caterpillar's value proposition to its customers is, "When you buy our machine, we'll do whatever it takes to keep that machine running." Many of Caterpillar's customers invest millions of dollars in their machines—and the machines typically generate thousands of dollars of revenue daily—so reliability is very important to Caterpillar's customers. To satisfy that need, Cat Logistics' infrastructure is designed to ship 99.8 percent of replacement part orders on the same day the order is received from the customer. There are 550,000 equipment part numbers serviced worldwide—330,000 of which are stocked day-to-day by dealers or Caterpillar warehouses—so 99.8 percent availability requires an extremely robust system.[2]

Organization

Cat Logistics is headquartered in Morton, Illinois. The company employs more than 8,000 people in 22 countries worldwide, and maintains more than 90 facilities with 18 million square feet of area for warehouses, shipping docks, and offices. Caterpillar does not break out the Cat Logistics business sales in its annual report. The company is a wholly-owned subsidiary of Caterpillar Inc., and includes four divisions:

Logistics Client Services was formed in 1987 to leverage Caterpillar's expertise in the service parts business to serve automobile maker Land Rover in the United Kingdom. It currently has more than 40 clients in several industries, including automotive (e.g., aftermarket replacement parts management for Land Rover, Ford, DaimlerChrysler, and several other car makers); aerospace and defense (SAAB Aerospace, U.S. Navy); and electronics (Ericsson, Sprint, US Cellular). In February 2002, the Caterpillar/Honeywell alliance went live with its system for the U.S. Marine Corps at Blount Island, Florida, to provide the system for their asset management and maintenance.

One of the company's current goals is to grow its aerospace business to the same size as its automotive business. In the aerospace government sector, for example, it is in a 30-year alliance with Honeywell to assure availability and delivery of auxiliary power units for the U.S. Navy's NAVAIR fleet and maintenance operations. Cat Logistics is managing all elements of the supply chain and retrogrades of F/A-18s, C-2s, P-3s, S-3s, and KC-130s.

Caterpillar Distribution Services supports Caterpillar's service parts business, servicing dealers worldwide. It has approximately 2,850 employees, of whom 750 are warehouse workers and 2,100 are in offices around the world. Customers order more than 50 million line items through this division per year.

Manufacturing, Logistics, and Transportation manages Caterpillar's inbound logistics to its manufacturing plants, overseeing a network of more

Figure 6.1: Caterpillar Logistics Services

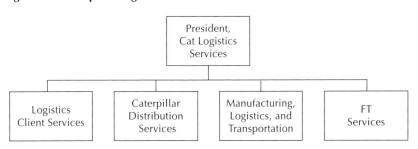

than 800 suppliers, as well as the parent company's outbound transportation. Caterpillar's network includes 200 internal facilities and approximately 1,850 dealer branches worldwide.

FT Services will work with Ford Motor Company to provide service parts distribution for various Ford automotive brands around the world. In addition, Caterpillar and Ford will collaborate with SAP to develop and resell a customized supply chain application based on SAP enterprise resource planning software. The application, Next-Gen, will be designed to "speed up the frequency and accuracy of spare parts logistics while cutting inventory costs. The software will also let Ford dealers see parts inventories and the status of customer orders via the Internet."[3] It will also benefit Cat Logistics' third-party clients and Caterpillar's Global Distribution Network.

System Description

Objectives

The objective of Cat Logistics' digital system is to enable the company to provide the following value-adding benefits for external clients and internal operations:
- Best-in-class client service
- Reduced operational costs
- Maximum end-user value

Architecture

Cat Logistics' client/server model, a 4-tier system, organizes the main components of the system architecture into user interface, business logic, database logic, and database tables.

An important part of Cat Logistics' architecture is its enterprise application integration (EAI) gateway in Tier 2. The EAI was deployed in the fall of 2000 to enable the company to integrate new, external applications more easily and cost effectively. Before the EAI, Cat Logistics would connect clients' legacy systems with its own applications via custom-built interfaces. With each client having several unique interfaces, development, time to market, and maintenance became expensive both for clients and for Cat Logistics.

The EAI provides a single point of exchange to connect clients' systems with Cat Logistics' applications. In essence, it is a "postal system" that manages messaging between disparate applications. It translates messages between software so that each tool can speak in its "native language." The

---

Cat Logistics' 4-Tier System

Tier 1 User Interface: Citrix, an application that essentially allows the client to access Cat Logistics' systems over a proprietary browser

Tier 2 Business Logic: Applications such as MIMS, SAP ERP, IM, SCPM (see the Technology/Applications section below) and the enterprise application integration gateway

Tier 3 Database Logic: Oracle/DB2

Tier 4 Database Tables: EMC

---

system was developed with IBM's WebSphere® platform product called CrossWorlds® InterChange Server, a business-to-business integration application. Figure 6.2 shows a top-level view of how the CrossWorlds application ties together internal and external applications.

Other benefits of the EAI include scalability, creation of a common integration environment, and simplification of future integration efforts. And with the number of entry points reduced, security of the system can also be managed more effectively.

Technology/Applications

The Cat Logistics infrastructure has several major applications that it uses internally for clients (proprietary) or is already integrated with:

- Planner Workbench is a proprietary tool that the company's inventory professionals use to help manage client inventory forecasting, especially to address atypical demand. For example, when a recall is made for a specific part, Planner Workbench can be used to override the normal forecasting of the part to ramp up its population in the supply chain prior to announcing the recall. The software enables the user to place new fixed requirements on the forecasting process. This is also a benefit for manufacturing, helping to smooth the demands from one period to the next—to keep the manufacturing burden as constant as possible.
- Supply Chain Performance Management (SCPM) is another proprietary application that Cat Logistics developed to monitor and manage clients' supply chains—from procurement of the part, to shipping, cross docking, receipt, inspection, put away, pick and pack, and then ship. It provides a graphical view of the supply chain to ensure that internal

Figure 6.2: Infrastructure Tools

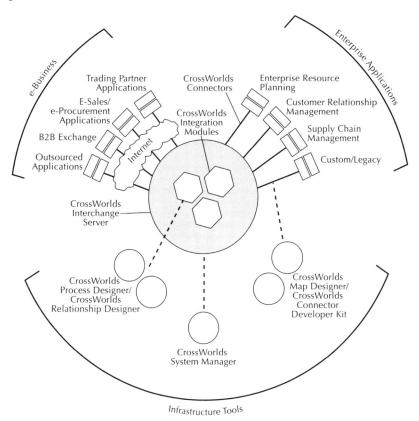

operations are meeting contracted performance metrics. Cat Logistics'
team creates performance metrics for each event and then electronically captures the execution times (start/stop) for each. These event data
are loaded into SCPM and are graphed, monitored, and "alarmed." The
alarms allow the company to see at a glance where operations are
below performance expectations—and then allow for modeling to
determine when and how operations should act to bring the event back
within tolerances. The system also does a failure analysis to determine
probable causes.

• Inventory Management/Distribution Requirements Planning is a proprietary system used to forecast replenishment based on demand patterns.
In addition, it enables modeling based on real demand data from clients.
For a new client, Cat Logistics typically will load upwards of three years
of real demand history of their entire supply chain and then run multiple simulations of various aspects of the operation—such as numbers of

warehouses, square footage, inventory requirements, geographic location, etc.—to map out the multiple scenarios that achieve the clients' supply chain specifications. The scenarios are priced with their associated inventory investments, capital investments, and any overhead burden to allow the client to calculate return on investment. The numbers generated from the simulation are the basis for the metrics that are written into the company's contracts and guaranteed to the client.

- Alliance Information Management System is an enterprise resource planning (ERP) suite of systems deployed for managing enterprise assets, specifically in terms of maintenance, repair, and overhaul. It is typically deployed for clients who have large capital investments in fleets (industries such as aerospace, trucking, mining, utilities, et al.). The system enables clients to monitor parts and system failures, schedule preventative maintenance around use, etc. By managing assets' maintenance, clients can maximize the time the individual parts are operating—thus maximizing their investments.

- SAP ERP is an ERP tool (developed by SAP AG) typically deployed by clients in industries with definable inputs required to produce specific outputs (manufacturing, supply chain management). As described previously, Caterpillar is developing a supply chain application with Ford Motor Company based on SAP's ERP system.

- Facility Logistics is a Cat Logistics proprietary system deployed atop a wireless infrastructure for warehousing management (pick and put away) within the company's worldwide facilities.

- TRACKS is a proprietary operations process that bundles warehousing events into manageable chunks of 15 minutes of work. The process allows the warehouse operation to keep the "high velocity" Cat Logistics warehousing model working smoothly.

- Schneider Utility for Managing Integrated Transportation is a system Cat Logistics licenses from third-party logistics provider Schneider Transportation to manage inbound and outbound transportation events. The system allows Caterpillar "to choose from among multiple modes of transportation to optimize costs for inbound and outbound shipments, while providing the ability to track and trace material in transit. The agreement will also allow it to have a centralized operation for managing its transportation requirements."[4]

Standards

Cat Logistics employs several standards that help the company control current processes and future system development. Three key standards that govern the company's digital logistics system include:

- **Guaranteed specifications:** The company's internal systems are designed to meet—and exceed—client specifications. Cat Logistics has a "fall on my sword before you don't get the part" culture that has allowed it to develop the internal ability to provide 99.8 percent of parts shipments within 24 hours of receiving the order.
- **Six Sigma[SM]:** "Six Sigma is a rigorous and disciplined methodology that uses data and statistical analysis to measure and improve a company's operational performance by identifying and eliminating 'defects' in manufacturing and service-related processes."[5] After two years of Six Sigma implementation, Cat Logistics saved over $40 million through several hundred projects in which they were forced to identify internal bottlenecks and find root causes.
- **Systems integration:** The company has standardized its EAI gateway to accept commercial off-the-shelf software. If a client wants to use a legacy system, Cat Logistics no longer buys the system outright. The client can implement systems that can be integrated with Cat Logistics' EAI.

Metrics

There are several metrics—such as financial, operational, procedural—used by management throughout the organization to gauge the effectiveness of their operations. Three major metrics include:

- **Ongoing investments:** Over the past 10 years, Cat Logistics has invested more than $400 million into its information system for executing and managing logistics—and currently spends an average of $100 million annually on the system. The system is supported by a staff of 700.
- **Automation:** One rule of thumb is that 95 percent of inventory is managed by automated processes, and the remaining 5 percent is managed manually by inventory professionals. The 5 percent of parts that don't conform to automation are usually subject to peculiar procurement or demand patterns that need to be managed on a special-case basis.
- **Continuous improvement:** Company management is always striving to improve operations. For example, 20 years ago, Caterpillar had more than 20 days worth of inventory in many of its factories. Through continuous improvement, many raw materials now come in multiple times per day to be used in production the same day. Overall, Caterpillar has cut inventory by half while improving the fill rate. Likewise, Cat Logistics will in some cases write specific improvement levels into client contracts, so that if Caterpillar can implement operational efficiencies, Caterpillar will get a share of the resulting cost savings.

Implementation of the Current System

Support for Cat Logistics' Mission

Cat Logistics' mission is to provide *top client service, reduced operational costs,* and *maximum end-user value.* Its digital logistics infrastructure enables the company to execute that mission in the following ways:

Top client service is built by increasing visibility, building partnerships, extending global reach, and decreasing back orders.

Having an integrated logistics solution—from supplier, to inventory, to warehousing, to transportation management and final sales data—increases visibility by giving the client and Cat Logistics the ability to see all the data that exists throughout the supply chain. By tying the whole process together through a digital logistics system, the client can analyze the data comprehensively and make the best business decisions.

Cat Logistics builds partnerships by working with clients to develop long-term relationships. Contracts typically last between five and 10 years, all the way up to 30+ years. Over 60 percent of company growth has come from existing clients. The company recognizes that it will succeed if its clients succeed.

The digital infrastructure that Cat Logistics has developed extends Cat's business around the world. It is used effectively by dealers on six continents. Likewise, Cat's international business gives the company deep knowledge and relationships in local markets worldwide. It has helped several clients grow across the globe.

Finally, Cat Logistics' system was developed to provide 99.8 percent fill rates for its original customer, Cat Inc., which lets the company offer to its own customers the value proposition, "You buy our machine and we'll do whatever it takes to keep that machine running." The only way to achieve that goal is to minimize back orders, which the Cat system achieved. That infrastructure is leveraged by CAT Logistics clients who have the same requirements of high-value, time-sensitive products.

Operational costs are reduced by reducing asset and inventory levels, using global economies of scale, and maximizing personnel productivity.

Visibility provides the ability to make predictions about supply and demand, which can then point to places in the supply chain where capital is being spent unnecessarily. This enables the asset and inventory allocations to be reduced, while remaining synchronized with service objectives.

At the same time, Cat Logistics' system provides a global network of IT, facilities, and management experience that a client can plug in to, rather than develop their own, less scaled operation. For example, the company has several facilities, centrally located throughout the U.S. and the world, that are leveraged by multiple clients.

Enabling employees to be more effective with the right mix of technology and automation can lead to reduced costs and higher productivity.

End-user value is maximized by linking supply chain specifications with customer expectations and anticipating part failures.

Cat Logistics' system helps clients identify, develop, and execute strategies to increase sales and customer retention. For example, some cell phone retailers do not carry inventory; the product is shipped directly to customers. The system can also be used to provide inventory to retailers so that customers leave the store with their cell phone in hand—enriching the customer experience and increasing retention.

Additionally, instead of reacting to failure, the logistics system can be set up to proactively order end-user parts before a customer's part fails and high-value equipment is inoperable. With the Cat system, for example, when the part fails, maintenance inventory already has it in stock to replace the failed part and keep the machine running.

Greatest Challenges to Change

Cat Logistics has a lot of experience in managing change—at client sites and internally—when implementing its digital logistics system. Key challenges include management of people, processes, and technology.

To change an organization, employees' functions and responsibilities must change—and in some cases even be eliminated. When new systems are implemented, all employees must understand why the systems are important. Management needs to instill a sense of urgency to develop supply chain efficiencies.

Traditional relationships among stakeholders do not necessarily foster the trust required among independent members of the supply chain. A third party provider can create new and more profitable relationships with its leverage and other partnerships. Then, by reducing logistics costs, a digitally integrated logistics system can lead to new market share gains.[6]

Finally, information systems must communicate across staffs, countries, and industries. Over the past two years, Cat Logistics has moved from developing customized IT solutions for each client to connecting clients via commercial off-the-shelf solutions that can interface directly with the Cat Logistics system gateway.

Security and Privacy

Cat Logistics leverages Cat Inc.'s systems network, which brings up contractual issues. How does the company ensure that it follows its agreements to keep client data separate and secure on a single network? Ensuring security is important for Cat Logistics, because its business model is based on trust that the company will deliver the highest customer service—even when the company simultaneously works for a client's competitors (e.g., automakers). Cat Logistics has several security measures to ensure that client data is kept secure.

First, the data is segregated into risk domains. Risk domains define where a client's information is located on Cat Logistics' network. Each domain is accessible only to people who have appropriate clearance within the organization. Typically, domains are separated by firewalls and passcodes. The company then develops information protection guidelines. This is the company's system for classifying information, i.e., spoken, written, and documented. The system classifies information with a red, yellow, or green color, depicting how confidential content is. For example, red is highly confidential, comprising 5 to 10 percent of Cat Logistics' total data. On an ongoing basis, the security team identifies relevant data and monitors that it is accurately classified. The guidelines also identify information owners and delegates. Often, a client manager within Cat Logistics will be identified as the information owner who will designate specific employees with access to certain forms of client data. The information owner works directly with a security custodian in the information technology department to put necessary digital rules in place (usernames, passwords, tags on documents). The system also prescribes security maintenance issues (e.g., ensuring that confidential data is marked and maintained as confidential).

The company has a dedicated security officer, with a staff of three, for overseeing security throughout the company worldwide. The security team reviews all software to ensure the application is safe for the existing environment, and to make necessary adjustments to firewall configurations (e.g., open up ports for designated information users). The security team also controls the identity management system, known as IMAP. IMAP is a major security implementation that allows the security team to identify everyone who accesses the Cat network and mainframes. Several types of users—external consultants, dealers, agents, employees, customers, suppliers—have access to the network, so IMAP provides a system of log-in identifications and passwords for tracking where users are in the network. The team monitors the company networks "24/7" for virus activities and access history. Virus protection is deployed at servers, firewalls, and desktops. Additionally, the system regularly undergoes independent audits by outside consultants.

The security is certified with a "Statement on Auditing Standards" (SAS) No. 70 for service organizations, an internationally recognized auditing standard developed by the American Institute of Certified Public Accountants. SAS 70 is the authoritative guidance that allows service organizations to disclose their control activities and processes to their customers and their customers' auditors in a uniform reporting format. An SAS 70 examination signifies that a service organization has had its control objectives and control activities examined by an independent accounting and auditing firm."[7]

As a final measure, Cat maintains a culture where information is controlled strictly. Previously there were many levels of protection, which drove up the cost in storage and management and decreased opportunities for employees to access data and make beneficial decisions for clients. With the simplified Information Protection Guidelines, the culture of keeping client information confidential—using a strict "need to know" guideline—is ingrained in all employee processes.

Lessons Learned

In Cat Logistics' ongoing development of its system and services, the company has made several key observations that will be helpful to government agencies looking to improve their logistics operations:

- **Define an accurate specification of logistics needs.** Many times, potential clients define their specifications one way, only to go with a lower bidder who cannot execute on the specs with the proposed bid.
- **Develop an infrastructure that allows an accurate view of overall channel performance.** Organizations should be wary of falling into the trap of viewing each part of its supply chain (i.e., inventory, warehousing, forecasting) as a discrete event. If the overall supply chain is not integrated effectively, it will cause significantly lower overall channel performance.
- **Have a true view of end-user service level requirements.** By understanding what the needs of end-users are, the supply chain upstream can be analyzed to find efficiencies that help to meet expectations.
- **Consider lifecycle cost of a fleet—not just initial capital cost.** Because of the severe conditions in which Caterpillar's construction equipment typically operates, up to 70 percent of a vehicle's total cost could be in maintenance alone. Agencies could reduce their asset investments, as well as improve their current fleets, by utilizing enterprise asset management systems within an integrated logistics system.
- **Develop contingency plans for atypical circumstances.** Cat Logistics has a "SWAT" team for overriding automated systems when special circumstances arise, ensuring customer satisfaction.

- **Cultivate long-term partnerships with companies that need high-end service.** Logistics can be a strategic differentiator for any company, if executed correctly. Developing a strong, working relationship with a third party logistics provider takes time. Cat Logistics has found that its long-term, high-quality service offering creates the best value for entities in industries such as durables, technology, and manufacturing.
- **Use private-industry management practices to develop systems and drive efficiencies.** Practices such as linking salaries with incentives and maximizing return on investment in a project can help agencies implement and maintain systems at lower cost.

Future

As Cat Logistics focuses future growth in automotive, aerospace, consumer durables, inbound manufacturing, and government sectors—becoming one of the largest third party logistics providers in the world by 2006—the company's digital logistics system will evolve to create new efficiencies and better service for clients. In the short term, the company will continue to incorporate new technologies into its infrastructure, as well as move to web-enabled, off-the-shelf software. In the long-term, Cat Logistics believes the global business community is realizing the power of a world-class logistics system to improve customer satisfaction while lowering costs and reducing assets. At the same time, government agencies and defense forces around the world are turning to improved logistics to help in areas such as improved weapons systems availability—reducing procurement spending while improving the readiness of the assets. A natural consequence is that defense forces are outsourcing a wider range of logistics functions to leverage commercial best practices and get better value from shrinking defense budgets.

Conclusion

Cat Logistics' digital logistics system has yielded success for its clients and Cat's own internal processes because it has afforded three key best practices:
1. **Integrate all aspects in supply chain.** By enabling the client to bring together suppliers, inventory, warehousing, and transportation management, efficiencies can be identified and realized, and the best business decisions can be made.

2. **Meet and exceed well-defined specifications.** The system should provide logistics services that reach accurate goals of end-user expectations and business necessity.
3. **Develop and maintain profitable, long-term partnerships.** In providing functionalities, management, and trust, you ensure your strategic partners can grow to meet future requirements.

By implementing these and other best practices in logistics, government agencies can improve their processes, lower their costs, and provide the country with better products and services.

Endnotes

1. Paul Joseph, Vice President, Client Services Division, Caterpillar Inc. Interviewed by William Lucyshyn and Dzintars Dzilna. Morton, IL., 27 July 2002.

Troy Avery, Senior Systems Analyst, Technical Services Division, Caterpillar Inc. Interviewed by William Lucyshyn and Dzintars Dzilna. Morton, IL., 27 July 2002.

Lisa Nethery, Technical Services Manager, Client Services Division, Caterpillar Inc. Interviewed by William Lucyshyn and Dzintars Dzilna. Morton, IL., 27 July 2002.

Dan Snell, Information Security Officer, Cat Logistics, Caterpillar Inc. Interviewed by William Lucyshyn and Dzintars Dzilna. Morton, IL., 27 July 2002.

2. Approximately 95 percent of orders can be satisfied from either the local dealer or facing facility; the dealer electronic search system brings the order fill up to 99.8 percent. The last 0.2 percent of back orders is usually filled by suppliers in 24 to 72 hours; the system takes the order and electronically routs it to the respective supplier. Estimated ship date for back orders is usually provided within 24 hours. Naturally, the company provides call centers with 24/7/365 service.

3. Marc L. Sonigini, "Ford, Caterpillar Team with SAP on Supply Chain Project," *Computerworld,* 5 August, 2002. Viewed at http://www.computerworld.com/softwaretopics/erp/story/0,10801,73207,00.html, August 2002.

4. Frontline Solutions, "Caterpillar Turns to Rival Logistics ASP," *Frontline Solutions,* March 2002.

5. Maqzen Maswady and Craig Tonner, "Six Sigma." Viewed at http://isixsigma.com/dictionary/Six_Sigma-85.htm, September 2002.

6. The first three points are adopted from a letter written (published Winter 2000) by Larry Newbanks of CAT Logistics to the editor of MIT Sloan Management Review, in response to an article (published Summer 2000) called "Saturn's Supply-Chain Innovation: High Value in After-Sales Service."

7. American Institute of Certified Public Accountants, "About SAS 70." Viewed at http://www.sas70.com/about.htm, September 2002.

Defense Logistics Agency's Business Systems Modernization: Delivering 21st Century Logistics

William Lucyshyn
and
Sandra Young

Introduction

The Department of Defense is in the business of supporting war-fighters, an industry where a competitive advantage in logistics literally can mean the difference between life and death.

The Defense Logistics Agency (DLA) is the combat support agency responsible for the supply distribution, reutilization, marketing, disposal, tracking, and storing of roughly 4.5 million items. DLA logistics processes impact a supply chain valued at close to $10 billion. For decades, DLA has coordinated logistics on a global scale. Managing the logistics of 89 percent of the consumable items in the Department of Defense (DoD), the DLA provides everything from toothpicks to tank parts for U.S. troops at home and abroad. In short, logistics is a huge component of everything the Department of Defense accomplishes.

The similarity between logistics in the commercial world and the world of defense goes further than impact, however. It is only very recently that corporations around the country have started to invest significant resources in logistics management. The Department of Defense, however, has not kept pace with logistics management software developments in the private sector. As a result, DLA's systems were not developed using an enterprise-wide approach. Over time, one of the world's largest and most complex logistical operations in the world became inefficient and costly.

In 1998, about the same time that corporations were awakening to the tremendous gains that could be made by improving logistical processes, the DLA tasked itself with completely renovating its logistics system—the result was the Business Systems Modernization (BSM) program.

In recent years, DLA has designed and launched a logistics modernization program that is completely reworking how it provides logistics support and the systems used to do so. Its goal is to turn DLA into a customer-focused, proactive agency capable of providing state-of-the art logistics support.

With the initiation of the BSM program in 1998, DLA began a process to restructure the agency, reengineer its business processes, and completely

---

"At the Pentagon, a lot of technology has been bought to upgrade weapons, but traditionally, not enough energy, attention, and money has been put toward upgrading and streamlining the level of back-office technology."

—Jay Farrar, former Marine and current vice
president for the Center for Strategic and
International Studies

"Before BSM, DLA had predominately an item focus. We bought items and you had them available. If someone ordered them, we had them on contract or in our warehouse to ship and that was it."

—Douglas French, Chief, BSM Office, Logistics Operations, HQ DLA

overhaul the information technology (IT) systems used to support its new focus. The program was on schedule and on budget. As of July 31, 2002, BSM is being used to manage 170,000 items and is scheduled to be fully operational for all 4.5 million DLA items by 2005. The total cost of the program is estimated at $700 million.

Once completed, BSM will replace legacy systems, including the mainframe-based legacy systems. It will allow DLA to track product deliveries, budgets, demand projections, and supply schedules in real time. It will accelerate the vendor payment process; align budgeting, pricing, and cost management; provide more efficient and reliable service; reduce the purchase of excess materials and parts; more accurately forecast material needs; and leverage purchasing power and logistical advantages to get the best value for items purchased in the market. DLA's vision is to provide the material that their military customers actually need, in the amount that they need, when and where they need it.

Background

DLA Process before BSM

Prior to the BSM reengineering effort, DLA maintained more of an arm's-length relationship with its military customers. The agency organization and focus was centered on supply items. They were grouped into Federal Supply Classes—ordered, stored, and managed by item managers (see Figure 7.1). The item managers made decisions on purchasing items based on the requirements provided by the military services and on how much of a given item was purchased in previous years. The item manager would give his/her purchase request to contracting, and contracting would order the materials from vendors and suppliers. Material would be purchased for direct delivery to the customer or for storage in DLA warehouses until ordered by the services.[2]

Figure 7.1: DLA Processes before Business Systems Modernization: Product/Function Focus

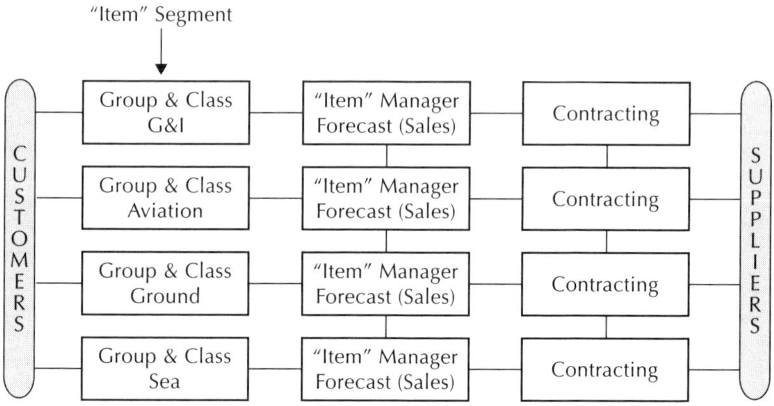

Built on two premises: item segments and forecasts (item focus);
little collaboration and planning

Process Problems

The arm's-length relationship that DLA maintained with the military services created numerous problems. Absent a good requirements communications network, there were often misunderstandings between DLA and its customers about when and how much of a given item would be required. Item managers made their ordering decisions based on existing stockpiles, budgetary constraints, and their estimates of true need. Inevitably, DLA would have available for some customers more parts than they really wanted (or expected), and for others fewer items than they really needed. "Today we're in kind of a guessing game. Our expectations could differ from customers' expectations because there's no mutual understanding. The result can be an unhappy customer."[3]

Furthermore, since customers are not charged until items are requisitioned and delivered, they do not suffer any penalty for inflated requests. DLA is forced to hold material it purchases, and is saddled with warehousing surplus inventory until the items are requisitioned or become obsolete. The process is not as efficient or cost-effective as it could be. In the 1990s, DLA officials began to acknowledge that they had to find a better way to service their customers' real requirements.

DLA Technology before BSM

Innovative reengineering was limited, however, by 20-year-old technology that had been designed to support the existing item-focused process.

Before BSM, DLA relied primarily on two legacy systems—the Standard Automated Material Management Systems (SAMMS) and the Defense Integrated Supply Management Systems (DISMS)—to monitor equipment, parts, and subsistence inventory. The systems were designed in the 1970s and 1980s, respectively, to help item managers maintain stockpiles based on estimates of military need.

Information Technology Problems

In the late 1990s, Y2K concerns mandated that the agency closely evaluate all of its IT systems. The existing systems were not Y2K compliant.

Initially, the DLA considered transitioning SAMMS and DISMS into a current IT environment and continuing with the same work processes, organizational structure, and skill sets.

However, in addition to Y2K problems, the evaluation showed that the legacy systems had not kept pace with current IT capabilities. "SAMMS has become an outmoded system based on old business practices and obsolete technology. It has become a system that is increasingly expensive to operate and maintain, based on excessive downtime, high operating costs, cumbersome system modification processes, and poor performance."[4] Both SAMMS and DISMS were batch systems and could not provide real-time access to logistics data. They required complex, special programs to extract data for any single purpose requirement.

DLA officials concluded that the shortfalls of the legacy systems caused "too many challenges to DLA personnel, customers, and suppliers."

The systems could be patched to function past New Year's Eve 1999, but they would not support DLA's customer-focused vision for the new millennium.

In 1998, the option of re-hosting the old systems was ruled out. DLA began to completely reengineer its business processes as well as the systems that supported them, and the Business Systems Modernization program was launched.

"To have put SAMMS 'on a life-sustaining system' to try to keep it going ... would have been a considerable investment. We looked at where we were going and decided we had to go beyond a technological substitution."[5]

—Jim Katzman, Process Reengineering

The BSM Solution

Objectives

BSM is three modernization processes in one. It involves the reengineering of the operational functions and the simultaneous development of a robust information technology platform that will enable and support those operational changes. And it involves the restructuring, retraining, and re-development of DLA employees.

The goals of BSM are to: 1) improve customer service, 2) provide best-value solutions, 3) provide training experience, 4) replace legacy systems, and 5) reengineer processes.

To accomplish these goals, DLA focused on four main functions:

- **Order Fulfillment:** Acquiring orders, maintaining customer relationships, and delivering material and services to meet customer needs.
- **Procurement:** Identifying and qualifying contracting suppliers, and obtaining their materials and services in accordance with customer needs.
- **Financial Management:** Defining and managing budgets, products, pricing, and operating costs.
- **Planning:** Understanding customer needs (demand) and the resources available to meet needs (supply), and implementing actions to match them.

In general terms, BSM's objective was to transform DLA from being a reactive, item-oriented agency to being a proactive, customer-focused agency.

Significant Changes

On the technical side, DLA officials wanted to move beyond the old system but also beyond the idea that they had to design new systems internally. The BSM program is a COTS (commercial off-the-shelf) software-based solution (see Figure 7.2). It uses the capabilities of a fleet of software that are commercially available, including SAP's Enterprise Resource Planning (ERP) system, which serves as the backbone. Then there are "bolt-on" applications such as Manugistics' Advanced Planning & Scheduling System (APS), and PD^2, the contract-writing software. Based on identified gaps in the commercial software, BSM systems also contain other COTS that are configurable to meet the needs of the specific logistics commodities managed by DLA.

In terms of structure and process, BSM changes the focus of DLA from items organized in classes to customers organized into segments: Aviation, Maritime, and Land and Troop Support (see Figure 7.3). Under the BSM sys-

Figure 7.2: BSM's Technical Blueprint

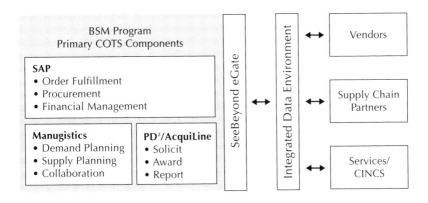

tem, the *item manager* position no longer exists. There are now *demand planners,* whose function is to work with their respective customers to analyze and understand what the customers' needs are and to process demand plans accordingly, and *supply planners,* whose function is to build a time phased inventory plan and have available material so that DLA can fill demand plans efficiently.

For example, the Air Force demand planner would meet with Air Force managers to determine what their depot maintenance plans and schedules are for the following year, and what parts and supplies will be required. The planner will then coordinate a demand plan that outlines all of the material requirements for all of the Air Force's maintenance plans. Rather than maintaining an artificially inflated quantity of parts and supplies, the Air Force demand planner, working closely with the Air Force, will determine realistic inventory quantities based on a realistic assessment of the planned activities and maintenance schedules.

The demand planner then submits the demand plan into the new logistics support software, which translates them into supply plans that are oriented by stock number. In laymen's terms, the new support software assesses the number of like parts the entire military will need by adding up the demands from all the different demand planners. The supply plan indicates how many of any one part DLA needs to buy to service all the military's needs.

If DLA is to successfully service its customers' demands efficiently and accurately and be cost-effective, the agency must develop a relationship with vendors as well. Once DLA enters the market with their supply plans, it becomes the customer. Under the BSM plan, the agency will develop long-term supplier relationships and work closely with vendors so that the

Figure 7.3: BSM Changes DLA's Processes: Customer Focus

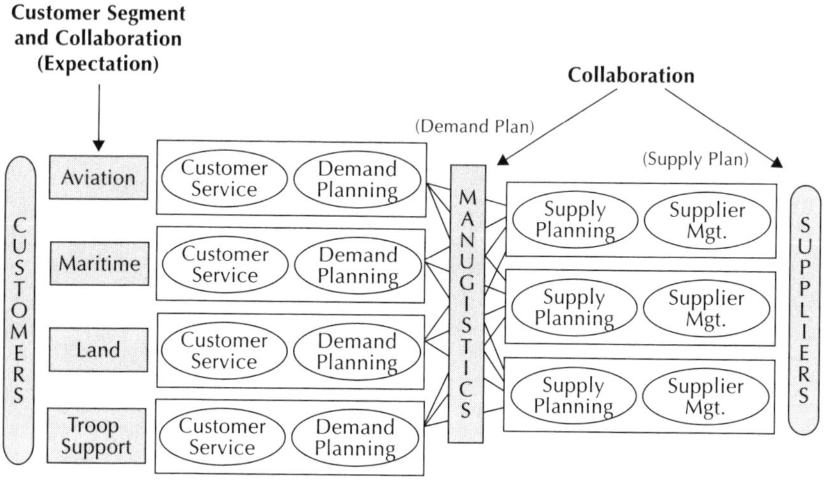

Built on two premises: customer segment and planning via collaboration

vendors can plan ahead and position themselves to better provide what DLA's customers' need.

Implementation

According to DLA, BSM is the sixth try in the last 20 years at changing DLA business processes. Even with the knowledge that the agency is 0 for 5, managers of the new system are confident that this time is different and that the agency will succeed. This confidence seems to be rooted in how the system has been implemented.[6]

Key officials point to the following implementation strategies and decisions as being critical to their success:

- Partnerships
- Involvement of senior officials and users
- Balanced input from IT Operations and Logistics Operations
- Decision to go with COTS
- Unique concept demonstration strategy
- Balance between automation and interaction

> "We are trying to all understand each other across the spectrum of the supply chain rather than having a series of arm's-length relationships."
>
> — *Douglas French, Chief BSM Office, Logistics Operations, HQ DLA*

Partnerships

Managers attribute a great deal of their confidence in the technological capacity of BSM to the fact that they worked *with* partners to create solutions at every stage.

DLA hired a contractor to help them run a competition to choose DLA's implementation partner. The implementation partner was selected. As integrator, the implementation partner introduced DLA to all the commercial and business best practices of logistics management, but DLA was involved at every level of solution development.

"[The implementation partner] did not just build a system and hand it over to us."[7] DLA officials recognized that the agency had to develop and maintain systems expertise so that once the contractor had implemented the BSM system, DLA would be confident that it included the solutions that the agency needed, and DLA would be able to maintain and utilize the system on its own in the future.

Managing and maintaining the partnerships is a crucial balancing act that must be managed constantly for success. According to BSM Program Manager Jim Kimberly, "you have to discipline yourself to be in control of your business rules, of *how* you conduct business, because that is what makes you unique."

Involvement of Senior Officials and Users

Previous attempts failed because they did not engage senior management or the workforce. In contrast, every two weeks almost every senior executive manager within the agency meets and talks about the issues facing BSM—sometimes for hours. According to David Falvey, DLA's program executive officer of Information Operations, they are actively working to remove roadblocks to implementation in their business units.[8]

Involving and engaging the workforce has also been a primary focus and a key to success. DLA has developed BSM on the premise that all DLA employees impact at least one subset of all processes.[9] "DLA leaders say they know that the success of BSM depends on the person who will be using the system. The leaders are committed to providing the training, experience, and opportunity to succeed."[10] BSM has focused on employee

"Even in DLA, we still have to be aware of the fact that we never
should give up the understanding of our systems to anyone."

—*Jim Kimberly, BSM Program Manager, DLA*
Information Operations

involvement and has incorporated employee training as one of its fundamental objectives.

To ensure continuity of the effort, DLA utilized a cross-functional executive board to oversee the BSM program. The Modernization Executive
Board adopted primary tenets (guidelines) for the program that cannot be
changed without the approval of the board. The board is composed of all of
DLA's senior executives, representing the human resources, financial operations, information operations, and logistics operations directorates. These
members are invested in the program and help to ensure that the program
receives the support needed and achieve the BSM program goals. The
unique authority to approve all changes to the primary tenets helps DLA
manage the challenges most agencies experience during leadership transitions when major projects can easily be sidetracked or changed mid-course.

Balanced Input from IT Operations and Logistics Operations:

In addition to senior support and involvement in the BSM process was
an effort to simultaneously reengineer processes and technology; it was the
first change that really sought balanced input from both the Logistics and IT
sections of the agency.

Previous SAMMS replacement attempts were technological changes. "We
wrote our requirements around the way we did business and handed them
over to automators to automate these processes to help us."[11] This time people, processes, and technology reengineering was consistently a team effort.

An internal structure was established for the development of BSM. The
structure formalized the need for balance between the IT group (internally,
J-6) tasked with IT solutions and the Logistics group (internally, J-3) tasked
with challenging the agency's logistics processes. As a result, both were
constantly and wholeheartedly involved in the process.

Decision to Go with COTS

One of the most significant changes that came about through this dia-
logue between the implementation partner, J-3 (Logistics), and J-6 (IT) was
the decision to abandon the "build-it-yourself" technology concept in favor
of COTS technology solutions.

Traditionally all IT systems implemented in the Department of Defense were designed in-house. The design, production, and coding processes could take years. So even if designers use state-of-the-art technology to develop IT systems for DoD, by the time that solution is implemented it is outdated.

By using COTS rather than designing the entire system in-house, DLA not only saves design expenses—and time—when it is implemented, the technology is also state-of-the-art. The decision to use COTS also addressed the question of BSM's ability to be a long-term solution for DLA. DLA will benefit from commercial sector development upgrades at no additional design costs. Not insignificantly, BSM's use of COTS is in line with the President's Management Agenda, which emphasizes reducing the overall design and maintenance costs of AIS, or automated information systems.

Unique Concept Demonstration Strategy

After testing, BSM was launched in a "concept demonstration" phase to learn operational lessons on a small group of items, prior to implementing for the bulk of DLA's business. The strategy was to select low-risk items that were representative of the broad types of products DLA supports, and switch those items over to BSM completely. The "concept demonstration" would test the entire network of reengineered processes, COTS technologies, staff training, and systems integration all at once, and live.

On July 31, 2002, DLA conducted its initial release of BSM. Some 170,000 items were switched from the legacy system and the old DLA process to BSM systems and process. "The items are a representative cross-section of DLA's product line," but none were critical weapons systems items.[12]

The goal of the initial release was to implement 80 percent of the requirements for 5 percent of the [DLA] users. "In the next release, in a year or so, DLA will try to use BSM to pick up the remaining 20 percent requirements."[13] After that, DLA will roll out additional items in batches over time. The strategic plan indicates that DLA will have implemented BSM across all items by 2005.

Balance between Automation and Interaction

DLA officials recognized that to *efficiently and proactively* meet the needs of the services, there had to be both automation and interaction. "So that when [DLA] collaborates with the Air Force on supporting the overhaul of an F-16 aircraft, everything associated with parts is automated,"[14] but customers can still interact with the system to determine when and how the overhaul should happen. The Advanced Planning and Scheduling system (APS) incorporated as part of the BSM process provides this capability. As the services plan the overhaul, they have a sense of what the bill of materials will look like and how it behaves. At the same time, BSM has an understanding of what has to be bought and delivered and when. "We believe that we can move into a proactive supply chain management the way Northrop-Grumman, Procter & Gamble, or an Oshkosh runs their operations today."[15]

Challenges

The greatest obstacles that DLA faced were the regulatory requirements placed on DLA (and all federal agencies) in regards to procurement. When asked if they would do anything differently, David Falvey and Jim Kimberly responded that they would have been more forceful in pursuing statutory and regulatory relief in the procurement process, so that they could have made more use of the commercial capabilities. During their preliminary analysis, the DLA modernization board identified 17 policy issues they had to address. Some were regulations, some laws, and others DLA instructions. According to Kimberly, "there is not an adequate procurement solution in the public sector" to address these requirements. DLA either had to get the policy changed or spend money developing supplemental systems to address the requirements.

Weaknesses

BSM seems to have made great headway in changing the way DLA views its customers, how it views itself and its purpose, and how it does business. The stockpiling of obsolete items will be reduced as BSM makes the supply chain more efficient and as customers become more confident in DLA. This is especially true for maintenance items. However, for operational supplies, DLA still faces the reality that it does not have complete control or insights into the entire supply chain. And, due to the nature of DoD, demands can be a lot more unpredictable than they are in the commercial sector. "Who would have known two years ago that we would be

---

"The hard part is how you better relate to one another to move the environment from one that is reactive to one that is proactive relative to managing the overhaul of an F15 airplane or other functions.... The biggest piece of the puzzle is APS."

—*Jim Kimberly, BSM Program Manager, DLA Information Operations*

having major operations going on in Afghanistan and that we would be consuming everything from helicopter parts to combat boots at a greatly increased rate? And that is where the inefficiency of what we do comes to bear compared to a commercial company. We have to be prepared to provide what the war fighter needs, when he needs it."[16] BSM does improve material estimates.

Future Prospects for DLA

Currently, DLA officials are looking to the future when independent testers are scheduled to do the Initial Operational Test and Evaluation (IOT&E) of the initial BSM launch. And they are working to ensure that the last of DLA's items can be switched to BSM and that the legacy systems can be switched off in 2005. In addition to rolling out the rest of BSM in its current form, DLA will be considering its role in retail-level logistics.

DLA has historically been associated with wholesale logistics. It manages DoD items until they reach the service. Each service actually owns and manages the items at the retail level. But as the services are trying to get more war-fighting capability, they are looking to DLA to take on more of the management and logistics of retail-level stocks as well.[17]

With SAMMS, that was not an option. DLA simply would not have been able to compute requirements at other than a systemwide wholesale level. DLA could compute only what was needed in the big warehouses. It could not "calculate how many widgets you needed at each customer installation," said Douglas French, chief of DLA's Business Modernization Office, Logistic Operations. With BSM technology, it is an option.

In fact, if the Office of the Secretary of Defense assigns responsibility to DLA for the retail portion of the logistics operation, it will give the agency a closer connection to the military needs on the ground. It may allow the agency to further narrow the gap between estimates of need and real need.

The Modernization Executive Board will help ensure the full implementation and long-term success of the BSM effort. Unlike other government organizations that often have projects redirected or sidetracked during leadership transitions, this management oversight structure requires approval by the board for any changes to the primary tenets (guidelines) for the BSM.

Endnotes

1. Douglas M. Lambert, James R. Stock, and Lisa M. Ellram, *Fundamentals of Logistics Management,* (Boston: Irwin McGraw-Hill, 1998), 10.

2. Douglas French, chief, Business Modernization Office, Logistics Operations, Hq Defense Logistics Agency. Interviewed by William Lucyshyn and Sandra Young. Arlington, Va., July 31, 2002.

3. Jim Katzaman, "Knowing Customers Better Than They Know Themselves." Viewed at http://www.dla.mil/j-6/bsm/html/core_messages/customer_serv.htm, August 19, 2002.

4. Defense Logistics Agency, Business Systems Modernization Program Office, "Frequently Asked Questions—Why do we have to get rid of SAMMS?" Viewed at http://www.dla.mil/j-6/bsm/faq/qsamms.htm, August 19, 2002.

5. Jim Katzaman, "Process Reengineering: Jump the 'Fence,' Enjoy the Ride." Viewed at http://www.dla.mil/j-6/bsm/html/core_messages/process_reeng.htm, August 19, 2002.

6. Ibid.

7. David Falvey, program executive officer, Defense Logistics Agency Information Operations. Interviewed by William Lucyshyn and Sandra Young. Arlington, Va., July 31, 2002.

8. Ibid.

9. Katzaman, "Process Reengineering."

10. Jim Katzaman, "BSM Leaders Commit To Workforce Training." Viewed at http://www.dla.mil/j-6/bsm/html/core_messages/workforce_success.htm, August 19, 2002.

11. Katzaman, "Process Reengineering."

12. Dan Caterinicchia, "DLA begins rollout of Modernization System," *Federal Computer Week,* August 6, 2002. Viewed at http://www.fcw.com/fcw/articles/2002/0812/news-dla-08-12-02.asp, August 19, 2002.

13. Falvey, interview.

14. Jim Kimberly, BSM program manager, Defense Logistics Agency Information Operations. Interviewed by William Lucyshyn and Sandra Young. Arlington, Va., July 31, 2002.

15. Falvey, interview.

16. French, interview.

17. Ibid.

CHAPTER EIGHT

General Electric Remote Monitoring and Diagnostics: Leveraging Technology to Automate Logistics

Brandon Griesel
and
William Lucyshyn

Introduction

Imagine a loved one who has a serious accident and needs an MRI (magnetic resonance imaging) to help diagnose his or her injuries. We expect that when we show up at the hospital emergency room, the MRI is operating. Even though it is a machine, we expect it to be up and running with 100 percent reliability. General Electric (GE) provides nearly perfect reliability with its remote monitoring and diagnostic capability. Remote monitoring and diagnostics (RM&D) is a great tool for equipment that needs to function at near 100 percent reliability or that has a high capital cost and life-cycle costs exceeding the purchase price.[1] It can diagnose the problem and, many times, can fix the problem remotely, thereby providing the highest reliability possible.

Now, imagine you are the maintenance manager responsible for the upkeep and timely maintenance of aircraft engines—you want to know how many engines will need maintenance in the next month and what parts you will need. With that information, you could replace a part or overhaul an entire engine immediately once needed. This could save hundreds of thousands of dollars by avoiding replacing parts before necessary or replacing them before they fail catastrophically and cause major maintenance problems.[2]

Although this technology, like that of the temperature gauge on your automobile, has been around for decades, new advances at GE have allowed them to get the most out of RM&D technology.[3] Advances in data storage and processing speeds have allowed GE to use new statistical modeling techniques to forecast failures better. This is done by identifying the most important factors that need to be examined in a failure.[4] This chapter will explain in further detail the background of GE, how RM&D helps automate logistics processes, the strengths and weaknesses of RM&D technology, results GE is seeing in the Jet Engine division, the lessons learned in developing the technology, and the future of RM&D.

GE has been in business for more than a hundred years. "GE is a diversified technology and services company dedicated to creating products that make life better—from aircraft engines and power generation to financial services, medical imaging, television programming and plastics, GE operates in more than 100 countries and employs more than 300,000 people worldwide."[5] GE, the only company that has been on the Dow Jones Industrial Index since 1896, continues to be a great example of a growth company. The GE Research and Development Center in Schenectady, New York, has been a catalyst for GE's growth. The Research and Development Center has developed products and services, such as the modern X-ray tube, the tungsten filament, the first television broadcast, and the basis for the microwave, as well as improvements in computed tomography (CAT) scanners, MRI, and RM&D devices.

GE's Corporate Research and Development department has many divisions, such as Energy & Propulsion Technologies, Chemical Technologies, and Information & Decision Technologies, under which remote monitoring and diagnostics is housed. The goal of the Information & Decision Technologies Laboratory is to find ways to turn data into vital business knowledge that GE can use to satisfy its customers' needs.[6] This is accomplished within a Six Sigma[SM] environment, using statistical modeling, case-based reasoning, data mining, various other labs, and sophisticated statistical techniques.

Remote Monitoring and Logistics

RM&D helps to automate logistics processes such as purchasing, transportation, storage, and repair. Remote monitoring can range from the simplest form of measuring and reordering supplies to the more complex function of tracking and forecasting when jet engine maintenance should be done. An example of a simple supply chain is displayed below with information on what remote monitoring and diagnostic tools could be used to improve that portion of the supply chain.

Suppliers	Manufacturing	Distribution	Customer/ Maintenance
Monitoring Raw Material Supplies:	Monitoring Manufacturing:	Radio Frequency Indicators (RFID Tags):	Forecasting & Diagnostics:
Allows for automatic renewals of orders.	Decreases downtime via devices that alert maintenance personnel to problems earlier and provide them with better information.	Allows for better tracking of parts and equipment, which helps decrease inventory on hand.	Provides vital information about when a part or piece of equipment might fail, sometimes fixing problems before they happen.

Suppliers

One of the simplest remote monitoring devices can be used to track when supplies need to be replenished at a customer's warehousing or manufacturing site. An example of this is the plastics manufacturers that GE supports. GE uses a vendor-managed inventory strategy for their plastics customers.

Customers can see silo-level data at any time via the web-based Global Vendor Management Inventory service. GE uses sound sensor technology and Six Sigma analysis to optimize the supply chain by lowering inventory levels, resulting in improved manufacturing stability.[7]

Manufacturing

Manufacturing equipment can be monitored to make sure that everything is running smoothly, and to check small problems that could become bigger problems if ignored. If done right, the manufacturing firm can save a lot of money because its equipment will become more reliable and they will not have to worry about costly work stoppages. GE uses RM&D technology to increase equipment productivity through lowering the elapsed time to repair in their industrial power systems.

By using RM&D technology, GE reduces to a few minutes the time from receiving information on a request to attaining an available engineer for the maintenance. This is because GE has been monitoring the equipment and can properly determine what type of engineer is needed to fix the problem quickly. Sometimes the necessity of bringing an engineer on-site is eliminated because the fix may be done remotely. If an engineer is required on-site, however, the time from the engineer's arrival to the solving of the problem also can be reduced because resources are more easily attainable and collaboration among engineers is easier.[8]

Distribution

Another technology used in the distribution portion of the supply chain under the remote monitoring and diagnostics umbrella is radio frequency indicator (RFID) tags. RFID technology helps track parts that are being distributed to help GE or its customers maintain equipment. For GE service contracts, GE is paid by how fast parts are installed into the product their customer is maintaining. GE uses these tags to track where their parts are and what parts they have available. By keeping better track of what parts they have and their location, GE can lower inventory and distribution costs.

An example of the use of this technology can be seen in GE Power Systems. A few years ago, the energy shortages on the west coast caused a major spike in demand for megawatts.[9] During this period of massive growth, tracking of supplies was done by pencil and paper. Using the pencil and paper method, GE found it hard to track efficiently when and where a part was located. With RFID technology, GE was able to know the quantities and locations of critical parts, thereby decreasing GE's need to carry extra parts in inventory.

Another example of RFID technology is tracking parts flow during maintenance procedures, such as the one GE uses for jet engines. By tracking the parts of a jet engine as they are processed through maintenance procedures, a maintenance analyst can spot potential inefficiencies in the process. By eliminating inefficient processes, the total cost of the maintenance of the engines can be lowered. In addition, this technology provides the valuable customer service tool of telling the customer exactly where the part is in the maintenance process. These RFID tags are now approaching a size (about as big as a grain of sugar) and a price (at high volumes, they will cost as little as a nickel) that may enable their application to extend to lower-cost items—from manufacturing to distribution and even to retail environments.[10]

Customer/Maintenance Process

Some of the biggest advances in RM&D have been in the area of maintenance for major industrial equipment for GE and its customers. RM&D is used to track when the equipment or part of the equipment will fail. This allows GE to get a replacement part ordered, delivered, and installed before the failure, thus reducing downtime. Two major functions are involved in detecting when a part will fail or when to overhaul complex equipment. The first is to detect the problems with the equipment, and the second is to forecast problems before they happen.[11] Of course, monitoring technology has been around for a while, a simple example of this being the oil light in your car. But only recently has this technology been taken to the next level.

Three advances have helped RM&D become more powerful and useful than it was in the past. The first advance was in the ability to design and build miniature, lightweight sensors. The second is the trend to transition from mechanical controls to digital controls, facilitating the collection of digital data. Finally, even though collecting a lot more data on complex equipment like jet engines is easier, the need for better ways of gleaning knowledge from the data remains. Increases in computing power and new statistical techniques improve researchers' ability to analyze the data and extract valuable information from it.[12]

With the increase in the speed and capacity of computers, engineers are now able to sift through many variables quickly, whereas, in the past, analysts and engineers made educated guesses using only a few variables and found only the most obvious problems. In addition, advanced statistical techniques have played a key role in making the collected data valuable business knowledge. One of the most helpful techniques, decision trees, goes further than the classical regression analysis. It does not assume a simple relationship among input variables—such as age, distance traveled, and operating temperature—and the output variable failure of the equipment. Given enough data, a decision tree can model almost any relationship, no matter how complex.[13] On the other hand, if regression analysis was used and the amount of data continued to increase, there would be a point of diminishing returns. With access to powerful computers and sophisticated statistics, scientists and engineers are able to collect and monitor data on many variables. This allows scientists and engineers to make more accurate forecasts and diagnoses of complex, sophisticated equipment like jet aircraft or diesel-electric locomotives.

One example of how GE is using these advances to improve the quality of their service is with the practice of maintaining and overhauling jet engines. According to GE's Aircraft Engines website, the main goals for the remote diagnostic service in the aircraft engine division are to:[14]

- "Reduce operational interruptions by avoiding major performance and maintenance issues."
- "Increase the time the engines stay on the wing, through better management and monitoring of engine temperature margins."
- "Provide better troubleshooting efficiency and speed by providing expert technical support, utilizing advanced diagnostics tools, and accessing information at our fingertips."

GE has long-term contracts in place with airlines such as Southwest and US Airways. Usually lasting about 10 years, these contracts are managed using the number of cycles[15] flown, combined with mandated part replacements (the FAA requires that specific parts on the engine be replaced after flying a specified number of cycles).[16] When GE decides to overhaul an engine, it must have a replacement engine to put back on the plane. Because GE is responsible for the capital costs of the engines, which can cost millions of dollars, and for parts, which can cost tens of thousands of dollars, it is very important that GE not have an excess or a lack of inventory for the engines on which it is currently working. If not carefully managed, these costs could easily skyrocket out of control.

This is where RM&D comes in. GE tracks exhaust gas temperature, fuel flow, core speed, and the number of cycles to determine when an engine will need minor maintenance or a complete overhaul.[17] With the data it gathers from these variables, GE uses advanced statistics to help predict what parts will be needed and the number of engines it will overhaul during the next planning period. RM&D is also used to avoid costly operational delays. "Just one delay can cost an airline $2,000 or more."[18] By reducing delays by 10 percent per year, GE's remote diagnostics has saved customers about $10,000 per aircraft annually.[19]

Getting the Most from RM&D Technology

RM&D technology is best used for high capital assets whose life-cycle maintenance costs exceed the purchase price, such as jet engines; or equipment that needs to have near 100 percent reliability, such as an MRI machine. This is because the technology has the ability to save hundreds of thousands of dollars for the company by avoiding downtime on their equipment like aircraft engines.[20] GE uses RM&D technology primarily in its industrial systems that match these criteria, such as power generation systems, and jet engines that GE maintains.

GE has tested RM&D technology on many of its short-cycle products like lightbulbs and coffeepots, but the business case for full implementation has not been made yet. Does a refrigerator need to be monitored if it already has 99.9 percent reliability? Is it worth the extra cost? GE has noticed that although some value can be created through the use of RM&D technology for household appliances, the greatest value comes either from equipment and machines that have a high capital cost and their high cycle cost is greater than the purchase price, or equipment that needs to have near 100 percent reliability.[21]

What Is Needed to Implement RM&D Technology

Three steps must be accomplished to implement this technology successfully: develop the ability to collect the necessary data, determine what needs to be measured, and determine how to analyze the data that are being measured. The first step is to find a way to get the data from the equipment to the computer that will help monitor and diagnose what is going on. Usually this is accomplished by using the Internet, but for equipment like jet engines, real-time, two-way satellite communication provides the means. The second main task is to find out what parameters to use and why. GE uses design of experiments, decision trees, and Weibull regression analysis[22] to estimate which parameters have the most effect on certain failures. The third process is to find out what statistical techniques to use to make the best decision on the data collected. GE uses neural networks[23] when they have a lot of data but do not have a lot of expertise. They use case-based reasoning when they have a lot of knowledge about the data and many documented outcomes. Fuzzy logic[24] is used when they receive conflicting information or the data are not black and white.[25]

Lessons Learned and the Future of RM&D

In his almost 20 years of working to develop this technology, Information & Decision Technologies Laboratory Global Technology Leader Rusty Irving has learned many lessons. Although the promise and potential of RM&D technology may be significant, the first lesson is to not oversell its usefulness. If a company "hypes" a new technology—as the answer to everything—the technology will have a tough time meeting expectations when it is developed and released.

The second major lesson is that scientists and engineers must have a business sense when developing products. There was a big push a couple of years ago to connect everything to the Internet because that was seen as the wave of the future. Some projects that GE looked at, such as connecting coffeepots and refrigerators to the Internet and monitoring them, did not have a solid business case behind them. These relatively inexpensive units are generally very reliable, so adding monitoring to them did not add much more value to the product.

The third lesson, and one of the biggest challenges to achieving the maximum benefits, is that it is imperative to evaluate and change the logistics processes as these new technologies are implemented. In addition, business managers who will benefit from the technology must take the lead in implementing the technology and make sure they change their management procedures and reengineer their business processes so they are not just automating poor, already existing processes. Finally, functional leaders must take the lead in communicating to their employees and other stakeholders why the change is happening and the benefits of the new technology. Doing this right will really facilitate the transition.

The future of RM&D is bright. Although GE will strive to build equipment and parts so reliable there will be no need for monitoring and diagnostics, in the meantime, they will continue working to develop and deploy RM&D technology to improve customer service. They are also researching new healing technology so that equipment can be not only remotely diagnosed, but capable of fixing itself when there is a problem. This technology is already being tested on MRI equipment with some success.[26] With new advances in technology and the focus on turning data into knowledge with statistical tools, remote monitoring and diagnostics will continue improving and automating logistics processes as well as lowering costs throughout the supply chain, well into the future.

Endnotes

1. Rusty Irving, Global Technology Leader, Information & Decision Technology Laboratories, GE Global Research. Interviewed by Brandon Griesel and William Lucyshyn. College Park, Md., August 13, 2002.

2. Robert Pool, "If It Ain't Broke, FIX IT," *Technology Review,* September 2001, 66-69.

3. Ibid.

4. Ibid.

5. General Electric Company, "Fact Sheet." Viewed at www.ge.com/company/companyinfo/at_a_glance/fact_sheet.htm, August 2002.

6. GE Corporate Research & Development, "Our Laboratories, Information and Decision Technologies." Viewed at http://www.crd.ge.com/wherewework/labsdetail.jsp?id-17, August 2002.

7. GE Plastics, "Vendor Managed Inventory." Viewed at http://www.geplastics.com/resins/devprod/vendormanagement.html, August 2002.

8. GE Industrial Systems, "Elapsed Time to Repair, ETTR." Viewed at http://www.geindustrial.com/cwc/services?id=2005, August 2002.

9. Irving, interview.

10. David M. Ewalt, "Pinpoint Control," *InformationWeek,* September 30, 2002, Viewed at http://www.informationweek.com/story/ShowArticle.jhtml?articleID=6503191, October 2002.

11. Pool.

12. Ibid.

13. Ibid.

14. GE Aircraft Engines web page. Viewed at http://geae.com/diagnostics/serv_fline_diag_ex.html, August 2002.

15. A jet engine cycle is defined as a takeoff and a landing.

16. Irving, interview.

17. Ibid.

18. GE Aircraft Engines. Viewed at http://geae.com/diagnostic/ serv_fline_diag_ex1.html, August 2002.

19. Ibid.

20. Pool.

21. Irving, interview.

22. The Weibull family of distributions is immensely popular in reliability theory because it includes distributions of decreasing, constant, and increasing failure rates.

23. A neural network is an information-processing paradigm inspired by the way the densely interconnected, parallel structure of the human brain processes information.

24. Fuzzy logic attempts to replicate human reasoning in its use of approximate information and uncertainty to generate decisions by providing formal tools for dealing with the imprecision intrinsic to many problems.

25. Irving, interview.

26. Irving, interview.

CHAPTER NINE

The Boeing Company: Launching an Integrated Financial Management System

Amitabh Brar
and
William Lucyshyn

Background

The Boeing Company is one of the leading aerospace companies in the world. In the year 2001, it was the largest U.S. exporter in sales terms, with total revenues of $58 billion, and had operations in 60 countries and 26 states of the United States. The design and successful implementation, in February 2002, of a company-wide digitally integrated financial management system has earned Boeing the distinction of being a world-class finance organization as well. The new system reflects Chief Financial Officer Mike Sears' vision of making the company "a world-class organization that drives value through leadership."

After successfully merging with two other companies—Rockwell International Corporation and McDonnell Douglas—between December 1996 and August 1997, the Boeing Company is now organized into six major Business Units (BU): Air Traffic Management (ATM), Boeing Capital Corporation (BCC), Commercial Airplanes (BCA), Connexion by Boeing, Integrated Defense Systems, and Boeing Technology Phantom Works. In addition, the Shared Services Group (SSG) provides common services to support the company's operations and advanced research and development, respectively. Overall, the Boeing Company employs close to 164,000 people worldwide, with customers in 145 countries and employees in 70 countries. The task of financial management of the company rests jointly with the Shared Services Group and the Boeing World Headquarters (WHQ). (See Figure 9.1.)

Description of Current System

Introduction

The need for a newer and more efficient financial management system, standardized across the entire company, was heightened after Boeing's merger with Rockwell and McDonnell Douglas. Serious inefficiencies resulted from running Boeing's existing financial management system (Timeline) in conjunction with the legacy systems of the acquired companies. This prompted the Corporate Headquarters to draw up a plan to restructure and develop a new financial management system as the first step toward integration of operations and control within the entire company. The move, in September 2001, of the Corporate Center (which handles finance) from Seattle to Chicago was part of the restructuring. Only limited support was provided to the existing Timeline system during the design and implementation of the new system.

Figure 9.1

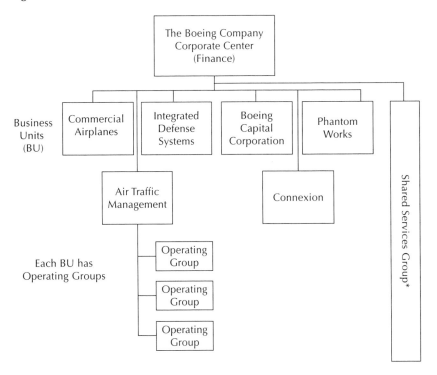

*The Shared Services Group business unit supports other business units and World Headquarters with common services such as computing resources, telecommunications, e-commerce and information-management security, and services including transportation, facilities, and purchase of non-production goods and services.

The proposed new financial management system was designed around the Corporate Center philosophy of decentralization of financial management functions to the Business Units to the greatest extent possible. Under the new system, BUs have to provide all required end-state final data to the Corporate Center. Additionally, the new system requires BUs to provide the final data via a single interface, as opposed to the multiple sources used earlier.

Objective

Besides decentralization, the main objective of the new system is to provide financial consolidation for Boeing's World Headquarters in the most efficient manner. The consolidated data is used by WHQ for two main purposes: (1) to produce corporate-level financial and tax statements, and (2) to perform financial analysis on the data collected from each BU, and to provide support based on the actual versus planned revenues, economic profit, and other parameters critical to the BU's operations.

To consolidate the financial data collected from different Business Units, the information system at each BU is required to integrate with the WHQ finance architecture. For this, an Interface Control Document (ICD) provided by the Corporate Center specifies the financial data required from the BUs. The final requirements would include all the data that was part of the General Ledger (GL) system such as expenses, cash, cost, etc. A Corporate Chart of Accounts defines this required data in more detail to support the ICD. Each BU is required to map its source GL accounts to the new Corporate Chart of Accounts before submitting the data (this function was previously performed by corporate staff in support of the legacy Timeline system).

Architecture

Overall, a modular approach has been adopted for the architecture of the new system. Based on the above proposal, a plan was set to adapt Boeing's existing business processes to match the new Corporate Center finance architecture. Prior to successfully reengineering the existing business processes at the Operating Group level within a Business Unit, they were documented and labeled "As-Is." The new, modified processes were documented and labeled "To-Be."

Many noteworthy differences exist in the features between the "As-Is" and the "To-Be" systems. The changes related to the three stages of the financial data collection and analysis are described in Figure 9.2.[1]

Design and Development

An in-house development of a new financial management system was considered but rejected because of concerns about a "scope creep" while designing the new system from scratch. The task of defining and finalizing the requirements for the new system to satisfy customers across the entire company was considered to be an endless one, and thus impossible to achieve efficiently.

In addition, the commercial off-the-shelf (COTS) software industry was thought to have matured to the point where it was now possible to buy an affordable software package that was less costly than developing in-house applications. The COTS software also could be implemented with limited modification, and the existing business processes could be reengineered to

Figure 9.2

	As-Is Business Processes	**To-Be Business Processes**
Load and Map Data	Operating Groups working directly in Timeline transform and load their own data. Corporate Center transforms and loads data for the remaining Operating Groups. The Corporate Center staff also performed inter-business unit allocations and supported business unit account reconciliation.	All Operating Groups map and load their own data, including production-related supply chain activity.[2] Operating Groups may submit as many feeds as necessary during the defined closing period. After that cutoff[3] date, any required changes will be approved by Corporate Center on an exception basis.
Post Journal Entries and Consolidate Data	Operating Groups work directly in Timeline to adjust online journal entries, perform consolidation activities, and produce their own trial balance for review. Corporate Center performs these activities for both the remaining Operating Groups and company-wide.	Corporate performs all consolidation activities and produces a trial balance. Operating Groups continue to review the trial balance and also provide approval to publish. If adjustments are necessary and made prior to the corporate cutoff date, they will be made via a new feed. After the corporate cutoff date, adjustment will be approved through WHQ.
Produce and Distribute Reports	Operating Groups who work directly in Timeline produce their own financial statements and internal reports. Corporate Center produces these reports for the remaining Operating Groups, as well as company-wide financial statements. In addition, all groups provide supporting data or reports for inclusion in the Corporate Financial Statements Report Package.	Operating Groups continue to provide specialized data and/or reports for inclusion in the Corporate Financial Statements Reports Package. These supplemental reports will be electronically published and staged on a web portal, along with the automated financial statement package generated by the new system. Corporate Center continues to produce segment Financial Statements and certain Internal Reports for the Operating Groups; however, the new architecture provides reporting templates, allowing each of the businesses to extract customized views of their financial data to meet their specific group needs.

fit the new software applications. Further, an added advantage of using a COTS package is that it is designed to include best practices.

Consequently, the company selected Hyperion Enterprise as the consolidation tool of choice after comparison of its requirements with the various COTS packages available in the market. Hyperion Essbase was selected as the financial database to store company-wide accounting actuals. Additional criteria used to evaluate the different software packages included the following: capability of the software package to meet the current needs of the company, ease of use of the software, quality of the reporting tool, capability of the tool for expansion into other functions (scalability), cost of purchase and maintenance of the tool and, lastly, recommendations from other users.

To support the installation of the Hyperion software system, the Corporate Center was directed to reengineer its existing processes and controls. The Corporate Center was given the responsibility to provide Business Units with interface control documents that contained the specifications for data requirements and information on tasks shifting to BUs described therein. The new system architecture is described in Figure 9.3.

Over a five-month period, between May 2001 and September 2001, the required changes to business processes were documented and presented to all the BUs, and validation was obtained on whether or not the BUs could meet the target dates for implementation of the new system. At the same time, a design review meeting was held with Hyperion to discuss the desired modifications to the existing software. Testing of the new system was held between October 2001 and January 2002. The new system went live in February 2002 using January 2002 data. The company reports good success with the new system so far.

Key Metrics

At Boeing, program managers use the Earned Value Measurement (EVM) process to track project cost and schedule. Although these are normally used at the BU level for high-value/high-visibility projects (e.g., development and production of the 767 aircraft), these are monitored at Corporate Headquarters. There are two performance indices that are commonly used for this purpose. One is the Cost Performance Index (CPI), which measures budget to actual cost, and the other is the Schedule Performance Index (SPI), which measures work scheduled to work performed.

In addition, to measure the performance records of different Business Units and their personnel, a balanced scorecard system is used within the company. The performance record is used to determine if a BU is on track with its measurable performance targets such as economic profit. The

Figure 9.3: WHQ Accounting Consolidation System Context Architecture Diagram

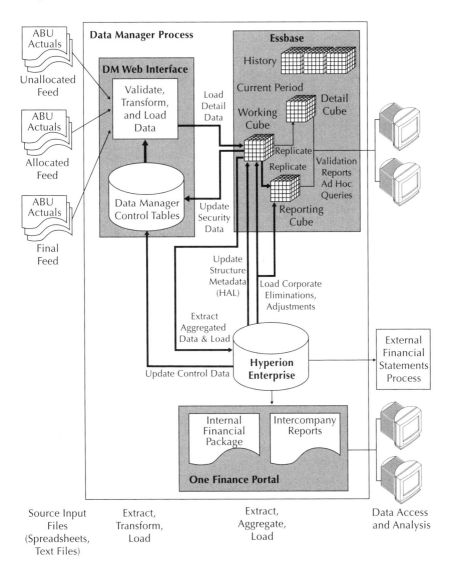

Source: Accounting Consolidation Presentation *Boeing Company briefing provided by Richard Smoski, March 7, 2002.*

scorecard is divided into five categories, each with a different weight attached to it. For example, in the scorecard used to track performance of finance systems within BUs, the five categories are Operating Plan, Customer Satisfaction, Quality, People, and Functional Unique Initiatives.

Performance criteria within each of these categories are measured either in terms of year-to-date relative to performance to plan (e.g., total overhead budget), a company-wide survey (e.g., customer satisfaction), or number of events reported (e.g., non-compliances). A sample scorecard used within the Shared Services Group for measuring the performance of its finance systems is shown in Figure 9.4.

Barriers/Challenges

As with the introduction of a major change within any large organization, Boeing's management had to overcome several barriers and challenges before the new financial management system could be implemented. The director of Finance Systems and Processes, Shared Services Group, shared the most significant ones:

- Coordinating the need for consolidated information and other details within the entire company into a single solution.
- Defining the new process for decentralization of financial management within the company, and transferring the workload from the Corporate Headquarters to Operating Groups within each Business Unit.
- Integrating operations within the various Business Units of the company, and ensuring adherence to the changes introduced in each BU.
- Meeting the complex needs of Boeing Space and Communications (S&C) Business Unit—comprising a group of seven different companies with a wide variety of products and allocation processes.
- Promoting a "new mind-set" of doing business within the company and managing the change associated with it.

Lessons Learned

The size, number of employees, and scale of operations of The Boeing Company are not too different from a typical government agency/department. For the design and development of a new digitally integrated financial management system in a government agency, the following best practices can be highlighted from the case of The Boeing Company:

- **Decentralization:** To ensure accuracy and efficiency in the supply of financial data, and to avoid duplication of effort, the Operating Groups

Figure 9.4: Sample Performance Scorecard Used within The Boeing Company Showing Key Metrics and the Technique Used to Measure Them[4]

Category	No.	Key Metric	Measurement
Operating Plan	1	Total Overhead Budget	Performance to Plan
	2	Company-Wide Economic Profit	Economic Profit
Customer Satisfaction	3	Support to Planning	Survey Results
	4	Support to Financial Accounting	Survey Results
	5	Support to Cost Accounting	Survey Results
	6	Support for Web Enhancements	Survey Results
	7	Support to Tax	Survey Results
	8	One/Finance Portal Usage	% Increase in Usage
Quality	9	Accounting Consolidation System	# of Problems Reported
	10	Cost Management System	# of Problems Reported
People	11	Performance Development Partnership	% Complete
	12	Employee Training Program	Training Hrs Per Employee
	13	Employee Involvement	Boeing Employee Survey
Functional Unique Initiatives	14	Accounting Consolidation System	Performance to Plan
	15	Cost Management System	Performance to Plan
	16	Web Enhancements	Performance to Plan

within each Business Unit must be responsible for providing all the end-state final data to the Central Headquarters. Also, the final data must be provided via a web-based single source instead of multiple sources.

- **Buy versus build:** To avoid the risk of running into "scope creep" while designing the new system, a commercial off-the-shelf software that requires limited changes to the existing business processes must be preferred over in-house design and development of the system.
- **Scalability:** The architecture of the new system must be modular to allow for future scaling up to include additional functions and operations of the organization.
- **Corporate leadership:** The corporate headquarters must provide clear, timely guidance to the Business Units to facilitate a successful implementation.

Conclusion

For the financial planners and managers at The Boeing Company, the financial management system is a steppingstone toward further integration of planning and operations within the entire company. The leap from a giant conglomerate running multiple legacy systems to a world-class organization utilizing a single, streamlined financial management system with state-of-the-art technology is no mean task. It could not have been achieved without a strong commitment to business process improvement by everyone involved, not just the senior-level management of the company. This commitment is expected to carry Boeing forward when the new system is expanded to incorporate the tax needs of the company and to continue with the integration of business planning within the company.

Endnotes

1. Richard Smoski, Director-Finance System and Processes, Boeing Inc. Interviewed by William Lucyshyn and Amitabh Brar. College Park, Md., March 7, 2002.

2. All non-production-based supply chain activity is currently handled through a separate system, "SPNN."

3. Between the first and second Monday of every month.

4. Smoski, interview.

CHAPTER TEN

Cisco Systems, Inc.:
The Building Blocks for a World-Class
Financial Management System

Brandon Griesel
and
William Lucyshyn

Introduction

This study offers an inside look at Cisco Systems, a company that has created what is widely recognized as a world-class financial management system. The idea to develop and implement this system began about six years ago to accommodate Cisco's rapid growth. Cisco had three main goals: to achieve a one-day close, to cut finance costs in half, and to transform the way the financial management system supported decision makers.[1]

Today Cisco has achieved all these goals and reaped other unanticipated benefits—including remaining agile and growing productively. Cisco has been and remains a leader in the constantly changing Internet market, growing sales at an annual rate of 70 percent per year throughout the 1990s.[2] Cisco created its new financial management system by using seven building blocks.[3]

- Having a strong management commitment to the creation of the system
- Building a reliable network infrastructure
- Standardizing and reengineering business processes
- Developing a strong link between the IT department and the rest of the company
- Skillfully integrating web-based applications
- Creating an Internet culture
- Continuing to review and improve processes

The new financial management system was pivotal in helping Cisco accomplish its goal of cutting the cost of finance as a percentage of revenue in half and, at the same time, achieving greater than 90 percent productivity improvement in the finance organization.[4] The new system also has helped transform the way management and analysts make decisions. Cisco empowers decision makers to make better decisions by providing them more accurate and up-to-date information from the system. Regional sales managers can compare daily sales forecasts versus actual sales and take action sooner than if they got the same information every month. Outside suppliers also get daily information about product backlogs and lead times, which allows them to make quicker decisions about adjusting manufacturing capacity.[5]

Background

Cisco Systems, Inc. is a worldwide leader in networking for the Internet. Founded by a group of Stanford computer scientists in 1984, Cisco went public in 1990. The company's core products are routers and switches—the hardware infrastructure that enables the Internet. The routers receive data from one network and route it in the most efficient manner to other networks. A switch is similar to a router in function, but it is used more for directing data within a network, not necessarily between networks. Cisco, however, is not just a company that sells routers and switches; they are a full-service provider for networking infrastructure. Other Cisco products and services are network and Internet access products, systems network architecture, Internet services, network management software, and customer advocacy.[6]

As of February 2003, Cisco had 34,986 employees worldwide, with its headquarters based in San Jose, California.[7] Its market capitalization, as of April 2003, is $92.7 billion[8] with revenue for Q2FY03 (ending January 2003) of $4.7 billion.[9] Not only does Cisco lead the market with the broadest portfolio of high-end switches and routers, but they also have a dominant position in the Voice Over IP market and other technology markets.[10]

It is estimated that more than 80 percent of Internet data traffic travels across Cisco equipment.[11] Cisco has become a technical leader in the research and development of new Internet technologies. It has acquired 63 companies since 1993, not only to increase its product line, but also to increase its intellectual capital.[12] To leverage its intellectual capital and help answer questions about Cisco's best practices, Cisco created the Internet Business Solutions Group. This group provides services for companies wanting to accelerate their e-business strategies and leverage the Internet for productivity gains.

Cisco has a fully integrated supply chain, which extends to their strategic partners, and directly manufactures only a small percentage of Cisco routers. After the institution of Cisco's networked supply chain, 81 percent of final product volume is now outsourced to partners and shipped directly to consumers.[13] Cisco has decided that its core competencies are in design and fulfillment processes, in addition to providing thought leadership and R&D for new technologies to drive the growth of the Internet.[14]

The supplier's information system and the financial management system are linked together for suppliers to view order demand and for financial managers to view production numbers. Cisco has chosen several major suppliers to be a part of its "networked ecosystem." The company has developed a strong partnership with these suppliers in the networked ecosystem so that both Cisco and the suppliers need to rely on each other for each to succeed. Because of this partnership, demand and supply information is very transparent between the suppliers and Cisco. In fiscal year 2001, Cisco attributed $284 million in cost savings to Internet technologies that increase the efficiency of the supply chain, with $75 million of that coming from cost savings due to electronic supplier integration and management.[15]

System Description

The financial management system is broken up into four sections: core financial processes, planning and analysis, treasury and revenue management, and electronic customer credit.[16] The core financial processes entail record keeping or general ledger activities. These include financial reporting consolidation, fixed assets, accounts payable, accounts receivable, tax accounting, and activity-based costing. The benefits provided by the financial management system for the core financial processes are increased accuracy, increased productivity, and reduced costs.

The planning and analysis function, the second part of Cisco's financial management system, entails forecasting, budgeting, cost analysis, merger and acquisition evaluation, and performance management. Cisco looks at several key financial metrics to measure performance and monitor budgets, including market share, order/revenue status, discounts, product margins, expense, after-tax profit, and cash position. Metrics such as market share, order/revenue status, and discounts are measured on an hourly basis. Product margins and expenses are measured on a weekly basis, and after-tax profit and cash position on a monthly/quarterly basis. Even though Cisco can view all its metrics on a daily and sometimes hourly basis, Cisco does not think that it is efficient to do so. A sample of the key metrics and time frames are listed in Figure 10.1.

Figure 10.1: Key Financial Metrics[17]

	Hourly	Daily	Wkly	Mthly	Qtrly
Market Share	X	X	X	X	X
Order/Revenue Status	X	X	X	X	X
Discounts	X	X	X	X	X
Product Margins		X	X	X	X
Expense			X	X	X
Headcount				X	X
Revenue per Employee				X	X
Business Unit Contribution Margin				X	X
Balance Sheet—Cash, Inventory Turns				X	X

Treasury is the third function of Cisco's financial management system. This function manages Cisco's cash position by minimizing financial risk.[18] Some of the activities that occur within treasury are risk management, cash management, lease/loan management, foreign exchange management, and electronic banking. The benefits of using the financial management system for this function come from providing timely information, which increases financial flexibility and provides a tool that helps to determine ways to decrease the risk of investments.

The fourth and final portion of Cisco's financial management system is revenue management and electronic customer credit. This entails areas that improve the revenue side of the income statement. The benefits from the financial management system through this function are a quicker order-to-cash cycle through electronic bill payment and electronic instant credit authorization. By implementing these four functions into its financial management system, Cisco was able to cut in half the cost of finance as a percentage of revenue, while achieving greater than 90 percent productivity improvement in the finance organization and improving the accuracy of all the major financial information.

Building Blocks

While transforming its financial management system, Cisco learned several lessons. The Cisco finance organization has molded these lessons into what it believes are the building blocks of a successful financial management system.

Having Strong Management Commitment to the Creation of the System

Management commitment is extremely important in the development of a large financial management system such as Cisco's. If there is not a lot of support for the project from upper management, then the chances for success will be limited.[19] The goals of the organization must be concurrent with the reasons for creating the system. If the technology or system that is being implemented does not help the company achieve its goals, then the company can easily fall into the trap of developing a new system just because it is the hottest technology out there. Larry Carter, the chief financial officer of Cisco Systems, challenged his team to provide such a system that matched the company's goals of lowering costs and positively transforming the way management makes decisions. He also provided the tools and resources needed to create the system because he had a strong commitment to the project. Once the managers of the project knew the value of the project and the reasons they were creating the system, the successful implementation was not far behind.

Building a Reliable Network Infrastructure

A reliable network infrastructure is a top priority in creating a stable system. Without it, either the system that is supposed to be reporting the needed information is down or the process of getting the information is too inefficient to use it properly. Carter has stated: "The infrastructure is the ante to get into the game. If a government wants to improve commerce in a country, it has to be able to support the traffic. It cannot do it without the infrastructure of highways, harbors, airports, and trains. The network infrastructure is the same in principle."[20]

Standardization is a key to developing a reliable network infrastructure. If companies and governmental agencies do not standardize, they will find themselves having "data traffic jams" or systems that cannot talk to each other. In addition, without standardizing, the costs of running the system increase and the process to get information out of the system becomes more complicated. Yet, a company or government entity does not want to over-standardize, leaving little room for flexibility or growth. Cisco has a saying of "Minimum Standards for Maximum Results."[21] It believes that many integration problems can be solved by standardizing a company's network, databases, and storage. The current primary technology standards for Cisco are listed in Figure 10.2.

Cisco believes that because of the company's standards philosophy, it has reduced time to market, reduced costs, and provided for easier data integration.[22]

Figure 10.2: Worldwide Standards

Network Protocol	TCP/IP
Database Management System	Oracle
Enterprise Servers	Unix
Workgroup Servers	Windows NT

Standardizing and Reengineering Business Processes

The next building block has to do with making sure that existing fundamental processes are the most efficient way of accomplishing the work. If the current processes are not the most efficient, they should be changed. An information system based on old, inefficient processes—because that is the way people are used to doing it—will not be as affected as an information system that is structured by using the most efficient processes, whether they are new or old. Automating flawed processes will not result in an increase in efficiency; it will result in flawed *automated* processes instead of a flawed manual one.

The most important steps to take for this process are standardizing financial definitions and systems, streamlining processes, eliminating unnecessary steps, and maintaining strong control.[23] It is important for the leadership to define financial definitions like bookings and backlogs, thereby avoiding disputes between sales, manufacturing, and accounting regarding order status.[24] As noted, Cisco has standardized its core network, databases, and storage systems to produce efficiencies with integration and to reduce costs. Cisco management started the process of streamlining processes by asking employees how it could shorten the period required to close its books. Management received an overwhelming response, which led to a significant decrease in the time required. Cisco has estimated that within two years of starting the process to shorten its close process, it eliminated 10 days from a 14-day process by streamlining and automating processes.[25]

Strong control over procedures and standardization must be maintained; otherwise, overcustomization can occur and gains in efficiencies can be lost. Without strong control, standardization can become customization as the company grows and changes.

Developing a Strong Link between the IT Department and the Rest of the Company

A strong link is needed because communication and efficient interaction between the IT department and the rest of the company is very important in developing successful information systems. Without a tight bond between the IT department and the other business units within the company, the business units that use the company's IT services might just think of it as a cost rather than an enabler for them to be more productive. In addition, the IT department could develop a system that does not meet the needs of the service department if communication is lacking between the two.

The way a company funds its IT projects also affects the way service departments look at the IT department. Cisco views the IT function as a strategic partner with other service departments like finance and marketing.

Rather than having the costs of IT projects counted as overhead, departments fund their own IT projects. This helps departments and the company to prioritize which IT projects will bring the most value to the department and allows departments more control over the types of projects that are being created for them. Cisco's finance department funded the IT costs for staff and software during the implementation of the financial management system.[26] Cisco's guidelines for all-company projects include the requirement that projects end in six months or fewer, the payback period be less than a year, and the system show how it will improve customer satisfaction.[27]

Skillfully Integrating Web-Based Applications

Web-based applications allow sales employees to check commissions and sales targets. They also allow customers to check order status and resolve payment issues. According to Carter, Cisco is saving an estimated $508 million per year because of such web applications.[28] In addition to the cost savings, the applications are improving customer satisfaction. Web-based applications can provide a lot of quality information in a quick, efficient, and less costly manner than paper reports. Cisco has two types of web-based financial applications: financial reporting tools for executives and productivity tools for employees.

Depending on an employee's position at Cisco, he or she will see a different view of the tools. Executives can view high-level detail about what is going on with the system's performance in terms of key metrics such as booking and discounts. On the employee productivity side, employee travel expenses are reimbursed within 48 hours because of the web-enabled travel expense application. In addition, employees also have a reporting system that details commissions and makes employees aware of any problems that might have arisen with a customer order. These applications have been the main driver of the cost savings, productivity, and efficiency that Cisco has seen over the past several years.

Creating an Internet Culture

Developing an Internet culture at Cisco has allowed the company to reap the maximum value out of its systems and applications. A properly implemented (fully supported and communicated) Internet culture can help increase flexibility, speed, bravery, and profitability.[29] Flexibility is achieved by creating a flat organizational structure and empowering employees. A flattening of a company's organizational structure allows the company to lower the number of organizational and functional obstacles that get in the way of great ideas from lower levels being heard by the decision makers. Empowering employees to take risks and implement new ideas creates a culture not afraid of change and increases employees' flexibility when things do change.

The speed at which a company does business is increased because decision making is pushed further down the organizational chart. In addition, processes such as procurement and bill payment are automated. When Internet-based solutions are created, the speed and richness of the information allow decision makers to receive more timely and accurate information. Therefore, companies will be able to manage risk better, be more decisive—the "bravery" benefit—and be less prone to make costly errors due to bad decisions. All of these benefits, in turn, will increase speed and accuracy.

Finally, a study by Adrain Slywotzy and David Morrison has shown that businesses such as Cemex, Charles Schwabb, Cisco Systems, and Dell Computer can produce profit margins and growth rates that are significantly higher than their competition.[30] This is because of the increased use of the Internet and automation, which could not occur unless support throughout the organization was behind the effort.

Companies can foster Internet culture through communication, learning, and leadership. To create an Internet culture you need great leadership. According to Cisco, "Leadership should be well informed and highly visible."[31] Cisco's leaders strive to be well informed through its financial management system and highly visible through live webcasts to employees. These webcasts also foster continuous communication between frontline employees and top executives.

The eExec system, the executive information system used by Cisco, also fosters communication and action through financial data alerts. This application offers communication portals where analysts and management from around the world can collaborate on financial results. A culture of learning and the benefits that e-learning bring has helped Cisco continually stay on top of current trends and take advantage of its internal capital by teaching others in the company. When Cisco needs to train employees on a new technology or application, it uses e-learning versus more expensive classroom learning.

Continuing to Review and Improve Processes

A company like Cisco can have outstanding processes now, but needs to continually assess its Internet capabilities to break away from its competition. Even great systems can become better. Rick Timmins, vice president of worldwide field op finance says, "A company can't improve what it can't measure." That is why Cisco uses the balanced scorecard approach when measuring the internal performance of the finance organization. Cisco uses four metrics for its balanced scorecard: quality, cost, cycle time, and client/customer satisfaction.

The finance department has several different metrics measuring the same end result of cost and customer satisfaction, but in different ways. For instance, the cost to process one invoice might be measured for accounts payable while the metric for corporate reporting might be the cost per report developed. Both metrics measure cost but in different ways. Review teams at Cisco study these metrics and work toward streamlining or solving any problems that occur in the Virtual Close process. If members on the review board notice that the cost per invoice is creeping upward, they will investigate it and then take action if necessary.

The Future

Cisco is continually trying to improve and update its financial management system. The finance department is working on two initiatives to accomplish this goal. The first is to view processes and systems holistically and to encourage more cross-functional cooperation.[32] The second is to maintain standardization in the back end while increasing personalization of information delivery to management and analysts. Timmins is leading Cisco into taking a more holistic approach to creating IT systems in the finance department. Cisco's client-funded IT model, where the "user" department funds and sets the requirements of the project, has worked well to maintain flexibility and customization for the department in the past, but overcustomization is beginning to cause problems with upgrades to new versions of application software.

To try to alleviate this problem, the finance department is moving toward concentrating more on how finance's IT projects will affect other departments like purchasing, sales, and manufacturing. Timmins also would like to continue to make sure that there are still strong controls over IT customization.

Although Cisco is trying to limit the number of back-end applications and customization of those systems, there is still a need for personalization. The company is looking for tools that will strike a balance between standardization and personalization. Such tools will help to cut through the information overload experienced by management but not overcustomize, which could cause future problems. Cisco is working on personalizing screen displays and data reports, but not necessarily back-end details of the system. The goal for Cisco is to have the same back-end system working for different departments, but different personalized settings that can be easily transferred from one software update to another.

Conclusion

Cisco has accomplished the goals it set for its financial management system. The system has the ability to close the books in less then a day, has helped to decrease finance costs as a percentage of sales by half, and has transformed the way management makes decisions. In summary, Cisco has accomplished its goals through these seven building blocks:

- Having a strong management commitment to the creation of the system
- Building a reliable network infrastructure
- Standardizing and reengineering business processes
- Developing a strong link between the IT department and the rest of the company
- Skillfully integrating web-based applications
- Creating an Internet culture
- Continuing to review and improve processes

Although no system is perfect, Cisco is continually improving and provides a great example of a world-class financial management system worth looking at for its best practices.

Endnotes

1. Larry Carter, "Larry Carter: Finance Takes the Lead in the Internet Economy," *Cisco IQ,* February 15, 2001. Viewed at http://business.cisco.com/prod/tree.taf%3Fasset_id =48793&ID=48295&ListID=85932&SubListID=44694&public_view=true&kbns=1.html, February 2002.

2. John A. Byrne and Ben Elgin, "Cisco Behind the Hype: CEO John Chambers still thinks his company can grow 30% a year. But critics question its aggressive accounting," *Business Week,* January 21, 2002, 54.

3. G. Patrick Pawling, "Virtual Finance: Moving Toward the One-Day Close," *Cisco IQ,* May/June 2001. Viewed at http://business.cisco.com/prod/tree.taf%3Fasset_id =47909&MagID =48175&public_view=true&kbns=1.html, February 2002.

4. Carter.

5. Larry Carter, "Cisco's Virtual Close," *Harvard Business Review,* Reprint F104A (April 2001):2-3.

6. George Herman and Stephanie L. Woerner, "Networked at Cisco", *Massachusetts Institute of Technology Teaching Case #1* (July, 20 2001): 2.

7. Cisco Systems Inc, "Fact Sheet." Viewed at http://newsroom.cisco.com/dlls/ corpfact.html, April 10, 2003.

8. Yahoo! Inc, "Quotes." Viewed at http://finance.yahoo.com/q?s=CSCO&d=t, April 11, 2003.

9. Cisco Systems Inc, "2Q03 Earnings Release." Viewed at http://newsroom.cisco.com/ dlls/fin_020403.html, April 10, 2003.

10. Ibid.

11. Cisco Systems Inc, "Internet Basics, Cisco's Role." Viewed at http://business.cisco.com/ prod/tree.taf%3Fasset_id=49620&public_view=true&kbns=1.html, February 2002.

12. Herman and Woerner.

13. Cisco Systems, Inc., "Industry Overview: Manufacturing, Leading by Example." Viewed at http://business.cisco.com/prod/tree.taf%3Fasset_id=48191&ID=48297&ListID= 44691&SubListID=44751&public_view=true&kbns=1.html, February 2002.

14. Don Tapscott, David Ticoll, and Alex Lowy, *Digital Capital* (Boston: Harvard Business School Press, 2000), 93-118.

15. Cisco Systems Inc, "Industry Overview: Manufacturing."

16. Cisco Systems Inc, "What You Need to Implement a Financial Management Solution." Viewed at http://business.cisco.com/prod/tree.taf%3Fasset_id=87439&ID= 44747&ListID=85925&public_view=true&kbns=1.html, February 2002.

17. Cisco Systems Inc, "EIS to eExec Evolution," *Cisco Presentation Executive Information System,* February 2002, p. 3.

18. Cisco Systems Inc, "What You Need to Implement a Financial Management Solution."

19. Pawling.

20. Ibid.

21. Susan Keys, Customer Solutions Consulting Manager, Cisco Systems Inc. Interviewed by William Lucyshyn and Brandon Griesel. Herndon, Va., February 20, 2002.

22. Richard L Nolan, "Cisco System Architecture: ERP and Web-enabled IT," *Harvard Business School Case Study 9-301-099,* (October 15, 2001): 8-14.

23. Pawling.

24. Ibid.

25. Ibid.

26. Ibid.

27. Ibid.

28. Carter, "Finance Takes the Lead."

29. Fred Sandsmark, "Culture Shift: Is the Internet a part of your company's culture? Here's how to tell if it is—what to do if it is not," *Cisco IQ*, March/April 2001. Viewed at http://business.cisco.com/prod/tree.taf%3Fasset_id=49804&ID=85947&ListID=85932& SubListID=44756&public_view=true&kbns=1.html, February 2002.

30. Sandsmark, p. 2.

31. Sandsmark, p. 3.

32. Rick Timmons, Vice President of Worldwide Field Operations Finance, Cisco Systems Inc. Interviewed by William Lucyshyn and Brandon Griesel. College Park, Md., March 15, 2002.

CHAPTER ELEVEN

Defense Finance and Accounting Service: Financial Management of the World's Mightiest Conglomerate

William Lucyshyn
and
Sandra Young

Introduction

The United States Department of Defense (DoD) is "the world's mightiest and messiest conglomerate."[1] Dwarfing the world's biggest multinational corporations, DoD's "2002 budget of $334 billion exceeds the annual revenues of the world's largest company, Exxon-Mobil, by more than $100 billion."[2] DoD processes 24 million commercial invoices each year and disburses approximately $1 billion a day. Over 100 million financial transactions are processed each month, affecting over 800 active appropriations.[3]

In terms of complexity, DoD oversees the four services—the Army, Navy, Air Force, Marine Corps, the Office of the Secretary of Defense; the Joint Chiefs of Staff; and 14 other defense agencies. "Daily, thousands of DoD personnel access and query financial systems from hundreds of world-wide locations in order to manage and carry out the department's financial and fiduciary responsibility."[4]

Even more significant than the size and complexity of DoD, however, is the fact that the department does *not* have a functioning, integrated financial management system in place to coordinate and account for its vast budget. DoD has not produced a department-wide auditable financial report in decades.[5] In January 2001, DoD's own auditors said that the department could not account for $2.3 trillion in historic transactions.[6] DoD was identified by former Congressman Stephen Horn of California as having difficulty accurately documenting the net cost of its operations and accounting for its assets—in particular property plant and equipment.[7]

In essence, DoD does not know with certainty what funds it has available. "Such information is essential for DoD and the Congress to determine if funds are available that could be used to reduce current funding requirements or that could be reprogrammed or transferred to meet other critical program needs."[8]

At a time when the country is attuned to accounting scandals and concerned with national security, it is imperative that DoD address the inadequacies of its financial systems. DoD officials are fully aware of the importance of timely action.

"Every dollar that is wasted translates into a bullet or a bomb or a weapons system that some [soldier] in Afghanistan needs right now."

—*Dov S. Zakheim, Under Secretary of Defense (2002), on why the war on terrorism makes financial management more important*

As with many government agencies, whose primary mission is not financial tracking, DoD developed its financial management system on an ad hoc basis. Each of DoD's departments and agencies developed their own financial management system over time, and installed applications and systems based on individually determined needs and business practices. "Systems requirements and functionality were based on local interpretations of financial management requirements and defense policy."[9] The long-term result was a convoluted financial management architecture consisting of 324 different, often non-compatible systems, many of which were redundant and did not meet general accounting standards.

Under this system, employees were often required to make formal requests for information from one another; they received the information in one form and would then have to translate it into their own system and, in some cases, reconcile it with data from a third system. Data was entered and re-entered multiple times. Hard copies of financial data had to be tracked and manually processed. Figure11.1 is a schematic of what system communications would look like if the old system had been maintained. Consider that in a non-integrated system, each line connecting two systems in the schematic would represent a manual transfer and a re-entering of data. It is easy to see how this system bred inefficiency, as data was transferred from one system to another, again and again.

As the department grew, the system proved to be costly as routine activities took more time to process. Analyzing data from this set of unique systems was also extremely cumbersome, and more often than not, financial reports were untimely and error prone. Furthermore, data provided was often that which was needed for budgetary accounting rather than information required for program management and cost controls. As a result, managers could not rely on financial reports when making financial management decisions.

From both a legislative and practical position, it was clear that changes had to be made. In January 1991, the Defense Finance and Accounting Service (DFAS) was established to perform and oversee finance and accounting

---

"More and more time is spent reconciling reports and correcting erroneous information because data shared between systems is dissimilar. Simple internal controls, such as pre-validating that an obligation exists in an accounting system before authorizing a disbursement, became expensive to implement."
— *Kathleen Noe, Director, Systems Integration*
Defense Finance and Accounting Service

Figure 11.1: Image from DFAS Financial Systems Strategic Plan January 2000 Section 2 *Standalone Operating Environment*

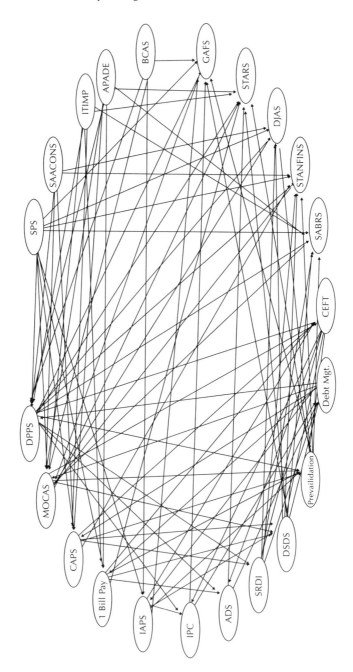

within the Department of Defense and, in many respects, to address the problems of the existing financial structure. Its formal mission is to "provide effective and efficient financial information, accounting, and payment services to the Department of Defense during times of peace and conflict."[10]

In addition to its own mission, DFAS was guided by a series of legislation passed by Congress that directed financial management improvements throughout government and by increasing expectations from within DoD for financial reporting "to support program managers and financial managers, as well as budget analysts."[11]

In order to meet the new congressional requirements, increasing demands for internal management support, and its own mission of providing "effective and efficient" financial services, DFAS focused on accomplishing two main objectives: systems reductions and systems integration.

Initially, DFAS pursued the idea of establishing a single, fully integrated system across all defense sectors. However, while DFAS had been charged with the responsibility of complete financial management reform, it was not given complete autonomy over the existing system. DFAS brought together the agency heads that controlled systems not under DFAS's direct authority. They discussed what a completely integrated system would entail, but could not agree to a single standardized system. DFAS would have to resort to a solution that would reduce the total number of systems but allow the different defense agencies to maintain some of their uniqueness.

It responded to the challenge by reducing the total number of unique systems from 324 to 65 (and has plans to further reduce the total to 32). While this reduction did a lot to make the entire management system less cumbersome, the remaining systems would still not be interoperable and as such it did not completely resolve the problems of system incompatibility and redundancy in data entry.

To address these concerns, DFAS designed a new financial data-management architecture. This architecture was to be implemented in three phases, with the final phase resulting in an integrated financial system by 2008. The cornerstone of this new plan was a centralized data system that would translate data from unique systems into standard data. The standard data could then be accessed by users from different systems according to rights granted and encoded into the user's access code.

System Description

The Structure

The following is a summary of the Integrated Financial System End State. Figure 11.2 gives a schematic overview of the key components of the system:

Figure 11.2: Summary of DFAS Integrated Financial System End State

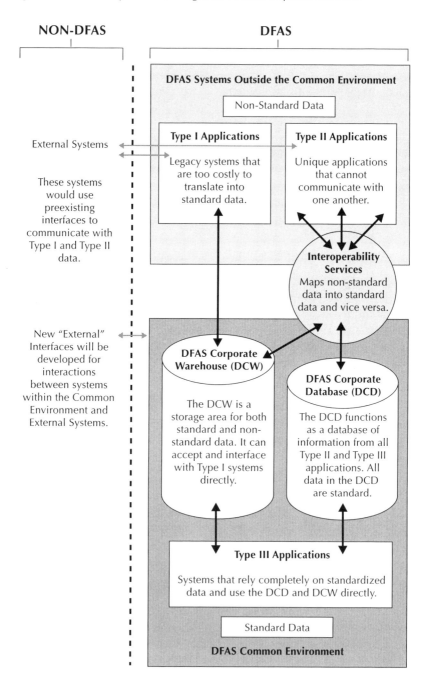

1. **Standard Data:** Data coded according to the Defense Data Account Finance Model (DFADAM), otherwise known as the defense data dictionary.
2. **The Common Environment:** The core of the new architecture is the Common Environment. This is the centralized area where data from the different defense agency systems are stored. All standardized data reside in the Common Environment. The primary components of the Common Environment are:
   – *DFAS Corporate Database (DCD)*—the centralized database. The DCD functions as a hub through which data move from one non-standard system to another and where data are gathered and analyzed for department financial reports.
   – *DFAS Corporate Warehouse (DCW)*—the central repository. The DCW functions as an archive for data from old applications. It is also the only place on the Common Environment that can receive and store non-standard data (usually from legacy systems that have not yet been replaced).
   – *Interoperability Services*—the translation or "mapping" function that re-codes unique system data into standard data and vice versa.
   – *Type III applications*—described under "feeder systems."
3. **Feeder systems:** A feeder system is a source of DFAS information. A defense agency system, an external vending system, or a DFAS-designed payment system would all be examples of different feeder systems. These systems use applications that are classified into types according to the degree to which the application is integrated with standard data and the Common Environment. There are three application classifications or "types."
   – *Type I applications*—legacy applications. These applications are the least integrated. DFAS has determined that it is too costly to map data from Type I applications to the standard. Data from these systems are stored in the DCW in their original form. These legacy applications will eventually be replaced by Type II or Type III systems. Once they have been replaced, data that are stored in DCW will be mapped to the standard and archived for future reference by other systems.
   – *Type II applications*—applications that are either too costly to replace with completely standardized systems, or applications that are not under the direct authority of DFAS and have not been replaced with standard systems by their controlling agencies. Data from these applications are mapped to the standard data through the interoperability services. Off-the-shelf applications are the most common form of Type II application. They come with their own database and standards. It is not cost-effective to build an entirely

new application using the standard data to accomplish a task that an off-the-shelf application can already accomplish. DFAS simply translates the data from the purchased application to the standard so that everyone else can access it.

- *Type III applications*—newly designed systems that are built to operate only with standard data. Many of these systems use the DCD as their primary database. Because the data coming from Type III systems is standard data already, there is no need for mapping Type III data. Type III applications reside in the Common Environment. They are linked directly to the DCD and do not go through interoperability services.

In the normal course of a transaction, data would come into the Common Environment via one of the feeder system applications. If the data enter through a Type I application, they are stored in the DCW; if data enter through a Type II application, they are mapped to standard data through the interoperability services and then stored in the DCD; and finally, if data enter through a Type III application, they are already in standard data format and go directly to the DCD. If a user needs to access data in the Common Environment from a non-standard application, data are translated from standard back into the non-standard code through the interoperability services.

Strengths of the System

1. **Gains in efficiency:** Once fully operational, the new architecture will allow users to obtain data from multiple unique systems by accessing the single central database, either the DCD or the DCW, where all data would already be translated and stored.

2. **Reduction in redundancy and increases in data accuracy:** There will no longer be a need for multiple inter-system interactions or for the duplicative manual entering of data. As a result, it will significantly reduce the human-error component in financial data management.

3. **Better financial reporting:** The centralized system will make it easier and faster to generate financial reports because data will not have to be tracked down from different systems; again it will all be centrally stored. Consequently, both Congress and Defense Department managers can get more timely and more accurate financial reports. Similarly, conversion into standard data will allow entities that fund multiple defense agencies to obtain comparative reports on how different agencies spend their monies for similar functions.

4. **Political feasibility:** The fact that the new architecture does allow for the existence of Type I and Type II (non-standard, unique) systems means that it is also a plausible solution despite the restraints on DFAS's

authority over the entire system. Unique systems can still be supported without completely sacrificing integration.

Weaknesses of the System

1. **Cost:** Cost is a significant weakness of this system. The development of a coding system that can translate data from a unique system to a standard and back again is extremely time-consuming and expensive. Many of the Type I (legacy) systems could not be mapped to standard data simply because the cost of setting up a translation code was too high. It was not economical to set up a code for systems that will one day be replaced.
2. **Lack of total standardization:** The translation architecture that DFAS is implementing is not the ideal system. A system involving only standard data would have been easier and more cost-effective to maintain.
3. **Lack of business process reengineering:** The translation architecture focuses on making data available across unique systems. It does not, however, assess whether or not the systems are tracking the most useful information. DoD has to submit financial reports to different "users," from financial analysts and budgeters to program managers and Congress. The integration approach has not addressed whether or not these people are getting the information they need. Since many of the processes were out of DFAS's control—i.e., services and defense agencies maintain some degree of autonomy—the focus was consolidation rather than process reengineering or data collection assessment.

Implementation

Tackling the challenge of financial reform for the entire DoD was an awesome task. DFAS faced the challenge by focusing on three distinct areas: the accounting system, the finance system, and security.

The Accounting System

Accounting was selected as a target area because it was one of the most convoluted and because it was a frontline system. It is also where most of the financial reports generated by DoD originate.

The Accounting Challenge: At the start of the project, some 600 different applications and 407 unique processing forms were in use across the

main defense agencies. Each of the branches used different coding structures for their respective accounting systems. And each accounting system
supported its own set of sub-departments—supplies, inventory, etc.—that
relied on that unique coding structure. Furthermore, in 1993, shortly before
DFAS began to look at reworking the accounting structure, the government
had made the shift from general accounting to cost accounting, so the
accounting staff was already trying to deal with a major transition. Finally,
defense agencies had autonomy over their accounting systems. DFAS was
limited in what restructuring it could accomplish.

The Accounting Approach: In order to develop a translation capability
in the interoperability services, DFAS deciphered the accounting codes from
all of the unique systems. This involved accessing codes and understanding
their corresponding functions. DFAS also tracked functions across unique
accounting systems so that similar functions occurring in different defense
agencies would be mapped to the same standard code. DFAS started with
the working capital fund (WCF) and divided it into nine business areas.
These business areas transcended service boundaries, but had a common
focus. For example, DFAS identified Depot Maintenance as an area with
common attributes, regardless of service identity, so they focused on establishing a standardized coding system for running that business area.

The Finance System

Unlike the accounting system, DFAS had direct control over most of the
finance components of DoD. As a result, DFAS could implement a higher
degree of standardization and could address some issues of business engineering in this area.

The Finance Challenge: The objective was to develop a single DoD-
wide finance system with standardized data that could deliver more accurate and timely information. To reach the objective, DFAS had to integrate
numerous and varied systems including military and civilian pay, disburse-
ments, department reporting, contract and vending services, and cash
accountability.

The Finance Approach: After extensive study and a competitive bid
arrangement, DFAS chose to implement an Oracle database prototype.
DFAS will be launching the finance prototype in different divisions
throughout 2003. These will be Type III systems and will therefore be fully
integrated with the common environment and will use standard data.

Security

Security is not specifically mentioned in the DFAS mission or in the legislation guiding financial management, but is nevertheless a critical function. The information that DFAS handles is unclassified, but there are privacy considerations as the records contain personal information, as well as operational security concerns. One could, for example, infer troop deployments and other operational information by aggregating the data held in DFAS systems. DFAS, therefore, goes to great lengths to secure access to system data. Security is simply considered a functional requirement of all DFAS systems.

> "Security is really a part of our business."
>
> —Audrey Davis, DFAS

DoD has security standards that every system must comply with. In addition, DFAS requires every financial management system to prepare a risk analysis and a security accreditation analysis as part of the implementation process. Once a security assessment has been conducted, and all weaknesses patched, DFAS will authorize a system for a maximum of three years only. If there is anything that changes the security posture of the system in that three-year period, it negates the system's authority to operate, and it has to be reassessed and re-accredited.

In the case of the new financial management system, the DCD and the DCW both had to go through this accreditation process. In addition, any system that is consequently added to the DCD or DCW will have to have an accreditation as well. A part of its accreditation will have to address how the new system will interface with DCD or DCW. Then the DCD and DCW accreditation becomes part of the new system's accreditation package.

So every new additional link has to have its own accreditation. And if any new changes impact DCD or DCW access controls, then DFAS will automatically have to redo the accreditation. If there are no changes to, or failures in, the system, it will still be reevaluated on a three-year cycle.

In addition to the accreditation system, DFAS has a small group of security personnel to "red team" its system. Their task is to perform vulnerability assessments and identify any weaknesses and get them patched before they can be exploited. In some cases, DFAS also hires independent third parties to test the system's security.

Lessons Learned

The implementation process has taken place in phases over the last 10 years. The following lessons have been learned from that implementation effort:

- **Be aware of political sensitivities and emphasize system improvement.** The new architecture involved a shift from field-controlled data systems to DFAS-controlled data systems, i.e., providing increased visibility into base-level activity. DFAS discovered that many people in the field felt threatened by the change. There was concern that individuals would be held accountable for any and all discrepancies found between the old and new systems. It is important to recognize and explain that with change, some discrepancies are inevitable. It is also important to emphasize that the goal is correcting problems in the system and improving the process, not blaming people for the failures of the old system.

- **Get buy-in from all levels early on.** If top management supports a change, it is far easier to get the assistance of field staff. Similarly, unless field staff understand and can see the benefits of change, they are more likely to hinder rather than help any change process.

  To ensure that the master interface and system translations would function, DFAS had to work closely with field experts from all of the defense branches to obtain coding data. Opposition to a "new" system and lack of perceived incentive on the part of field personnel made obtaining the necessary access difficult. Consequently, transition management created a huge obstacle to the restructuring and integration of the financial system.

  Eventually top-level involvement and support was obtained and access was achieved. However, if DFAS had secured the support of agency heads first and had approached the field staff earlier in the process, many months of delays and frustration might have been avoided.

- **Deliver prototypes and involve clients in the design of programs from the beginning.** It is important to recognize that one can spend forever trying to make a system that meets all of the requirements of a customer but is still not necessarily what the customer needs. Often customers need to see a system to properly evaluate it and their needs. They need to use it and see it and see how it is going to look in their environment.

  Inevitably there are going to be changes after a system is initially launched because the customer did not realize that the system was going to do this or look like that. So, it is important to get clients involved up front. If they are not involved until the implementation stage, then requirements have to be met and problems have to be addressed from the back end, which is invariably harder to accomplish.

"That is probably the big lesson learned over the last two years. We are finally getting the customer involved up front as well as getting them to sign off on requirements," explains Audrey Davis, chief financial officer for DFAS.

- **Do not address security as an afterthought.** Security should be considered a determining factor rather than a limiting factor when deciding what capabilities to bring on board. DFAS considers security equal to any functional requirement of a new system in terms of importance. Security addressed after the fact is much harder to implement and often more costly. DFAS goes to great lengths to prevent having to make such back-end security adjustments.

- **Process reengineering is the best type of system reform.** DFAS made the decision that process reengineering was not feasible. DFAS does recognize, however, that had they been able to address fundamental process changes, more dramatic improvements would have been possible. There is a sense that better practices, not just better systems, would have led to a more complete reform and that over the long run a business process reengineering approach would have been a much better solution for DoD.

Vision for the Future

For DFAS, 2001 brought with it a new administration, continued budgetary pressures, increased emphasis on financial management, and a new direction. There seems to be far more agreement that the more effective reform would be to require all defense agencies to agree on and use standard data instead of investing resources into mapping unique systems to the central database. The new administration has placed a renewed emphasis on integration and process reengineering.

In addition to political support from the administration, it seems that DFAS is getting the clout it needs to make reengineering and standardization a reality. The under secretary of defense (comptroller) and CFO, Dov S. Zakheim, was granted the centralized authority over all financial management decisions that DFAS previously lacked. He commented that since the announcement, "All of sudden the [Army, Navy, Marine Corps, and Air Force] financial management was ringing my phone off the hook because they realized they couldn't do a thing without my say."[12] Additionally, the Office of the Comptroller is getting ready to award a contract for a 12- to 18-month study to develop a DoD-wide enterprise architecture. After that, if the decision is made to implement this new architecture, it will be five to 10 years before it is fully functional. Since DFAS does not know what the new system will entail, there is a reluctance to continue devoting resources to mapping non-standard data to standard data. "We don't want to continue to invest a lot of dollars now that may get thrown away when the new architecture is put in place."[13]

Conclusion

The recent private sector accounting scandals have emphasized the need for transparency, accuracy, timeliness, and control over finances and accounting. Obtaining all of those things in a government agency that literally dwarfs any corporate entity in both size and complexity is, however, no easy task. DFAS used tremendous ingenuity to develop a solution that would work within the political and financial limitations it was operating under at the time. The architecture that DFAS created and implemented over the last decade was a successful attempt to reform DoD's financial system, to meet new legislative requirements, and to advance the mission of the agency. The result of DFAS's efforts was an overall increase in efficiency and effectiveness. "The cost of Finance and Administration is steadily decreasing."[14] In fact, since its inception in 1991, DFAS has achieved "93 percent reduction [through operations and systems consolidation] and an annual savings of $120 million through FY98."[15]

The change in the political climate, however, has altered the array of feasible options available to DFAS; it seems that the agency will be heading in a new direction. As Dr. Zakheim said, however, "each effort is a learning experience." Hopefully the lessons that DFAS has learned over the last 10 years will make the implementation of the new architecture smoother and faster, whatever that architecture may entail.

Endnotes

1. Tim Reason, "Federal Offenses: A dozen years after passage of the CFO Act, the U.S. Government still struggles to close its books," *CFO Magazine,* March, 6 2002. Viewed at http://www.cfo.com/article/1,5309,6768,00.html, March 2002.

2. Ibid.

3. Kathleen Noe, "DoD's Future Integrated Financial Systems Architecture," *Armed Forces Comptroller,* Winter 1999, Vol. 44, Issue 6:18.

4. Ibid.

5. Gerald W. Thomas, "DoD's Critical Feeder Systems: Achieving Compliance With the Federal Financial Management Improvement Act of 1996," *Armed Forces Comptroller,* Winter 1999, Vol. 44, Issue 1.

6. U.S. Senate, Senator Robert Byrd speaking on the nomination of Donald Rumsfeld to be Secretary of Defense to the Senate Armed Services Committee, January 11, 2001.

7. Steve Horn. *The Department of Defense: What Must Be Done to Resolve DoD's Longstanding Financial Management Problems?* Oversight hearing before Subcommittee on Government Efficiency, Financial Management, and Intergovernmental Relations. 107th Congress, May 8, 2001.

8. Gregory Kutz. *The Department of Defense: What Must Be Done to Resolve DoD's Longstanding Financial Management Problems?* Oversight hearing before Subcommittee on Government Efficiency, Financial Management, and Intergovernmental Relations. 107th Congress, May 8, 2001.

9. Noe.

10. "Foundation for the Future," *DFAS Financial Systems Strategic Plan,* January 2000. Version 3.1.

11. Noe.

12. Reason.

13. Audrey Davis, Defense Finance and Accounting Service. Interviewed by William Lucyshyn and Sandra Young. Arlington, Va., March 8, 2002.

14. Department of Defense, Defense Finance and Accounting Service, *DFAS Financial Systems Strategic Plan,* Washington, D.C.:GPO, January 2001.

15. Department of Defense.

CHAPTER TWELVE

The National Science Foundation's Centralized Management: Driving Financial Management Successfully

Dzintars Dzilna
and
William Lucyshyn

Introduction[1]

Whether a federal agency performs procurement, manufacturing, or grant procedures, supply chain management can help conduct those processes more effectively. But no organization can apply supply chain management procedures without having its own financial house in order. Managers must have timely, relevant, and accurate data about their own budgets and expenditures to find areas for improvement. Financial management is the foundation upon which efficient supply chains are built.

The National Science Foundation (NSF) is widely recognized for its fully integrated financial management system and serves as a model for other government agencies. The Foundation has demonstrated several accomplishments through its financial management systems, including:

- **Green light:** The NSF's financial management initiative received the only "green light" from the Office of Management and Budget (OMB) in the President's 2001 and 2002 Management Agenda evaluation. The evaluation examined five initiatives at each of 26 federal agencies.[2,3]
- **Overhead control:** The NSF spends only 5 percent of its budget on overhead. Over the past decade, the Foundation's budget has increased over 80 percent—and with it, new challenges such as funding international, multi-disciplinary, and inter-agency research projects, without raising staffing levels.
- **E-grants:** The NSF is one of the few federal research agencies that receives and processes proposals and payments to grantees electronically on a production basis—increasing operating efficiencies as well as services to grantees.

The agency's financial management system has been an integral part of keeping its costs down and productivity growing. This case study provides insight into the NSF's financial management systems and explores its best practices for planning, implementing, utilizing, maintaining, and growing a strong financial management system. The discussion examines how the financial management system acts as the basis for the Foundation's supply chain management strategy.

Background

This overview of the mission and organization of the NSF gives a point of reference for comparison with other agencies and demonstrates how NSF's structure and history have influenced the development of its financial management systems.

Mission

Statutory mission: To promote the progress of science; to advance the national health, prosperity, and welfare; and to secure the national defense.

The NSF executes its mission by providing funds—in the form of grants, contracts, and cooperative agreements—to schools (K–12), students, teachers, colleges and universities, researchers, scientists, small businesses, and others. Grants are made in three strategic areas:

- **Research:** The bulk of NSF's budget (52 percent) goes to supporting ideas that are tested and examined by scientists. These grants are made mainly to university researchers—i.e., professors and graduate students—who explore new technologies, applications, and theories. Money is directed into new areas of technology development to generate academic and business interest in specific promising fields—developing workers with expertise and motivating private companies to enter those new fields. One recent example is nanotechnology, where microscopic tools and mechanical processes are being developed for applications such as removal of cholesterol from arteries.
- **Workforce:** One fifth of NSF's budget is spent on developing and maintaining science, engineering, and teaching workforces. This role helps to ensure that industry and government will have the workers they need for current and future projects. A recent example is when the NSF provided an emergency $200,000 grant in November 2001 to researchers who sequenced the anthrax bacterium when the virus scare hit the nation.
- **Tools:** The Foundation provides a range of equipment and facilities to scientists and engineers across the country. Examples include telescopes, accelerators, underwater vessels, aircraft, and earthquake simulators.

Organization

The NSF's centralized organization has been highly conducive to developing an integrated financial management system. Three key elements include:

- **CFO:** The chief financial officer, or CFO, has direct charge over the following departments in the NSF:
  - Budget, Finance, and Award Management
  - Grants and Agreements
  - Contracts, Policy, and Oversight

The Scope of the National Science Foundation

- Grant funds are distributed among 35 branches of science, including physics, chemistry, biotechnology, and engineering fields.

- 30,000 proposals for grants are received annually.

- 40,000 peer reviewers conduct over 200,000 merit reviews on the submitted proposals.

- Grants are awarded on a competitive basis; only about a quarter to one-third of all proposals receive funding per year.

- Almost 90 percent of NSF's funding is allocated through its merit-based review process.

- The Foundation accounts for about 20 percent of federal support to academic institutions for basic research.

- **Bottom line:** During FY 2001, NSF invested a total of $4.2 billion in the country's scientific and education communities.

By overseeing all the financial functions throughout the agency, the CFO's office has been able to implement systems integrated in all departments, and thus track every dollar from when it comes through the door to when it's spent—whether for multi-million dollar grants, procurement of office supplies, or employee salaries.

- **IT Group:** The agency also has a centralized Information Technology Group, which allows for standardization of systems (hardware and software), upgrades, maintenance, and timetables across all departments. By maintaining IT standards, applications such as financial management can be applied across the organization efficiently. Many agencies face challenges in implementing enterprise-wide financial management systems because their departments or offices have disparate IT systems that are too expensive to standardize. Additionally, NSF's IT Group has historically been aggressive in adopting new technologies, such as a PC on every desk in the mid-'80s and client-server technology in the '90s. Scientists and researchers who have served at the NSF have also set high expectations for the organization to use technology for operations. The IT Group is part of the Office of Information and Resource Management, and thus separate from the CFO's office.

- **Location:** All of NSF's 1,200 employees are located at its Arlington, Virginia, facility. This centralized location helps management roll out new systems and workflows more easily than agencies that are, by contrast, large and geographically dispersed.

System Description[4]

Objectives

The effort at the NSF to develop a robust financial management system has been an ongoing endeavor. Historically, the Foundation has consistently upgraded its information technology systems since the early 1970s, following its agency role as catalyst of technology development.

NSF's management has been driven by the vision to use technology to optimize its main function of grants disbursement. A significant goal has been to develop an electronic grants system. By automating its financial functions, it has been able to successfully generate operational efficiencies and build a web-based, electronic grants system known as Fastlane.

The NSF's Financial Accounting System (FAS) is the core technology of the Foundation's financial management. Development of the FAS has been driven by key objectives including:

- Accountability and transparency
- Performance
- Customer service

Architecture

Financial management at NSF is enabled by the agency's Financial Accounting System. Figure 12.1 is a schematic of the system. The FAS provides a full spectrum of financial transaction functionality. It operates with the agency's Enterprise Information System (EIS), which provides real-time replication of finance data and performance data. The EIS is accessible to all managers, and information can be used to manage programs for decision-making purposes. The FAS is made up of several financial functions including:

- **Financial input:** All commitment and obligation transaction input is online, real time. Most of NSF's expenditure transactions are generated from the Fastlane input of the Federal Transaction Report. All other expenditures are entered directly into the FAS system. (Currently, travel orders, requisitions, and purchase orders do not have an integrated electronic interface with the FAS. Management plans to make these functions completely electronic in the near future.)
- **Inquiries/reports:** Extensive reporting capabilities, including daily, weekly, monthly, and quarterly reports.

Figure 12.1: FAS System Procedure and Interface Diagram

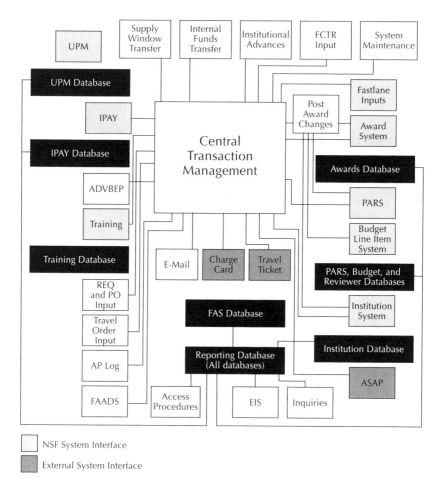

- **Budget execution:** Planning, commitment, and obligation management.
- **Administration:** Each of NSF's seven operating directorates manages parts of their payroll, overtime, and cash awards administration.
- **Procurement:** Office supplies.

One of the FAS's key components is the agency's Standard General Ledger. (The Foundation implemented the General Ledger in 1987, following the mandate of OMB and Treasury for all agencies.) The FAS's General Ledger is a report, not a separate file, so that when a transaction is input into FAS, it is applied to all the appropriate General Ledger accounts. Other systems force users to summarize input data and selectively enter it.

The FAS also integrates with non-financial, operational divisions:

- **Proposal and Reviewer:** Processing of proposals submitted.
- **Awards:** Monitors ethics codes, appropriate management systems of grantee institutions.
- **Fastlane:** NSF's web-based channel.

Grant budgets are developed and allocated to each program branch, and program managers oversee those budgets. The FAS allows program managers to follow, on a real-time basis, how much grantees have spent and how much they have left in their grants.

The following is an illustration of how FAS integrates with the operations side of NSF. When a proposal is awarded, called a division director concurrence, the Proposal system checks with the FAS to ensure that there is money to be allocated. If the FAS finds that funds are available, it creates a commitment transaction and the Proposal system's proposal data is updated to indicate a committed status. The information is then sent to the Awards system, where internal controls such as ethics forms are done. When the Awards system checks the information, the grant is awarded and the FAS system makes the obligation and keeps track of ongoing changes.

Technology/Applications[4]

There are three applications that are useful for understanding the NSF's financial management system and what it can provide for the agency and its customers. The applications include FAS, Fastlane, and IPAY.

- **FAS:** The system incorporates much of its financial editing in a process called the "post routine" so that any financial request—whether generated from the financial system or by an external system—is verified against all of the internal rules of the system before it can be posted to the database. The system is on a client-server architecture. It uses a Sybase database and was written in-house using PowerBuilder and C++. The system's user interfaces have a Windows look-and-feel.
- **Fastlane:** Fastlane (www.fastlane.nsf.gov) is NSF's website that allows researchers, scientists, reviewers, and all other NSF customers to interact electronically with NSF staff and departments. The site has several tools for submitting proposals, receiving notifications, reviewing proposals, etc. The Fastlane site is connected with FAS through middleware, which sits between the Fastlane server and FAS server. The site is maintained by NSF's Operations department. In terms of financial management, Fastlane uses the FAS as a foundation to provide grantees with significant financial applications:
  - *Cash disbursement requests and updates.* By integrating with the FAS, Fastlane is able to let grantees access their grants like at an

ATM—i.e., with a username and PIN number, the grantee can make cash requests. The request is received by the Grants system, which then checks against FAS to see if the money is available from the grantee's account. Given that the account is not overdrawn, the transaction will be certified for payment and the request will be sent to Treasury. Treasury will issue an EFT (electronic funds transfer) payment to the account online.

- *Efficient turnaround.* Within 48 hours, grantees will have their cash on hand. No one has been on the phone, nor has any paper been shuffled. The NSF issues up to $3.5 billion annually in this workflow with four grant accountants.
- *Federal Cash Transaction Report access and submission.* Grantees are required to submit expense reports on how they've spent their grant money. Each quarter the NSF sends grantees an electronic spreadsheet which, when filled out, can be automatically loaded into FAS to post expenses.
- *Timely availability of money.* Grantees don't have to wait for months for agency representatives to evaluate and check reports that may come every month or so. They can use the money that they have allocated on a timely basis. Although grantees are provided with only three days' worth of cash for expenses, they can get access to additional funds through the "ATM" if their reporting is up to date.
- **IPAY:** NSF's integrated payroll system interfaces with FAS, as well as the agency's timecard and human resources modules. The employee self-service module in IPAY allows employees to electronically manage their payroll information, e.g., federal and state tax withholding, direct deposit, mailing address changes, and purchases of federal savings bonds.

Guidelines

NSF has developed the following guidelines that provide a framework to make ongoing decisions about system development. By defining these guidelines, management is able to communicate its goals and how to reach them.
- **Federal compliance:** Chief Financial Officers Act, Federal Financial Management Improvement Act, Government Performance and Results Act (GPRA), Government Management Reform Act.
- **Input once/use many:** The development of NSF's financial management system has been based on a strategy to have financial information entered once, and then utilize IT to distribute that data to the appropriate systems and databases. The practice reduces redundancies and errors significantly.

- **Hardware and software:** Virtually all employees at NSF are armed with an Internet-enabled personal computer.

Metrics

Metrics provide benchmarks to measure system performance. In developing its financial management system to its current performance level, the NSF has used the following metrics:

- **Timely and accurate:** Information must be timely and useful for management decisions. FAS is real time for all finance-related data posting.
- **Accelerated reporting:** Produce financial statements, budget execution data reports, and cash reports on demand.
- **Security:** Sufficient layers of internal controls ensure proper separation of functions and reduce the chances of error through seamless integration.

Implementation of Current System

How Does Financial Management Support the NSF's Mission?

Financial management lends crucial support to NSF's mission. Most important, the integrity of the system translates into a higher perceived integrity of the Foundation. By being able to produce accurate and verifiable financial reports on a timely basis, the NSF keeps the focus on its agency mission, not on its financial management practices. Unlike some agencies, NSF does not have to "engage in 'heroic efforts'—whereby they [spend] millions of dollars and thousands of person-hours … adjusting journal entries and reconstructing the books."[5] Consequently, the NSF continues to develop a strong reputation for providing a valuable service to the country.

By utilizing electronic workflows and moving to a more paperless office, the system also helps the agency to control overhead costs. As pointed out in the introduction, the NSF has been able to grow its financial scope and reach without increasing staff levels. The financial management system improves overall performance and efficiency, with functions such as the automation of General Ledger entry and timely report generation.

Thirdly, the system supports the agency's customer service function by keeping costs down and providing applications its customers want. Because the financial management system is electronic, the agency was able to "build" its website, Fastlane, on top of it. Fastlane provides its customers (scientists, researchers, reviewers, etc.) with tools so they can access the information they need, rather than call agency staffers or program managers. For example, instead of having scientists call the agency to confirm a grant balance, scientists simply access Fastlane and get the information they need. NSF's customers are largely technically sophisticated and web savvy, and they, indeed, want a web-based system that provides these interactive tools that allow them to handle routine transactions by themselves.

NSF's financial management system also demonstrated a critical operational attribute during the anthrax scare earlier this year, which stopped the flow of physical mail in some areas. Because the financial management system is digitized and paperless, it does not rely on physical mail delivery. While other agencies could not work without their mail delivery, NSF's systems could continue providing uninterrupted service.

Integration with the Supply Chain

In private industry, supply chain management is commonly applied to procurement and production workflows. While NSF does relatively little of what might be generally considered procurement, its grants management workflow is analogous to a procurement cycle, where it is procuring services (scientific research) and producing products (reports, trained workforce, etc.). To procure the right services, the agency puts out solicitations in the areas of science and research it wants to develop, and scientists submit proposals. These proposals are evaluated, and then awarded or denied an award. The agency then takes on a customer service role, helping researchers use their award or getting their proposal approved the next time around.

Supply chain techniques are applicable to NSF's workflow, including:

- **Forecasting:** NSF's continuing grants allow researchers to mortgage up to 65 percent of next year's budget. They can go up to five years ahead. Likewise, because the NSF has its books up to date on a real-time basis, it can allocate budget rescissions that may come from Congress. This allows the agency to make appropriate changes to its "procurement schedule."
- **Streamlining:** FAS allows for strategy and operations decisions not only in terms of what grants may be funded but also in terms of administrative resources available to support the operations function of the flow of grant work. Because of the complexity and time to award some larger grants, bottlenecks in the chain management of awards are easily avoided because of the high integration of the systems from solicitation, proposal, merit review, award, post-award, and closeout. Large grants turn out to be just as easy to manage through the chain as smaller ones.
- **Customer satisfaction:** Helping researchers change their grant proposals is a form of feedback that helps them to develop better proposals the next time around. They must understand what is important to the customer—how the agency can make its operations better for the sectors

it serves. By having the FAS in order and being able to build applications like Fastlane on top of it, NSF has enabled researchers to help themselves in the proposal process—and help the agency save money on customer service expenditures over the long run. For example, submitting Federal Cash Transaction Reports directly into the finance system helps researchers with an efficient electronic form and avoids duplication of information since it is fed directly into the FAS.

- **Collaboration:** The NSF often provides grants with other agencies. When those agencies' financial systems are made fully electronic, the NSF will be able to obligate money from the other agencies more effectively.

Greatest Challenges to Change

One major obstacle facing most agencies on an annual basis is the uncertainty of funding levels. Because an agency may not know whether it will get as much or more funding next year as this year, it is difficult to make realistic capital budgeting decisions. Agencies that need to revamp their financial management systems are especially burdened by the need to build within their capital spending plan a transition to keep old systems going while getting the new one developed. Finance infrastructure investments in other agencies may take a backseat to programs that are a higher priority in the short term.

Change Management Issues

One of the most important aspects of deploying new technologies in an office is change management. By implementing new processes and tools, people can be made to feel irrelevant and unnecessary, or may be forced to do a job they do not want or like. It is critical to gain buy-in from employees and management when rolling out a new system such as electronic financial management.

The NSF already has a long history of new system implementation, so it has entered into the Foundation's overall culture. One way that NSF continues to manage change is by including employees in the technology development process. Systems are highly advertised—i.e., NSF's management effectively communicates the value and importance of any new system—and tested with input from many users. People will support what they help to create. Systems are brought up through marketing, implementation, recovery, and risk management strategies.

Another change management issue for the Foundation is that the systems throughout the organization are now so highly integrated, that all the departments need to work together whenever something needs to change. For example, what if there was a desire to create a subentry on General Ledger accounts? Adding two characters to account entries would mean that the changes would affect system subroutines used by Proposal, Department of Information Systems, and executive information interfaces.

To work on issues related to interconnectivity, the agency has formed an overarching group of administrative services (e.g., property system, visitors' system, payroll, time and attendance, HR, awards, Fastlane maintenance, etc.) to bring together a cross-functional team of executives and users who convene regularly to communicate needs and planned changes. Currently, all NSF systems and interfaces with other systems are replicated into a test environment, using the same type of server and enterprise architecture as the live production environment. Division of Financial Management staff and computer programmers rigorously test interfaces before they are implemented throughout the agency.

Security and Privacy

One of the main requirements of financial systems by the Federal Financial Management Improvement Act (FFMIA) is for automated systems to develop robust security measures. Information security weaknesses are one of the primary causes for agencies' systems noncompliance with FFMIA.[6]

NSF's Division of Financial Management oversees security of the FAS by using a user profile system. The division controls individuals' access to accounting procedures—for example, contracting officers, who are allowed to obligate certain amounts of money. The division does not control how much the officers can allocate, but it does control whether the allocations can be added to the FAS. Most accounting transactions are not entered by division management, so user profile maintenance is a key part of the system.

Finally, a yearly review of NSF's security program planning and management is conducted in conjunction with the Foundation's Office of Inspector General. This security review follows current guidance (including the Government Information Security Reform Act of 2000, OMB Circular A-130) and the General Accounting Office Audit Guide. It includes the following:

- Conduct risk assessments of all mission-critical systems and certify for operation.
- Publish policies documenting security program.
- Establish a security management structure and assign security responsibilities.
- Incorporate security-related issues into personnel policies and provide ongoing training of staff.

Lessons Learned

As a leader of financial management in the federal government, the NSF can provide fellow agencies with some valuable insights about how it has been able to develop a robust system. The most important takeaways include the following:

- **Top-down leadership:** It is imperative that agency leaders like the CFO take a lead role in using technology and new processes to implement sound financial management. Top executives must take ownership of the process and communicate to the whole agency that financial management systems development is a priority.
- **Centralization:** NSF has the luxury of having all its employees under one roof, with relatively small divisions that are organized in a way to give the CFO control over financial management. To develop a sound financial management system, decision making for financial and technology decisions from a central group can be critical. A central decision-making body, such as a financial IT council, involving executives from different divisions, could be developed to champion a new system.
- **Focus on the long term:** Instead of using resources in the short term to get a clean audit bill, agencies should focus on updating their systems—so that they can do the proper planning and be realistic that a new system may take three to five years of development.
- **Stretch:** Instead of undertaking dozens of performance goals, agencies should focus on five to seven stretch goals—for example, developing an IT standardization plan that will allow the agency to implement the hardware and software systems needed for an enterprise-wide financial management system.
- **Capture once:** A key element of the NSF financial management system is using IT to reduce the redundancies that are associated with paper-based workflows. IT allows organizations to capture once and then reuse data effectively.

Future Vision

As the federal government moves to more fiscally responsible government, there are several possible outcomes that will affect the NSF, its systems and agencies in general. Some high-level outcomes include:

- **Federal standardization:** The federal government may step in and force all agencies to use one or more standard systems for financial management. For example, the government may have all agencies use the same payroll system. The government may realize economies of scale with the move, but individual agencies like NSF may wind up needing to update several other systems integrated with payroll—at a high cost in new development and training.

- **GPRA:** The results orientation of GPRA does not mesh with the NSF's merit-based system of finding projects to invest in. Currently, the NSF has an independent audit done of its operations. It has a panel of external experts called Committees of Visitors, which are convened to review the technical and managerial stewardship of NSF programs on a three-year cycle. The NSF is currently looking at ways to automate further the process of tying results from research with expenses and funding.
- **Verification:** Currently, there are no standards across agencies for verification of how funding is being spent by grant recipients. As agencies develop better financial management, verification may become more important for all agencies.
- **Move to web:** NSF's next technology move is to bring its administrative systems from client-server to web architecture. The change will allow the agency to standardize maintenance of its system and provide access from anywhere.

Conclusion

Information and communication technologies promise to help enterprises find new sources of value by better integrating their internal operations with their supply chain. Internal financial management is the foundation upon which to develop this integration. Without clear and current visibility of revenues and costs, an enterprise cannot manage its relationships with suppliers, vendors, and customers effectively.

Integration between financial management and supply chain is especially important for grant-making operations, where its raw materials and end products are themselves financial in nature. The NSF has recognized this and focused on developing—on an ongoing basis—a robust financial management system. The NSF's success can be attributed to several best practices, perhaps the most important being centralized management of financial functions and technology implementation. Centralized organization in these areas allows the NSF to design systems that utilize the capture-once strategy to generate efficiencies and reduce costs. Underlying this practice is NSF's top-down leadership of improving infrastructure with new technologies and workflows.

With a robust financial management system in place, the NSF has been able to utilize supply chain processes such as forecasting, streamlining, and customer service. By generating these and other operational efficiencies, the NSF continues to provide visibility of its operations—and ultimately prove its integrity to Congress and the American people.

Endnotes

1. Except where noted, information for this report came from interviews with Thomas N. Cooley, chief financial officer, and Donald G. McCrory, deputy chief financial officer, conducted on March 11, 2002; and with Donald G. McCrory, Carrie Gail Dira, chief, Financial Systems Branch, and Vincent Yoder, head, Systems Development & Review Section, conducted on February 28, 2002.

2. National Science Foundation, *FY2001 Management and Performance Highlights,* February 2002. Viewed at www.nsf.gov/pubs/2002/nsf02099/nsf_return.pdf, February 2002.

3. *Office of Management and Budget Performance and Management Assessment for FY 2001.* Viewed at www.whitehouse.gov/omb/budget/fy2004/pma.html, March 2003.

4. Internal documents from NSF's Office of Budget, Finance, and Award Management: *Financial Accounting System (FAS), Financial Accounting System Overview, Implementing Electronic Grants, IPAY/ESS: The New NSF Integrated Payroll/Employee Self Service.*

5. Tim Reason, "Federal Offenses: A dozen years after passage of the CFO Act, the U.S. Government still struggles to close its books," *CFO Magazine,* March 6, 2002. Viewed at http://www.cfo.com/article/1,5309,6768,00.html, March 2002.

6. General Accounting Office, *FFMIA Implementation Critical for Federal Accountability,* GAO-02-29, October 1, 2001, 34.

CHAPTER THIRTEEN

Covisint:
Driving the Auto Industry

Amitabh Brar
and
William Lucyshyn

Introduction

The Covisint story is compelling not only because it involves a new and exciting technology but also because the company was formed as a result of an unprecedented collaboration between rival automotive companies. In the spring of 2000, Ford, General Motors Corporation, and DaimlerChrysler shocked the business world when they decided to join hands to respond to the suppliers' call for a common e-business platform for the entire automotive industry supply chain. The result of this unique partnership was Covisint, a company focused on meeting global automotive industry needs with Internet-based tools and services, particularly collaborative product development, procurement, and supply chain management solutions.

Covisint yielded significant results for its stakeholders early on. First announced in February 2000, Ford Motor Company estimates it saved $70 million in 2000, and forecasted a further $350 million in savings during 2001 through use of the exchange.[1] According to *InformationWeek*,[2] the total value of transactions managed through August 2001 by Covisint has exceeded $129 billion, including $96 billion worth of raw materials and parts purchased by General Motors Corporation for future auto models.

Background

Typically, more than 50 percent of an automobile's parts are supplied to an Original Equipment Manufacturer (OEM), such as Ford or DaimlerChrysler, by an outside vendor or supplier. Procurement of these parts has been traditionally handled via phone, fax, or e-mail between the OEM and its suppliers. Any modifications in production schedules resulting in a change in the demand or supply of the parts to be supplied were communicated through all the links in the supply chain until they reached the lowest-tier supplier. Predictably, the inefficiencies built into a system relying on these methods resulted in poor inventory and time management, causing substantial material and manpower waste. More recently, EDI (Electronic Data Interface) systems between an OEM and its suppliers were deployed to reduce this time lapse in communication. However, the point-to-point communication design of an EDI system, though much faster than legacy systems, is still limited in that it fails to link across the entire network of suppliers and OEMs (see Figure 13.1).

In the 1990s, it became increasingly evident that an open information exchange network, such as the Internet, could bring significant reduction in costs and improve the efficiency of the traditional procurement methods. Recognizing this, Ford and General Motors (GM) both sought to leverage

Figure 13.1: Covisint's "Hub & Spoke" Model Improves Communication Efficiency

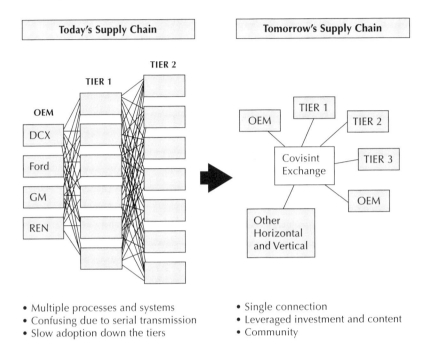

- Multiple processes and systems
- Confusing due to serial transmission
- Slow adoption down the tiers

- Single connection
- Leveraged investment and content
- Community

the power of the Internet for the supply chains that supported them by announcing their own e-procurement initiatives in November 1999 called "Auto-x-change" and "TradeXchange" respectively. Ford chose Oracle as the technology partner for Auto-x-change, while GM selected Commerce One to set up TradeXchange.

Soon, however, these exchanges ran into the same hurdle that they were meant to overcome. Large suppliers in the automotive industries serving both GM and Ford were faced with two different e-procurement systems, which meant that they had to support the distinct protocols of each system. To make matters worse, there was the prospect of other OEMs, like DaimlerChrysler, setting up their own separate systems. It was evident that supporting multiple proprietary electronic exchange programs would lead to the original problems of extra costs and inefficiencies in the supply chain—the same maladies that the exchanges were designed to alleviate.

In response, Ford, GM, and DaimlerChrysler announced in February 2000 the formation of a single global Internet exchange aimed at serving the entire automotive industry. This new organization, called NewCo, relied upon both Oracle and Commerce One as technology partners. The company was renamed Covisint in May 2000 and, by then, counted Renault, Nissan, and PSA Peugeot Citroen among its OEM partners.

In September 2000, Covisint obtained the critical clearance from the Federal Trade Commission, followed soon after by approval from the German Bundeskartellamt. In December 2000, the formation of Covisint, LLC was announced. Kevin English was appointed chairman and CEO of the company in April 2001. The opening of offices in Europe, Asia-Pacific, and Japan in May 2001 has ensured Covisint a presence in the global market of automotive parts and services.

Current Situation

Management and Organization

Although the company began with an emphasis on procurement applications—mainly auctions—it became clear that auctions alone would have a limited impact on improving efficiencies within the auto industry. As a result, collaborative e-commerce and supply chain management gained increasing visibility in the company's strategic focus.

In less than two years since its inception, Covisint has evolved into a global application service provider, occupying a prominent place in the entire B2B e-commerce arena. The company now partners with a majority of the automotive OEMs in the United States and around the world. Additionally, 15,000 companies worldwide (including the top 100 to 150 in sales figures) are registered with Covisint. A customer sitting anywhere in North America, Europe, or Asia equipped with a PC and access to the Internet can connect with Covisint.com and have access to the broad suite of applications offered at the website. For instance, a supplier of braking systems for a new vehicle can use Covisint to view, in real time, parts inventories, forecasts, shipping receipts, etc., and determine the next action.

There are four main product families within the Covisint e-business solution—Portal, Collaboration, Procurement, and Supply Chain Management. Figure 13.2 graphically depicts the Covisint architecture. The following provides a brief description of each of these tools:[3]

Portal: Covisint Portal uses a single sign-on to allow access to all Covisint products and services. The portal environment provides a gateway into the full family of Covisint procurement, supply chain, and product development applications, as well as other features, such as third-party news and automotive-specific content.

Figure 13.2: Covisint Architecture

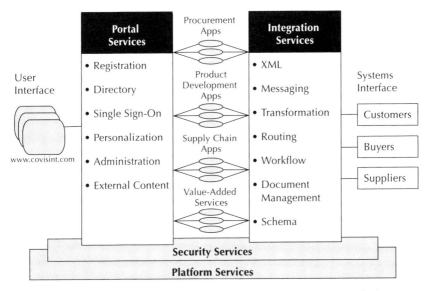

Design Criteria—Best of Breed, Scalable, Secure, Based on Internet Standards

Collaboration: Covisint Collaboration facilitates communication across corporate boundaries. Collaborative virtual teams formed between trading partners can use this tool to increase the innovation, speed, and effectiveness of core functions such as product development, program management, and strategic sourcing. By using the Covisint Collaboration Manager, designers at an OEM can share their two- and three-dimensional drawings with the suppliers in real time, resulting in a faster turnaround time from the concept phase to the market. MatrixOne and Engineering Animation are the technology providers for this platform.

Procurement: Covisint Procurement is aimed at reducing the time needed to complete sourcing activities. Covisint Quote Manager allows electronic transmission of RFQs (request for quote). Customers can use the Auction tool to hold one-to-many online auction events for products and services they wish to sell or buy. Buyers have the option of limiting their auction to a few qualified suppliers or having it open to all. The online Custom Catalog tool allows for sale/purchase of automotive parts ranging from the basic to the highly engineered. Covisint Asset Control can be used to re-allocate resources or buy and sell them online.

Supply Chain Management: Covisint's supply chain applications are targeted at operations in the production process and are considered to be a major step toward the realization of the build-to-order vehicle. Through tools such as Covisint Fulfillment and Covisint Supplier Connection, trading partners in a supply chain can collaboratively communicate, and develop production and ship schedules using standardized information and common systems, as necessary.

A business model based on these tools and services helps Covisint generate multiple revenue streams. The collaborative and supply chain management applications raise subscription-driven fees, whereas the procurement applications generate event-driven fees. In addition, licensing and hosting fees, and consulting and deployment services are also expected to contribute to overall revenue generation in the future.

With the automotive industry in particular, where things have been done a certain way for years—maybe decades—accepting the changes Covisint offered in the supply system was a serious challenge. Personal interviews with the Covisint management team highlighted several best practices within the organization that have led to what they believe is a viable business model. Foremost among them were the clear identification of existing industry challenges and the development of a strategy that specifically addresses them through Covisint's services and then marketing the services to those targeted areas. The company's mantra, "one customer at a time," illustrates the targeted marketing strategy necessary in this industry.

Second, Covisint attempted to put to rest the apprehensions and concerns that they would be biased toward a particular customer because of the close ties to particular companies. The first CEO appointed to head Covisint, Kevin English, had no prior affiliations with any one automotive company or supplier. Third, Covisint is staffed with "experts" from the automotive industry who bring with them a solid understanding of the intricacies of the automotive manufacturing and supplying world.

Finally, Covisint created a forum, called Covisint Customer Council (C3), to stay in tune with all of its OEM customers and to ensure greater supplier participation. C3 includes representatives from the top 40 automotive suppliers and all the OEM partners of the company. C3 receives customer feedback, tests products, and mobilizes a larger audience for Covisint's products.

There are, however, several challenges facing the company's management. Initially, Covisint focused entirely on engaging the auto-industry heavyweights, leaving the bulk of the lower-tier suppliers off the "radar screen" of the company. A concerted effort is now being made to engage and include these lower-tier suppliers in its services and business strategy.

Additionally, Covisint managers learned of supplier community worries that Covisint was just another "slick trick" by the OEMs to squeeze them further by driving prices down through increased competition. The marketing team at Covisint is faced with the crucial task of educating its customers about the benefits that this electronic exchange can offer them, their customers, and their suppliers in the automotive supply chain.

Covisint is also threatened by automotive e-business exchanges created by other OEMs such as Volkswagen and BMW of Germany, albeit the main purpose of these exchanges is for internal communication and collaboration. Japanese car manufacturers, such as Honda and Toyota, prefer to establish closer relations with a few long-term suppliers in an off-line manner, which further compounds the challenge to Covisint. The absence of a single standard for Internet-based procurement is one of the hurdles Covisint faces in convincing suppliers to use the exchange. The company is trying to address this in talks with Volkswagen, BMW, and others, aiming to draft a common industry standard for Internet-based multi-company collaboration.

After two years of operations Covisint was not, however, achieving the planned growth. Mr. English resigned in June 2002 and was replaced by Harold Kutner, a former vice president from General Motors, who reorganized the operation—reducing the emphasis on design-collaboration efforts and refocusing on e-procurement and supplier integration.[4] Covisint still seems committed to the value its suite of solutions offers and has shown a strong growth of its registered users in 2002 (up 253 percent to 77,000).[5]

More broadly, as noted earlier, Covisint believes a key success factor has been the involvement of automotive industry specialists from the start. As the company seeks to expand its service in the future to non-automotive manufacturers, it will be faced with the crucial task of learning the nuances of these industries in order to be attentive to their needs.

Technology/Security/Confidentiality

Covisint's information security is critical to its objectives. Its security mission aims to ensure:

- Protection of customer information from unauthorized users (confidentiality)
- Exchange of information resources only in a specified and authorized manner (integrity)
- Proper operation of systems and service to authorized users (availability)
- The same level of security to each and every customer's data (neutrality)

Covisint utilizes a three-stage process to ensure a robust security framework. First, key business processes and initiatives are identified. This calls for an understanding of the nature of the industry and of the core processes and transactions within the business, as well as the role of information in these business processes. This helps to determine the extent to which information security is critical for Covisint's business.

Second, the current and future types of technology being implemented within Covisint are assessed. It is important to understand the nature of the technology as it relates to centralization, automation, connectivity, and other core control functions. This helps to determine how reliant on technology Covisint's services are.

Finally, the assessment of state-of-the-art technology within the company then helps to determine risks to the business. Vulnerabilities and weaknesses that constitute a threat to the business are identified. Prioritization of information protection needs can be achieved by assessing the business impact of different risks. Both quantitative and qualitative measures are employed for this. Quantitative measures include a ranking of each risk according to potential dollar loss by evaluation of its impact on business activities. Qualitative measures such as customer perceptions, business needs, and user culture and other intangible aspects of information value can also be utilized. Such a thorough understanding of business and technical risks enables the security team to prioritize protection needs and evaluate the cost and impact of countermeasures.

At Covisint, all site content is documented in XML. Secure Sockets Layer (SSL) enabled Internet browsers are used to enable identity verification of both external users and computers. User identity is ensured via a unique ID and password—a 1024-bit Public Key Infrastructure (PKI) certificate is issued and token-based identification is used. Identity of external computers is verified using 1024-bit PKI certificate for signature and encryption. Industry standards are used for these purposes.

The Covisint website construction uses a three-tier network. Tier 1 is the public Internet, to which external users connect. The web server resides in tier 2, which can be accessed by anyone using a computer with an Internet Protocol (IP) address. The database servers for the company, which contain all of the private, critical information, reside in tier 3. The private data is encrypted before it is released for public viewing at the tier-2 level, which is then decrypted at the customer site after verification of signature and non-repudiation.

There are two main best practices followed at Covisint for information security purposes. First, there is a separate information security division within the organization responsible for the definition and execution of the security vision and strategy for the company. Second, the mission of information security staff is to serve as consultants to meet the core needs of the business and not merely as security auditors who keep an eye on it.

Due to the complex nature of business interchanges taking place through its website, Covisint must be diligent about information security. Proof of a safe and secure information system is provided via customer audits, an external audit, and "ethical" hacking undertaken twice a year. The company's European operations just announced the creation of a security audit committee, overseen by an independent consulting firm to protect confidential information between carmakers and suppliers.

Information security employees of the company interact with information security officers at the OEMs and suppliers in monthly meetings. Even more challenging, the global nature of the company involves differing laws related to information technology business. For example, the European operations of the company must work with the European "safe harbor" laws that mandate different handling of data collected from users than do the laws existing in North America.

The selection of technology partners for each of the core applications offered by Covisint is based on expertise, market leadership, and customer penetration. Covisint management is faced with the task of building and maintaining a successful business relationship with its multiple technology partners, who otherwise compete with each other in the open market.

Return on Investment/Stakeholder Issues

For its OEM customers, the value that Covisint brings is seen in terms of cost savings in the procurement of parts or commodity items, as well as reductions in production time cycles from design to manufacturing. Customers using the collaboration tools report savings of 4 percent to 17 percent, and those using the procurement tools reported savings of 7 percent to 16 percent.[6]

For suppliers, Covisint offers the opportunity to access the global automotive market, enabling them to expand the customer base for their products. It makes procurement and collaborative tools available between a primary and a lower-tier supplier, similar to those used between an OEM and a primary supplier. Thus, the company caters to the entire automotive supply chain, from the OEM at the top to the smallest supplier at the bottom of the supply chain. It enables the lower-tier suppliers to obtain a better price for their products if the market rate is higher. Additionally, it makes the supply chain transparent, allowing the lower-tier suppliers to view inventory levels in real time and respond quickly to any changes in demand. For its owners, the company expects to build on its current momentum to boost revenue and reach profit-making status. During 2002, Covisint is estimated to have brokered between $50 and $60 billion worth of sales in online bidding events.[7]

Future

The long-term vision at Covisint is for the company to become the e-business operating system of the automotive industry. It plans to continue to make strides in establishing a greater presence within the global automotive manufacturing industry. The vision is that this could be achieved by including exchanges currently being run by other OEMs, such as Volkswagen in Europe, and by inclusion of those OEMs and suppliers currently not on the Covisint roster, such as Toyota and Honda of Japan. Competition from other Internet companies has, however, forced Covisint to reduce the fees they charge well below what they had planned. The reduced revenues have forced the company to reduce staff and cut other costs.[8]

The company aspires to expand its services to include non-automotive manufacturers. Covisint's suite of applications is seen as scalable to other manufacturing industries worldwide such as heavy equipment, farm equipment, marine, trucking, and motorcycles. Exchange-to-exchange connectivity is seen as another avenue for extending the company's presence beyond the automotive industry.

Conclusion

Indeed, significant lessons can be learned from the Covisint story, and highlighted for the successful launch of a future e-business venture in the private or public sector:

- In any sector of the industry, the successful business model for an e-business venture provides complete solutions instead of limiting its offering to a few select services.
- To truly meet the needs of potential customers rather than pushing a solution at them, a clear identification of current industry challenges, and a marketing strategy based on targeting them, is formulated.
- To ensure that the e-business will remain neutral and unbiased toward particular customers or individuals, the e-business must remain independent of the other companies and stakeholders in the market.
- An e-business must be driven by, and cater strongly to, the needs of the customers in the market. Since Covisint was established based on the demand of the suppliers, it was assured of their support when it came into existence.
- The e-business venture must have experts from within the industry on its staff to learn the nuances of conducting business in a certain industrial sector or market.
- To help formulate its business strategy plan and to remain in tune with its customers' needs in the long run, a focus group of customers and other industry advisors (C3 in the case of Covisint) should be created.

Endnotes

1. Carlos Grandy, "Ford Recoups Its Investment in Covisint," *Financial Times,* July 2, 2001, 23.

2. Steve Konicki, "GM Buys $96 Billion in Materials Via Covisint," *InformationWeek,* August 16, 2001. Viewed at http://www.informationweek.com/story/IWK20010816S0001, September 2001.

3. Covisint, Inc., "Covisint Services." Viewed at http://www.covisint.com/solutions, September 2001.

4. Antone Gonsalves and Steve Konicki, "CEO Quits as Covisint Restructures," *InformationWeek,* June 28, 2002. Viewed at http://www.informationweek.com/story/IWK20020628S0005, April 10, 2003.

5. Covisint press release, viewed at http://www.covisint.com/about/pressroom/pr/2003/2003.MAR.10.shtml, April 10, 2003.

6. "Detroit-Area Internet Auto-Part Venture Hits Turbulence as Business Falls Flat," *Tribune Business News, Detroit Free Press,* December 9, 2002.

7. Covisint, Inc. Viewed at http://www.covisint.com/about/pressroom/speeches/oesa_10_22_01.shtml, October 22, 2001.

8. "Detroit-Area Internet Auto-Part Venture Hits Turbulence as Business Falls Flat."

CHAPTER FOURTEEN

Defense Medical Logistics Standard Support: The New Department of Defense Medical Logistics Supply Chain

Douglas Chin
and
William Lucyshyn

Introduction[1]

The Defense Medical Logistics Standard Support (DMLSS) system is an integrated system for use by medical logisticians throughout the Department of Defense to improve medical logistics responsiveness at reduced costs. Excessive medical supply inventories at facilities are replaced by just-in-time inventories. By using the tools of business process reengineering to implement business innovations and e-commerce practices, overpriced pharmaceuticals, medical, and surgical items have been replaced by competitively bid and regionally awarded pharmaceutical contracts with guaranteed delivery and availability. Excessive order and ship times, measured in days and weeks, are now replaced by times measured in hours. The excessive time spent by health care providers on medical logistics functions is now being spent devoted to patient care. DMLSS has standardized military treatment facility logistics within each military branch of the armed services (Army, Air Force, and Navy) and among the services. When fully implemented, DMLSS will replace the functionality of nine legacy systems, saving the costs of maintaining these stand-alone, non-integrated systems.

Background

In early 1990, it became obvious that medical logistics business processes within the Department of Defense (DoD) were outdated, costly, and inefficient. Large inventories of pharmaceuticals and medical/surgical items were maintained at the wholesale and retail levels within DoD because it took so long to get needed supplies—the cycle time from order to receipt of materiel and supplies was excessive. Government prices for pharmaceuticals and medical/surgical items were high, and health care providers were spending too much time on medical logistics matters. This condition prompted the establishment of an intense business process reengineering effort. Thus, the Defense Medical Logistics Standard Support (DMLSS) system was born in May 1990.

At about the same time, DoD's medical supply chain was called into action during Operation Desert Shield/Desert Storm. Based on an organizational structure in place for over 50 years, medical readiness items were inventoried, boxed, and shipped from existing depots to DoD warfighters throughout the Saudi Arabian peninsula. Unfortunately, when they reached their destination, no one wanted the equipment and supplies because the medical supply chain had not kept pace with technological advances. Many of these items were outdated and not the products demanded by the physicians and clinicians sent to practice medicine in the Gulf War. Large numbers of acquisition requests were sent back to buy the latest products and therapeutics. By the time the auditors finished adding up the bill, 92 percent of all items used by the medical team in the Gulf War were bought specifically for that event. Only 8 percent of the supplies came from the existing depot stock, which had cost DoD millions of dollars to procure and maintain.

Objective

The DMLSS reengineering effort was designed to support the Military Health System's (MHS) health care delivery mission in providing timely materiel, facilities, services, and information resources essential to patient care during both peacetime and wartime. In an environment of shrinking military budgets, escalating costs, and inefficiencies in distribution (circa 1990), the military health care community recognized that a fundamental change from the traditional methods of doing business was necessary. Process operations were consuming 43 percent of the operating budget of typical medical treatment facilities (MTFs)—(19 percent in product costs and 24 percent in overhead costs). Lead times of 30 to 60 days for product procurement and delivery were common. On-hand inventories equaled six months of stock for a typical MTF. Complex and antiquated medical logistics systems took much time from the health care providers to manage medical logistics needs. The lack of integrated, automated information systems to research medical/surgical item availability through the requisitioning, receipt, redistribution, and disposal of an item necessitated the time-consuming use and maintenance of multiple information systems.

System Overview

The DMLSS program is a unique partnership engaging the wholesale medical logistics, medical information management, medical information technology, and user communities (see Figure 14.1). The mission of the DMLSS program is to dramatically improve the responsiveness of medical logistics support through the implementation of business innovations that significantly increase effectiveness of logistics support while reducing costs. In addition, the program seeks the development of a high-quality, integrated medical logistics automated system for use by all Army, Air Force, Marines, and Navy forces in both peacetime and war.

   The vision of DMLSS is to meet the peacetime and wartime requirements of MTFs and field medical units at an affordable price through inno-

Figure 14.1: DMLSS Brings Electronic Commerce to Health Care Operations

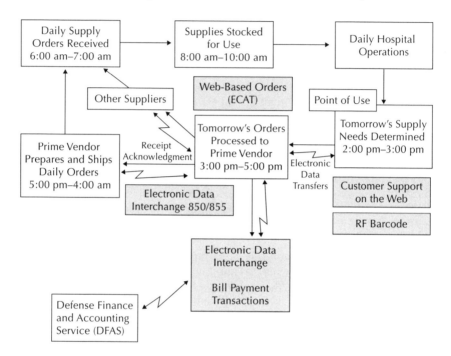

vative ideas and reengineered business processes. The system will also provide the best medical logistics Automated Information System (AIS) in DoD and U.S. health care. According to its website, DMLSS will reduce the time that health care providers spend on logistics, and support the Defense Supply Center Philadelphia (DSCP) in its efforts to supply materiel to U.S. operational forces better, faster, and cheaper. Readiness is its primary reason for being.[2]

The DMLSS AIS provides materiel management, facility management, and equipment and technology management capabilities for its users. It relies on e-commerce to speed delivery of pharmaceutical and medical/surgical items to customers, negating the need to stock a large inventory at depots and military treatment facilities. It provides automated product and price comparison tools that ease the ordering process and encourage customers to purchase the most cost-effective products. The DMLSS AIS provides an assembly management capability that ensures deployed forces are provided the right mix of equipment and materiel consistent with the current practice of medicine in fixed military treatment facilities and the commercial health care sector.

In support of readiness, the DMLSS program relies on commercial and military asset visibility. Using knowledge of pharmaceutical and medical/surgical pricing and fulfillment in the commercial sector, DMLSS supports deployed forces using the right mix of modern materials and equipment known to be available in the commercial sector in sufficient quantities to meet requirements. Additional DMLSS goals are presented in the box entitled "DMLSS Goals."

DMLSS Goals

- Lowest prices for supplies and drugs in U.S. health care
- 80% of items received in less than 24 hours
- 20% of items received in 48 to 72 hours
- DoD inventories of supplies and drugs nearly eliminated
- Contracting, ordering, and bill payment are totally electronic
- Supplies and drugs go to deployed units directly from commercial vendors
- One standardized medical logistics Automated Information System

---

Organizational Issues

The DMLSS program, co-sponsored by the assistant secretary of defense (health affairs) and the deputy under secretary of defense (logistics), is a partnership involving the wholesale medical logistics, medical information management, medical information technology, and user communities. (See Figure 14.2.)

The Military Health System (MHS) Information Management/Information Technology (IM/IT) program's organizational structure provides the governance for the oversight and management of the MHS portfolio. This governance process is also intended to ensure compliance with the Government Performance and Results Act (GPRA), Clinger-Cohen Act of 1996, and DoD acquisition and management regulations. Critical elements of this structure include senior management oversight, MHS chief information officer (CIO) leadership, and senior managers for both IT and IM who are responsible for executing and monitoring the portfolio investment plans and are accountable to senior managers and the MHS CIO.

Senior executive oversight is provided by the assistant secretary of defense (health affairs) [ASD (HA)], the service surgeons general (SGs), the Joint Staff deputy director for medical readiness (see Figure 14.2), and the executive director of the TRICARE Management Activity (TMA). This senior management structure ensures that the IT portfolio supports the mission, vision, and strategic direction of the MHS.

Mission area analysis is conducted by the services on a continuing basis to ensure that medical logistics support for deployed and deploying forces is adequate. The Medical Logistics Proponent Subcommittee (MLPS) represents the unified medical logistics needs of all services to the TRICARE Executive Committee. For the DMLSS program, the MLPS effectively serves as the board of directors and approves the functional capability description that defines the user's requirements for a given release. Membership includes the chiefs of medical logistics from each service, the director of medical materiel at Defense Supply Center Philadelphia, the staff director of the Joint Readiness Clinical Advisory Board, and the director of health services and operations support, TMA.

Figure 14.2: DMLSS Management Organization

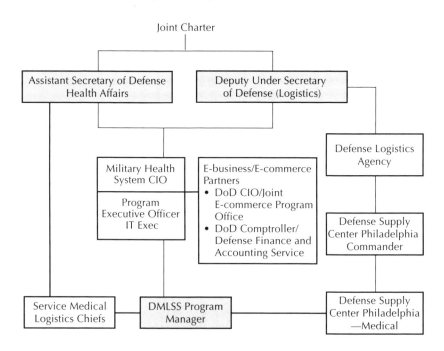

E-Commerce

In 1996, recognizing the importance of information technology for effective government, the Congress and President enacted the Information Technology Management Reform Act and the Federal Acquisition Reform Act. These two acts together, known as the Clinger-Cohen Act, require the heads of federal agencies to link IT investments to agency accomplishments. The Clinger-Cohen Act also requires that agency heads establish a process to select, manage, and control their IT investments. In addition, the act called for the appointment of a chief information officer for each federal agency with responsibility for coordinating electronic efforts.

The Clinger-Cohen Act was designed to help ensure that investments in IT provide measurable improvements in mission performance. A key to using IT to enable improvements in DoD's operations and procedures is establishing processes through which executive leadership can align business processes and resources to mission goals and strategic objectives. Other key factors are for a capital planning process and a portfolio management strategy that allow executive leadership to manage IT and IM resources throughout their life cycle. Through such activities, executives periodically assess all projects—proposed, under development, and operational—and then prioritize them and make funding decisions based on such factors as cost, risk, return on investment, and support of mission-related outcomes.

In addition, the Government Paperwork Elimination Act of 1998 and digital signature legislation of 2000 promote the advancement of e-commerce by streamlining processes and reducing paperwork while allowing agencies to use an "e-signature" rather than pen-and-paper signatures. These actions helped shape the current e-commerce systems within the government.

Implementation

The DMLSS AIS is being developed and deployed in three major releases. This is a departure from an earlier program acquisition strategy that called for deployment of five releases. The decision to deploy three releases instead of five was influenced by the costs associated with additional deployments as well as the potential interruption that is caused at a military treatment facility when a release is deployed. (See Figure 14.3.)

Release 1.0, consisting of the first increment of materiel management and the first increment of facility management, was deployed to 110 sites worldwide. Development of DMLSS Release 2.0, consisting of the second

Figure 14.3: DMLSS Release Objectives

DMLSS Release 1.0	Facility Management Version 1 Forward Customer Support Standalone Prime Vendor Interface	Joint Medical Asset Repository (JMAR)
DMLSS Release 2.0	Customer Area Inventory Management Facility Management Version 2 System Services Customer Support Including Web Version Integrated Prime Vendor Interface	DMLSS Echelon 1/2 MEDLOG Component of TMIP for Echelon 2 and Below (TMIP Block 1)
DMLSS Release 3.0	Customer Area Inventory Management Facility Management Version 2 System Services Stockroom Readiness Inventory Management Assemblage Management Customer Support Including Web Version Integrated Prime Vendor Interface Contract Services Equipment Management Equipment Maintenance	MEDLOG Component of TMIP for Echelon 2 and Above (TMIP Block 3)

increment of materiel management, the second increment of facility management and business process reengineering enhancements, is complete. Formal operational testing and evaluation (OT&E) for DMLSS Release 2.0 was conducted in January 2000. Clinger-Cohen certification supported the Milestone III approval for worldwide deployment of DMLSS Release 2.0.

Release 3.0, which incorporates the final increment of materiel management and equipment and technology management, will include an assembly management module. Deployment of Release 3.0 enables the services to turn off service-unique medical logistics legacy systems at medical treatment facilities worldwide. The goal is to have legacy systems such as AMEDDPAS, BIOFACS, CPD, MEDLOG, MICRO-MICS, TAMMIS (MEDSUP, MEDASM, MEDMNT) off-line by 2007.

In addition to containing all functionality of Release 1.0, DMLSS Release 2.0 provides complete inventory management (receipt, storage, and issue) of pharmaceuticals and medical/surgical items for customer areas such as wards and clinics. Release 2.0 also provides electronic ordering and financial management capabilities and provides facility managers with space management, life safety, utility management, housekeeping, and contract management capabilities. The two major modules of Release 2.0 are the Customer Area Inventory Management (CAIM) module and the Facility Management (FM) module. With DMLSS Release 2.0, the Prime Vendor (PV) Electronic Commerce (EC) initiative allows DoD medical treatment facilities to communicate with their commercial trading partners using a single standard Tri-Service online medical purchase order. Electronic Catalog Web-based Ordering expands the medical logistics just-in-time inventory management program to allow customers to place orders by way of the web using medical logistics inventory management systems and summary billing. With EC, DMLSS has developed an automated interface between retail DoD medical logistics systems and the electronic catalog, and incorporated a fully automated bill payment process. Electronic Commerce Support to Deploying Units ties the prime vendor and the electronic catalog projects directly to support of military personnel in the field. It generates electronic orders to vendors based on shortages in deploying units, uses leading-edge e-commerce business practices to submit orders once commercial assets are known to be available through asset visibility, and integrates e-commerce with asset visibility of contracted and non-contracted commercial peacetime and wartime stocks.

DMLSS Release 3.0 will include the Stockroom Inventory Management (SRIM) and Equipment and Technology Management (E&TM) modules. SRIM has two main components: inventory management and readiness management. E&TM will replace all legacy systems for organization-level property accountability and equipment maintenance and includes Customer Support for Equipment, Equipment (Property) Management, Maintenance Management and Administration, and Contract Services Management and Administration.

E-Commerce Applications

Prime Vendor Electronic Commerce

The DMLSS Prime Vendor Electronic Commerce/Electronic Data Interchange initiative converts over 300 DoD medical prime vendor program ordering points from a myriad of proprietary vendor order-entry systems to an e-commerce/e-data interchange environment. With the implementation of DMLSS Version 2.0, all DoD medical treatment facilities will communicate with their commercial trading partners using a single standard Tri-Service ANSI X.12 medical purchase order. Reengineering of the communication interchange loop has eliminated communication bottlenecks. Ninety-five percent of the orders placed on the system are confirmed within 45 minutes. This initiative totally reengineers and standardizes the paperless computer-to-computer exchange of purchase orders across all military medical treatment facilities. As of September 30, 2000, DMLSS was generating electronic purchase orders from 416 ordering points at 121 medical treatment facilities to 11 commercial trading partners.

Prime Vendor Business Management Application (PVBMA)

PVBMA streamlines and manages the Prime Vendor Program by providing automated support and much-needed information to various functions including contract negotiations, program marketing, customer service, program management, and invoice processing. PVBMA allows for online access to Prime Vendor data through predefined, customized, and ad hoc queries. Information is available on product demand, Prime Vendor performance, financial status, fill rate/supply availability, and response time.

Electronic Catalog (ECAT) Web-Based Ordering

Through the use of an Internet browser (Internet Explorer 5.X or Netscape Navigator 4.6), ECAT is the e-commerce business solution for the next millennium, providing paperless contracting, electronic ordering, electronic invoicing, and electronic payments. ECAT allows users to do web-based research, place web-based orders, and make payment for optical, laboratory, and dental items. The first product of this project, the Laboratory Integrated Delivery System (LIDS), uses web-enabled technology to accomplish multiple online catalog ordering of clinical and research laboratory products. ECAT Web-Based Ordering system accepts both Military and Federal Requisitioning and Issue Procedures (MILSTRIP and FEDSTRIP) transactions and government-issued credit cards for payment. The Web-Based Ordering System's features include multiple catalog ordering, browser-based application, acceptance of credit card payment, application of cumulative discounts, capturing of demand history, a robust search engine, reordering templates, fully supporting e-commerce, and is scalable to meet future needs. ECAT is another opportunity for users to automate supply chain activities and minimize provider intervention in medical logistic matters.

Medical Electronic Commerce Assistance (MECA)

MECA is an online repository of product and pricing comparison data for a broad range of medical items. The information link between the DoD medical wholesale and retail system, MECA provides product and price comparison needed by the customer to make the best value decision when ordering medical supplies. This database contains nearly 500,000 pharmaceutical and medical/surgical items accessible with speed and convenience using client-server technology through a Windows-based user interface. MECA enables users to access its database, which provides online, detailed descriptive data and pricing information to view and compare medical/surgical and pharmaceutical items. MECA is the cornerstone on which the military health services community bases its e-commerce business practices. Future planned enhancements include web access, catalog updates through Electronic Data Interchange (EDI) transactions, expansion to include commercial databases of medical equipment comparison data, and computer aided design (CAD) drawings.

Electronic Commerce Support to Deploying Units

This project ties the other e-commerce projects, such as Prime Vendor and the electronic catalog, directly to support of soldiers in the field. It shows how e-commerce solutions can work in both peacetime and war, and is a vital component of DoD's ability to deploy medical forces successfully at a time when the supply chain has been radically reengineered. This project responds to the Tri-Service medical community requirement for e-commerce materiel acquisition capabilities integrated with commercial asset visibility to rapidly plan, acquire, and distribute materiel to deploying forces. It generates electronic orders to vendors based on shortages in deploying units, uses leading-edge e-commerce business practices to submit orders once commercial assets are known to be available through asset visibility, and integrates e-commerce with asset visibility of contracted and non-contracted commercial peacetime and wartime stocks.

DMLSS-DFAS Streamlined Financial Interface

This continuing project reengineers the financial transaction business practices and processes between the medical logistics system (DMLSS) and Defense Finance and Accounting Service (DFAS) using standard ANSI X.12 transaction formats for EDI. The complexity of the logistics-financial interface has been reduced by 98 percent.

Customer Support on the Web (CSW)

CSW is a web-based application providing web-based access for users located within the facility as well as users located in geographically separated units. CSW provides users with the ability to perform catalog research, place replenishment orders to restock, submit New Item Requests (NIRs), electronically process NIRs, submit Facility Management Work Requests, and review the status of previously submitted NIRs and work requests. CSW also provides enhanced NIR processing, the automatic creation of customer catalogs for items stocked by the medical treatment facility, and secure access via Internet Explorer or Netscape web browsers.

Assemblage Management

Assemblage management is a government off-the-shelf application that provides automation support for the management of medical assemblages (equipment and supplies) and electronic replenishment ordering.

Universal Product Number

The DMLSS initiative to establish a universal product number system within the government and industry will do for medical and surgical items what National Drug Codes have done for pharmaceuticals. No comparable code exists for medical and surgical items, which complicates attempts to compare products and prices, and creates an environment where unscrupulous parties could take advantage of the government through improper billing practices. In addition to solving a DoD medical logistics problem, the Universal Product Number initiative promises to save the U.S. health care industry $11 billion per year and Medicare over $1 billion per year.

DMMonline

DMMonline provides the customers and commercial trading partners of the Medical Directorate, DSCP, with a convenient, state-of-the-art, readily accessible web portal that enables them to accomplish their business efficiently and effectively. By using the services available through this e-portal, DoD is saving taxpayers millions of dollars a year while improving the ability of its health care providers to service DoD beneficiaries throughout the world.

DMMonline hosts innovations developed by the DMLSS program, providing both the tools and intelligence necessary to efficiently do business in a totally web-centric environment. Major capabilities housed within the site include Web-Based Ordering, Trading Partner Data Exchange, and Business Intelligence.

The **Web-Based Ordering** function features the Electronic Catalog system, which enables the Directorate's customers to browse, compare, and purchase over 650,000 medical items. The system conveniently interfaces with the customer's legacy supply and accounting systems, simplifying its integration into the customer's existing business practices and encouraging its use. At over $2.3 million, ECAT's monthly sales exceed those of its counterparts in the commercial sector. Web-based ordering saves DoD customers approximately 25 percent of the product and handling costs involved in obtaining items through comparable processes like local purchase, MILSTRIP, etc. Since its inception, the savings from using ECAT have exceeded $8 million.

The **Trading Partner Data Exchange** enables the Directorate's trading partners, including commercial vendors and federal customers, to exchange critical product, price, and standardization information. This web-based functionality is a significant improvement over the previous modem-based method of downloading vast files to each of the 20 vendors and requiring them to sift through the entire array. The new process reduces cycle time from days to minutes. DMMonline also provides a secure information exchange for standardization intelligence among the 11 TRICARE regions located across the country. This functionality incorporates multi-dimensional database technology with On-Line-Analytical-Processing (OLAP) to enable the user to quickly drill down and obtain detailed intelligence. The Trading Partner Data Exchange promotes information sharing and eliminates duplication of effort by enabling regions to efficiently exchange business intelligence on their completed or in-process standardization initiatives.

The **Business Intelligence Area** provides a series of convenient reports that alert federal customers to potential savings. The Best Pharmacy Report lists the top 100 pharmaceutical purchases made by the customer in the previous three months, offers less expensive alternatives when available, and estimates the savings that would accrue if the alternatives were purchased. Similarly, the National Contracts Report alerts customers whenever they buy pharmaceuticals outside the price-favorable National Contracts negotiated by the Defense Logistics Agency and the Department of Veterans Affairs and estimates the savings that would accrue if the customer were to purchase the products covered under National Contracts. DSCP customers consider these reports invaluable aids in their efforts to obtain the best value for their pharmaceutical dollar.

Benefits

The DoD medical user community has reaped tremendous benefits from the e-commerce efforts of the DMLSS program. Prime Vendor e-commerce sales exceeded $1.23 billion in FY 2000 and are forecasted to exceed $1.35 billion in FY 2001. In April of 1999, the first month in which ordering from ECAT included orders in dental, optical, and laboratory supplies, ECAT sales totaled $204,000. For November of 2000, sales were $1.7 million. Prime Vendor capitalizes on the efficiencies of commercial distribution channels, reduces procurement times from up to 45 days to two days or less, reduces inventory by up to 85 percent, and has a 95 percent fill rate in less than 24 hours.

Web-based ordering provides customers a wide variety of commercial items at negotiated and very competitive prices and expedites payment through the acceptance of MILSTRIP and government-issued credit cards. The PVBMA provides a more efficient compilation of Prime Vendor data, enhanced Prime Vendor Program planning activities, negotiation of lower product prices and distribution fees, and improved Prime Vendor performance (e.g., fill rate, supply availability, delivery times). MECA provides the user a tool for fast product and price comparison, streamlines catalog

---

Benefits

With the completion of worldwide fielding of DMLSS Release 1.0 in November 1996, DMLSS:
- Reduced order to receipt time from 20 days to 24 hours.
- Reduced days of inventory in the Department of Defense from 380 days to 10 days.
- Reduced the medical inventory at Department of Defense depots by $429 million (65%).
- Reduced medical inventory at Department of Defense hospitals by $130 million (81%).
- Reduced the cost of drugs by $389 million.

In addition, DMLSS:
- Achieved price discounts of $136 million in fiscal year 1999.
- Achieved cumulative estimated savings through the end of 2000 of more than $1.253 billion.

research, simplifies product identification by cross-referencing with multiple search criteria, decreases customer inventories and overhead processing times, and facilitates the leveraging of lower item prices. As a result, the DoD medical user community now has at its fingertips a fully automated and integrated inventory and information management system ready to meet the medical logistics needs of the military services in the 21st century.

For the period between 2000–2012, it is estimated that every U.S. taxpayer will benefit from the DMLSS system, as every $1.00 invested in DMLSS will return a benefit valued at $5.92. In 2001, over 8 million active military personnel and retirees whose care providers use the suite of applications and systems under the DMLSS umbrella benefit from the DMLSS system. As caregivers spend less time on the medical logistics arena, more time can be given to those men and women seeking their medical expertise.

Overall, the DMLSS program benefits the medical logisticians at military medical treatment facilities around the world, whose jobs have been simplified through improved business processes and automated tools. Health care beneficiaries enjoy a much greater selection of pharmaceuticals and medical/surgical items, greater availability of items normally stocked, and greater and simplified access to health care. In addition, the DMLSS program has garnered several prestigious awards. (See box entitled "DMLSS Program Accolades.")

Challenges

Through the use of best-of-breed commercial applications (e.g., Business Objects), the DMLSS program has been successful in narrowing inefficiencies in the DoD logistics management process. However, as the program moves forward, it faces additional challenges.

One major challenge is the sustainability of the program as it becomes the standard for medical logistics. Technology will continue to advance, and what was best of breed in terms of application packages today may not be best of breed in the future. Introduction of new best-of-breed applications may be hindered by current system design. That may present some organizational challenges, since there are many stakeholders who use and benefit from the system. However, it is not clear who, if anyone, believes that they have "ownership" of the DMLSS system. In addition, as systems users become savvier, the large process-inefficiency gains of the past will be diminished. Users will demand more to achieve smaller efficiencies.

DMLSS has had process reengineering as a prime objective from its inception. However, continuously evaluating and reengineering the business process takes time. Some managers may be tempted to allow the technology

DMLSS Program Accolades[3]

2003 • E-Business Transformation Award

• Excellence.Gov Award

2002 • 2002 Federal Acquisition Award

• FGIPC Intergovernmental Solutions Award

• 2002 Accenture and MIT Digital Government Award

2001 • Pioneer Award for Electronic Commerce

• The Federal 100 Award

• E-Gov 2001 Award

• Government Computer News Agency Award for Excellence

2000 • E-Gov 2000 Award

1999 • Pioneer Award for Electronic Commerce

1998 • The Federal 100 Award

• Computerworld Smithsonian Award

• The Hammer Award

• DM Review Award

1997 • 1997 Government Information Technology Leadership Award

• 1997 Government Information Technology Services Award

to drive the reengineering or to simply automate existing business processes, rather than improving the process before applying the best technology. Program managers may be pressured to produce results and either attempt to or perform a cursory business process reengineering effort. Risk-averse managers may be reluctant to invest funding in an expected outcome and then be obligated to manage the program to achieve that expected outcome.

Conclusion

Within the past 10 years, the DMLSS program has completely reengineered the $2.3 billion Department of Defense medical logistics supply chain (see Figure 14.4) through the use of e-commerce. Every portion of this chain has been dramatically improved. Leading-edge e-commerce solutions have radically transformed the distribution of medical supplies to both peacetime hospitals and deploying forces, and are held as models for the entire DoD. No longer does DoD hold massive amounts of medical inventory in its depots and retail activities. Today, a modern just-in-time inventory system, the first of its scope in DoD, provides medical supply support with response times measured in hours, not days or weeks, and with high customer confidence. Medical supplies are not only delivered faster and more reliably today, but also are substantially less expensive. DMLSS's development of automated tools and comprehensive databases, integrated with the best commercial purchasing and e-commerce practices, have driven down the cost of medical supplies for all of DoD, and these savings will continue to grow each year. Bill paying is being streamlined and made more accurate through a model e-commerce reengineering project with the Defense Finance Accounting Service. Using DoD communications capabilities, forward medical units are now able to order materiel directly from commercial distributors using standard e-commerce transactions in a fraction of the time, at a fraction of the cost. The web-based ordering initiative allows customers to electronically browse, compare, select, and order non-prime vendor items via the web, while retaining the ability to electronically interface with both service legacy medical and financial systems. This last element is critical for user acceptance, as it enables this tool to work for both human-machine and machine-machine interactions.

Figure 14.4: Medical Logistics Business

Purchase Category	Approximate Annual Cost in FY 2002
MTF Pharmacy	$700 million
TRICARE Pharmacy	$300 million
Equipment Purchase	$200 million
Medical-Surgical/Other	$600 million
Facility Maintenance	$390 million
Deployable Units Supply/Equipment	$150 million
Annual Purchases	**$2.34 billion**

Endnotes

1. Except where noted, information for this report came from the following: Colonel Dan Magee, Program Manager, DMLSS; John Zurcher; John Saikowski, Program Consultant; Gary D. Duvall, DMLSS Deployment Manager; and Gary L Rebholz, Senior DMLSS Navy Representative. Interviewed by William Lucyshyn and Douglas Chin at Headquarters, DMLSS Program Office, Arlington, Va., October 2001.

2. DMLSS website viewed at http://www.tricare.osd.mil/dmlss/org.cfm DMLSS on April 14, 2003.

3. DMLSS website viewed at http://www.tricare.osd.mil/dmlss/awards.cfm on April 14, 2003.

CHAPTER FIFTEEN

Department of Defense EMALL: Bringing E-Commerce to DoD

Wesley Johnson
and
William Lucyshyn

Introduction

The DoD EMALL is an ambitious online catalog—a one-stop electronic marketplace for the federal government and armed services offering information technology, training, and operational supplies. Though functionally an e-procurement platform, the DoD EMALL facilitates online order management by streamlining and automating much of the paper-based and serial-intensive purchasing processes that government customers have been accustomed to in the past. Currently there are 13 million items, including 5 million National Stock Numbers available via its website. The DoD EMALL bridges traditional procurement processes with 21st-century technologies, aiming to "meet the operational requirements of the armed services, providing support in hours or days versus weeks."[1] The EMALL target market for equipment and supplies within DoD was estimated to be in excess of $4 billion in FY 1999. DoD Government Purchase Card sales represent 84 percent ($3.6 billion) of the potential markets, with the remainder made up of purchases made with traditional purchasing methods.[2] The EMALL hopes to capture some significant percentage of these purchases.

Background

The Department of Defense has been undergoing a "Revolution in Business Affairs." Throughout the late 1990s, DoD took significant steps to adopt commercial best practices and apply them to its processes. One of the objectives was to develop a useful e-commerce capability to reduce the costs and inherent time delays with the existing paper-intensive processes. Ultimately, the goal was to develop such a capability and "reduce the costs of non-warfighting tasks and apply the savings to the acquisition of new weapons systems."[3] This objective could be achieved by enabling the Defense Department to leverage its buying power through volume discounts and by streamlining the procurement process.

The emphasis on adopting commercial best practices and e-commerce capabilities has its roots in the Federal Acquisition Streamlining Act of 1994 and the Clinger-Cohen Act of 1996, which called for business improvements and singled out technology as a vehicle for making needed improvements. The 1995 and 1998 Government Paperwork Elimination Acts added emphasis to this effort, as did the 1997 release of the chairman of the Joint Chiefs of Staff's *Joint Vision 2010*,[4] which called for the adoption of "Focused Logistics"—the fusion of information, logistics, and transportation technologies in order to provide a rapid response that could meet the asymmetrical threats of the future. In 1997, the Defense Reform Task Force (formed by the Secretary of Defense) completed its review and released the Defense Reform Initiative (DRI) Report. The DRI Report identified four pillars, or major areas, of Defense reform:

- *Reengineering*—adopting best practices;
- *Consolidating*—reorganizing;
- *Competing*—applying market mechanisms; and
- *Eliminating*—reducing excess support structures.

The task force also developed specific Defense Reform Initiative Directives (DRIDs), which included a number of reforms designed to exploit both information and Internet-based technologies that would rapidly move the Department of Defense toward an efficient use of e-commerce.

Specifically, DRID #43 established the Joint Electronic Commerce Program Office (JECPO), with the objective of developing and executing an e-commerce strategy that would expedite the application of Internet-based technologies within the Defense Department. This strategy included revamping the procurement process by taking advantage of advances in paperless contracts and shared data sources such as online catalogs, while providing a vehicle to assure compliance with federal regulations. Toward that end, the DoD EMALL was established in 1998, on the foundation of the Defense Logistics Agency (DLA) Research and Development program's DLA EMALL.

These efforts were reinforced the following year with the release of the 1999 Defense Authorization Act, which called for the development of a "single defense-wide electronic point of entry," one that might provide an "electronic window" across all electronic sources and throughout individual suppliers' virtual inventories.[5] The key federal laws and policies that led to the development of the DoD EMALL are highlighted in the box entitled "Federal Policy Context."

DoD EMALL

Description

The DoD EMALL is a one-stop electronic marketplace that grants users the ability "to search, locate, compare, and order material armed with near real-time visibility into public and private sector inventory levels and lead times."[6] Through the DoD EMALL, users have access to more than 13 million items, with plans to continually increase the number of items available for purchase through the site.[7] The DoD EMALL provides access to 5 million National Stock Number (NSN) items that include both DLA and General Services Administration managed items. Additionally, millions of commercial part numbered items are available through 180 contracts written specifically

Federal Policy Context

- **The Federal Acquisition Streamlining Act of 1994 (FASA)** made a number of changes in the way goods and services, at or below $100,000, are acquired. The act replaces the $25,000 threshold with a new "Simplified Acquisition Threshold" (SAT) of $100,000 once an agency (or procuring activity within the agency) has achieved certain electronic commerce (FACNET) capabilities, is using them, and certifies that it has met the criteria. Until that time, the threshold is only increased to $50,000.

- **The Government Paperwork Elimination Acts of 1995 and 1998** laid the groundwork for Defense Department innovations in e-commerce applications by directing efforts to streamline government processes and reduce the associated paperwork.

- **The Information Technology Management Reform Act of 1996 (Clinger-Cohen Act)** designates a chief information officer within each executive federal agency and sets out some requirements for federal procurement.

- *Joint Vision 2010* **(1997)** called for the adoption of "Focused Logistics"—the fusion of information, logistics, and transportation technologies in order to provide a more rapid response, one providing support in hours or days versus weeks.

- **President's Management Council's Electronic Processes Initiatives Committee, March 1998, "Electronic Commerce for Buyers and Sellers: A Strategic Plan for Electronic Federal Purchasing and Payment"** outlines strategies for government e-commerce applications—"customer-friendly electronic purchasing tools integrated with end-to-end commercial processing of payment, accounting, and performance reporting information."

- **The 1999 DoD Authorization Act** directed that DoD create a one-stop electronic marketplace where suppliers and their goods could be consolidated.

- **The Electronic Signatures in Global and National Commerce Act** ("E-SIGN") was enacted on June 30, 2000. E-SIGN eliminates legal barriers to the use of electronic technology to form and sign contracts, collect and store documents, and send and receive notices and disclosures.

for the DoD EMALL. There are currently 18,000 registered users, with 5,300 placing orders within the last six months. DoD EMALL is organized into four corridors:

- **The Part and Supplies Corridor** provides over 12 million consumable items from DoD inventories at Defense Supply Centers (Columbus, Philadelphia, and Richmond). All items are backed by a Department of Defense contract. Users are allowed to carry out cross-catalog product searching for supplies ranging from clothing and textile items to electronic components. There are 350 vendors in long-term contracts and 2.5 million National Stock Numbers from the DLA-managed catalog.

- **The On-Demand Manufacturing Corridor** allows customers to initiate contact with potential suppliers for products that do not have a finished-goods inventory. Suppliers include both commercial vendors and government organic suppliers. Customers can transfer information to the suppliers via online communication to order individually manufactured low-use items.

- **The Information Technology (IT) Corridor** provides commercial IT products like hardware, software, and replacement parts. This corridor allows users access to commercial vendors' websites to utilize special features such as custom hardware configurations, individual software licenses, and special IT packages.

- **The Training Corridor** gives users the ability to enroll in training classes. Current approval-authority standards are maintained. Future releases of EMALL will offer classes on a variety of topics across the country including IT (software and hardware), government/defense specialty, continuing education, and leadership.

Using only their Internet browser, users are able to access and browse multiple, certified vendor electronic catalogs simultaneously; users can access technical data, specification sheets, images, and product availability, and perform product comparisons and more right from their desktop in real time.

Although this is a Department of Defense program, it is open to all federal agencies. In FY 2001 DoD purchases accounted for approximately 70 percent of the $6.7 million total. The next three largest users were the Department of the Interior with 6 percent, the Department of Justice at 5 percent, and the Department of Transportation at 2 percent.[8]

Concept of Operations

The EMALL's concept of operations is to be the "single entry point for DoD customers to find and acquire off-the-shelf, finished goods and items from the commercial marketplace and government sources, while shifting the acquisition paradigm away from repetitive small purchases." To meet these objectives the EMALL's Program Office strategy includes:

- Utilizing the Internet market space;
- Providing a single access point to access all stores and catalogs available to the Defense Department;
- Allowing cross-searching for product comparisons, which will ultimately allow the customer to make "best value" decisions;
- Providing a single view of status for all orders; and
- Providing a vehicle to maximize the use of the government's purchase card.

To orient users to the site and make it as user-friendly as possible, the site provides both online demonstrations as well as briefings, which can be downloaded, that provide an overview of the EMALL and its capabilities. Included here are glossaries of terms, links to related sites, and other information detailing the procurement processes involved. Potential users can peruse EMALL's features as a "guest" without having access to pricing information. The site also prominently features information about "green" products as well as safety information about products.

Ordering

The DoD EMALL provides users direct access to 36 complete supplier catalogs. These catalogs include the Federal Logistic Information System (FLIS), vendor/supplier and third-party hosted catalogs, and catalogs hosted by other government agencies. All of the catalogs that are accessible through the EMALL are managed and hosted either by the suppliers themselves or a third party. In addition, another 400 suppliers with contracts through the Defense Supply Centers that have subsets of their product lines are available and represented on the site. Users have access to all of these electronic sources when logged into the site.

To log into the EMALL, users are given a unique user ID and password. Once logged into the system, users can search for items under a number of parameters. These include National Stock Number (NSN/NIIN), Supplier, Manufacturer, and Manufacturer Part No., Universal Product Code (UPC), and keyword. Searching under a return query, users have the ability to sort under additional parameters that include price, quantity available, and Days After Receipt of Order. Users choose items to add to their shopping cart, save items for when they return later to the site, and save lists of items.

As noted, users have the ability to view product specifications and other documents before purchase and can perform product comparisons. Users can pay for their purchases using either their Government Purchase Card, like a credit card, or through the Interfund Billing Process. Following receipt of their order, users respond to an electronic Material Receipt Acknowledgement message, providing information on quantity received and, and if they desire, submitting questions or comments about their order.

System Architecture

Using a distributed architecture, the DoD EMALL integrates user registration, item search, order management, and order tracking capabilities across its entire interface. The advantage of a distributed architecture as used by the DoD EMALL site is that its online catalogs and information databases are maintained entirely by the *vendor*. The user logs on to the site and views catalog product information as if it were coming from a single, unified source. In reality, product information is maintained entirely by the vendor—allowing vendors to better manage and update their own product description (which includes product specifications, drawings, photographs, and applicable software) and pricing information.

DoD EMALL requires registration if the user intends to select items for purchase or make a purchase through the system. Users who are not registered can see items in the EMALL, but will not be able to see product prices or quantities. Once a user has registered, a customer ID and password is used to log on to the system. Transaction security is then maintained while users are logged on to the site utilizing Secure Socket Layer (SSL) technology. SSL is a protocol that was developed by Netscape for transmitting private documents via the Internet. Both Netscape Navigator and Microsoft Internet Explorer, the two most common Internet web browsers, support SSL.

The EMALL consists of four component subsystems:

- MOMS—the Modular Order Management System
- PartNET and eBroker—the search engine and catalog
- ODM—an On-Demand Manufacturing module that allows orders to be placed for custom items
- The Rules Engine—agency-specific rules that are applied to the order management process (The Rules Engine is useful in cases of tracking or monitoring specific types of purchases within a specific agency.)

These component subsystems are accessed during the course of a transaction, as are the Defense Logistics Agency requisition and ordering system. Encrypted e-mail and ordering is used to transmit information throughout the transaction process.

The distributed architecture of the DoD EMALL allows the online electronic marketplace to continue to expand as the Program Office contracts with more vendors and suppliers to make more catalogs available. Accessing the information from each vendor directly eliminates the need for replication of data already maintained elsewhere. This, in turn, limits the degree of error in transcribing information from one source to another since all vendor data that the user is able to access through the site is acquired directly from the vendor's own hosted commercial business databases.

Challenges and Benefits

Users

A continuing challenge for the EMALL program is increasing the number of users and, ultimately, the total number of transactions. The Program Office's approach has been to provide a user-focused capability without making anyone feel like he or she is being coerced into using the EMALL (there is currently no directive mandating its use). The EMALL's targeted users are what the Program Office refers to as "artisans." In most cases, these buyers will actually use the equipment or suppliers they procure. Previously, purchases were typically made by procurement specialists for use by others. Targeted purchases are:

- Items not readily available through the normal, automated logistics system, including items not immediately available and specific rather than generic parts
- Items not available in the Federal Supply catalog—only a small fraction of the items offered in the commercial marketplace are available in the Federal Catalog system
- Items that require an interaction to identify the specifications in order to make a best-value decision

The Program Office has implemented a strategy that includes an active marketing program, coupled with providing the best possible service to the end user.[9] For the DoD or other government user searching for the best

Figure 15.1: EMALL by the Numbers

	FY01	FY02
Sales	$6 million	$13.7 million
Registered Users	4,400	18,000
Orders	5,000	36,338

Source: DoD EMALL Program Office, June 2003

EMALL Benefits

The DoD EMALL's goal is to provide the following benefits to the military service customer buying commercial and military items needed to accomplish their mission:

Customer Benefits
- Assurance of ordering against established contractual vehicles and compliance with federal regulations
- Desktop access to product information (i.e., technical data, spec sheets, images, etc.) and product availability
- Single point of entry, search and order across all electronic sources
- Convenient payment mechanisms
- Increased buying office productivity
- Security

Vendor Benefits
- Uses the vendor's business data: no need to update government databases
- Lowers the transaction cost of vendor and customer transactions
- Uses the vendor's commercial business practices
- Uses familiar commercial payment mechanisms
- Provides visibility of products and services to a large buyer community

value, which can be a combination of price, quality, and availability, the EMALL provides the best alternative. "For those many times when the buyer has to interact with the seller to make informed best-value judgments—the DoD EMALL is the best place to do those efficiently," noted Donald O'Brien, program manager of EMALL.[10] This is the direction that the DoD EMALL seems to be taking—using the web as a means to advance that interactive process.

Currently the largest user base on the site is the Navy and the Reserve Components. These users are and will continue to be targeted in the near future to encourage and facilitate increased use. "We're working right now to see what we can do to increase use and what we can do to get others at these locations to use the DoD EMALL," O'Brien said, "and so I think ultimately we'll continue to work where we've been a success."[11]

Finally, there are also more subtle reasons some users are reluctant to use the EMALL. On military installations in smaller communities, buyers have a strong incentive to "buy locally" to maintain good relations and support their local communities. Using the DoD EMALL generally means those orders will not go to businesses in the local community. The Program Office has responded to this concern with their Regional EMALL initiative, which should allow customers to shop from local vendors once contracts are established with them. Additionally, there are a number of restrictions placed on users by their agencies regarding what may and may not be purchased. The Rules Engine can be set up for each agency to track purchases and to notify users when they are violating procurement procedures. However, it does not enforce them. The Air Force, for example, does not allow any purchase for what it categorizes as "weapon system" related (the intent is to restrict any non-approved substitution of critical weapon system parts). This has the unintended consequence of, for example, restricting the purchase of "D cell" batteries, since they are used in flashlights on aircraft. The user can override these restrictions, but since the military services can monitor these overrides, users may be reluctant to make these purchases.

Return on Investment

Although one of the primary objectives of the EMALL is to provide the best possible service to the user, the Program Office can also make a compelling business case. **The principal cost savings comes from cutting transaction costs on what DLA refers to as "manual buys."** A "manual buy" is defined as the traditional paper-intensive procurement activity that starts with the user manually filling out a requisition form. DLA specific transaction costs for manual buys averaged $146.00 per transaction for FY 1999. The cost for the same transaction carried out on the EMALL averaged $11.31, a cost avoidance of $134.69 for each manual buy item. The other type of transaction is the Government Purchase Card. For purchases under $2,500, authorized users can purchase items directly (much like a consumer credit card purchase). Transaction costs for these Government Purchase Card orders averaged $25.62 per transaction in FY 1999. On DoD EMALL, those same transactions averaged $11.31, a cost avoidance of $14.31 for each credit card purchase. If the EMALL site had been used as the standard during FY 1999, the potential savings for micro-purchases (purchases totaling less than $2,500) could have amounted to more than $90 million dollars.[12] Clearly, the potential exists for significant cost savings.

DLA and the Program Office currently use the sales figures for its registered users as a metric. In FY 2002, DLA began phasing in tools to track additional leading indicator metrics, to include item cost, cost recovery,

DoD EMALL operating costs ($1.025 million for FY 2002), ease of use and reliability, number of items available, wait time, interoperability, customer care concerns, and percent of orders with order status reported. Although originally there may have been a vision to make the EMALL self-sufficient, there is currently no charge levied on transactions to cover operating expenses. The only associated cost recovery is set by the contracting office (at a 3 percent rate) to offset the expense of the DLA contracting function.

Current Developments

The U.S. Navy recently decided to abandon its two-year effort to build its own online capability and became the first service to incorporate its online procurement effort in the EMALL in 2002. With a modest investment of $500,000, the EMALL will develop a separate area dedicated to the Navy to accommodate service-specific procurement rules, and add service features and electronic catalogs now unavailable to Navy purchasing agents. This will significantly increase EMALL participation while increasingly leveraging the DLA investment. Once the capability to integrate with the EMALL, while maintaining service unique requirements, is demonstrated, resistance from the other services should fade.[13] Additionally, the Army recently designated the DoD EMALL as the "preferred" ordering site for all office supplies, and the Program Office believes an announcement from the Air Force and Marine Corps will be forthcoming soon.

The Program Office is also focused on continuous improvement and currently has two major initiatives to improve the utility and the quality of service of the EMALL. The first is to increase the quantity of parts available to users. In addition to negotiating contracts with new vendors, the Program Office is actively pursuing agreements with electronic trading exchanges. These initiatives will work to leverage the investment made by the exchanges and expand the DoD EMALL's reach throughout industry by linking EMALL users to additional catalogs through the trading exchanges site. These exchanges include:

- Air Transport Association's (ATA) SPEC 2000,[14] an online exchange for buying and selling aircraft parts and repair services, because of the similarities that exist between ATA's commercial parts and many of the armed services' military parts
- Ariba, an online exchange where businesses can search an open directory of trading partners, including over 20,000 suppliers worldwide
- Aero Exchange, Cordiem, and Exostar—three other aerospace exchanges

Another area for improvement that the Program Office has identified is coordination with the Government Purchase Card program. Currently there is no automated mechanism for reconciling and tracking invoices. Users have to manually work with both their invoices and purchase card statements. DLA is currently working with the Government Purchase Card Program Office (GPCPO) to examine the feasibility of linking the databases and automating that process. This will require working closely with two banks— U.S. Bank and Citibank—to allow EMALL users to access more detailed records from their orders.

Finally, on an organizational level, the management of the DoD EMALL transitioned from JECPO to DLA during 2001, in an effort to provide tighter control of operations, greater integration, and a more focused marketing strategy.

Barriers to Expansion

The DoD EMALL has made a great deal of progress, shows much promise, and has specific plans for continued expansion, yet its future is far from certain. There exist a number of external barriers to increasing the use and growth of the DoD EMALL. Most notably, Congress has passed several laws that promote social and economic contracting goals. These laws can add to the complexity of negotiating the broad agreements[15] required to place an entire vendor's catalog on contract. The small-business protection acts, designed to increase competition and improve opportunities for small and disadvantaged businesses, require the rotation of the supplier base and ultimately make it more difficult to procure specific goods from specific manufacturers. The Javits-Wagner-O'Day Act identifies federally mandated sources of supply for a variety of office products. These products are manufactured by nonprofit agencies throughout the United States that employ people who are blind or have other severe disabilities. The Buy American Act[16] requires that the federal government buy only American-made goods. This places severe restrictions on suppliers to account for the origin and content of all of the items in their catalogs—or requires the Program Office to get an exemption from these provisions. The end result is that the process for establishing the underlying contracts is difficult and slow.

Conclusions

The DoD EMALL is a work in progress and offers a number of lessons for other government e-procurement efforts. It was initiated and developed in response to two DoD initiatives. The first was a desire to adopt commercial best practices and make greater use of Internet-based electronic shopping catalogs to help improve the purchasing process. According to the 1997

Defense Reform Initiative report, such catalogs could help by putting buying decisions in the hands of the people who actually need the items. The second was in response to the concept of "Focused Logistics," which the chairman of the Joint Chiefs of Staff outlined in *Joint Vision 2020*.

The DoD EMALL has created a capability where customers can make their own best-value decisions and can efficiently locate and order items from the electronic catalogs of qualified vendors through a "point, click, and ship" system. This automated process provides a better service to the user and reduces transaction costs significantly. It is also a step in the direction of the integrated supply chain envisioned in *Joint Vision 2020*. Clearly, much progress has been made toward introducing e-procurement to federal agencies through the DoD EMALL. There are, however, challenges and more work that needs to be done to achieve the full potential of this system.

The Program Office recognizes that the key to a successful program is increasing the number of transactions. The Program Office is pursuing a two-pronged approach to achieve that end. It is continuing to negotiate new contracts to increase the total number of parts available and, at the same time, undertaking a more active marketing campaign to both increase the number of users and increase the volume of sales. The Program Office believes that if it can do that successfully, the EMALL will succeed.

Endnotes

1. *Joint Vision 2010,* p. 24.

2. Personal interview with Donald O'Brien, Program Manager, EMALL, November 2001.

3. Defense Reform Initiative Directive 43.

4. *Joint Vision 2010* is the conceptual template of the chairman of the Joint Chiefs of Staff for how America's armed forces will achieve new levels of effectiveness in joint warfighting. *Joint Vision 2020,* published in 2000, builds upon and extends the conceptual template established by *Joint Vision 2010.* The concept of focused logistics remains essentially unchanged.

5. 1999 Defense Authorization Act.

6. Joint Electronic Commerce Program Office, Standard DoD EMALL Briefing, September 2001.

7. Personal interview with Donald O'Brien, Program Manager, EMALL, October 2001.

8. Based on data provided by the Program Office, November 2001.

9. Most recently, DLA has begun to work more closely with the U.S. Department of State to encourage and facilitate use of the DoD EMALL site from overseas embassies, primarily for their civil engineering programs.

10. Donald O'Brien, EMALL Program Office, November 2001.

11. Ibid.

12. For FY 1999 there were 698,000 micro-purchase transactions totaling $458 million.

13. Karen Robb, "Navy Buys Into DoD's E-Mall," *Federal Times,* February 4, 2002.

14. The SPEC 2000 Aviation Marketplace hosts over 6 million records of part pricing information, surplus availability, repair capabilities and pricing, and tools, test, and ground equipment availability.

15. These contract types include Blanket Purchase Agreements and Indefinite-Delivery Indefinite-Quantity.

16. The Buy American Act gives preference to domestically produced articles, materials, or supplies purchased for use by the federal government. Enacted March 3, 1933 (41 U.S.C 10a et seq.), it stipulates that federal agencies buy only articles, materials, or supplies "mined, produced, or manufactured in the United States except in cases where (1) U.S. goods are not available in sufficient quantity and satisfactory quality; (2) the cost is unreasonable; or (3) it is inconsistent with the public interest to purchase U.S. articles, materials, or supplies." There are additional Buy American restrictions contained in provisions of the Berry Amendment (DoD Appropriations Act, 1993).

Appendix:
Forum Participants

E-Procurement Forum Participants
Affiliations current at the time of the forum: December 2–4, 2001

Speakers
Mark Forman
Associate Director
Information Technology
and E-Government
Office of Management
and Budget

Jacques S. Gansler
Professor and Roger C.
Lipitz Chair
Center for Public Policy
and Private Enterprise
School of Public Affairs
University of Maryland

Ronald Kerber
President
SBDC Corporation

Shankar Kiru
Director of Business
Development
Covisint

Claudia "Scottie" Knott
Executive Director
Logistics Policy and
Acquisition Management
Defense Logistics Agency

David Levine
Director of Global
Alliances
GE Global eXchange
Services

Colonel George (Dan)
Magee
Program Manager
Defense Medical Logistics
Standard Support

Participants
Mark A. Abramson
Executive Director
PricewaterhouseCoopers
Endowment for The
Business of Government

Rear Admiral Raymond A.
Archer
Vice Director
Defense Logistics Agency

Julie Basile
Procurement Policy
Analyst
Office of Federal
Procurement Policy
Office of Management
and Budget

Jerry Cooper
Vice President
Information Technology
Development
AC Industrial, Inc.

G. Edward DeSeve
Professor of Practice, and
Director, Management,
Finance and Leadership
Program
School of Public Affairs
University of Maryland

Susan Pompliano Keys
Customer Solutions
Consulting Manager
Cisco Systems, Inc.

Marvin Langston
Senior Vice President
SAIC

Deidre Lee
Director
Defense Procurement
Office of the Under
Secretary
of Defense
(Acquisition, Technology
& Logistics)

Robert E. Luby, Jr.
Partner
PricewaterhouseCoopers

William Lucyshyn
Research Scholar
Center for Public Policy
and Private Enterprise
University of Maryland

Tom Luedtke
Associate Administrator
Procurement
National Aeronautics and
Space Administration

Christine Makris
Director
Acquisition Policy and
Programs
Department of Commerce

Jim Newman
Director of E-Supply
Chain
Raytheon Company

Colonel Jeffery P. Parsons
Assistant Deputy Assistant
Secretary
Contracting Operations
Division
U.S. Air Force

William R. Phillips
Partner
PricewaterhouseCoopers

Rear Admiral Thomas
Porter (RADM USN, Ret.)
Director
PricewaterhouseCoopers

Kimberly M. Ross
Executive Director
Center for Public Policy
and Private Enterprise
University of Maryland

Eleanor Spector
Vice President
Corporate Contracts
Lockheed Martin
Corporation

Robert C. Taylor
Program Manager
Small Business
Administration

Marty Wagner
Associate Administrator
Office of
Governmentwide Policy
General Services
Administration

Research/Coordination

Amitabh Brar
Graduate Research
Assistant
School of Public Affairs
University of Maryland

Douglas Chin
Graduate Research
Assistant
Robert H. Smith School
of Business
University of Maryland

Wesley Johnson
Graduate Research
Assistant
School of Public Affairs
University of Maryland

Guarav Kapoor
Graduate Research
Assistant
Robert H. Smith School
of Business
University of Maryland

C. Dawn Pulliam
Program Coordinator
Center for Public Policy
and Private Enterprise
School of Public Affairs
University of Maryland

E-Finance Forum Participants

Affiliations current at the time of the forum: April 28–30, 2002

Speakers

Thomas R. Bloom
Director
Defense Finance &
Accounting Service

Andrew Cailes
Director of Finance
Cisco Systems, Inc.

Thomas N. Cooley
Chief Financial Officer
Office of Budget, Finance
and Award Administration
National Science
Foundation

Mark W. Everson
Controller
Office of Federal Financial
Management
Office of Management
and Budget

Jacques S. Gansler
Professor and Roger C.
Lipitz Chair
Center for Public Policy
and Private Enterprise
School of Public Affairs
University of Maryland

John J. Hamre
President and CEO
Center for Strategic and
International Studies

Richard M. Smoski
Director
Finance Systems and
Processes
The Boeing Company

Participants

Mark A. Abramson
Executive Director
PricewaterhouseCoopers
Endowment for The
Business of Government

Karen Cleary Alderman
Executive Director
Joint Financial
Management
Improvement Program

Owen F. Barwell
Principal Consultant
PricewaterhouseCoopers

Julie Basile
Procurement Policy
Analyst
Office of Federal
Procurement Policy
Office of Management
and Budget

Lieutenant General Roy E.
Beauchamp
Deputy Commanding
General
Headquarters
Army Materiel Command
U.S. Army

Allen W. Beckett
Principal Assistant Deputy
Under Secretary
(Logistics & Materiel
Readiness)
Department of Defense

Ronald S. Brooks
Director
Business Modernization
and Systems Integration
Office of the Under
Secretary of Defense
(Comptroller)

Bonnie L. Brown
Partner
PricewaterhouseCoopers

Audrey Y. Davis
Chief Information Officer
Defense Finance and
Accounting Service

G. Edward DeSeve
Professor of Practice, and
Director, Management,
Finance and Leadership
Program
School of Public Affairs
University of Maryland

Dennis J. Fischer
Vice President Sales
VISA U.S.A.

Kevin Fitzpatrick
*Assistant Deputy
Commander for Fleet
Logistics Operations
Naval Supply Systems
Command*

Luke J. Gill
*Vice President
Joint Strike Fighter
Integrated Customer
Support
Lockheed Martin
Aeronautics Company*

Donald V. Hammond
*Fiscal Assistant Secretary
U.S. Department of
Treasury*

Susan Pompliano Keys
*Customer Solutions
Consulting Manager
Cisco Systems, Inc.*

Robert E. Luby, Jr.
*Partner
PricewaterhouseCoopers*

William Lucyshyn
*Research Scholar
Center for Public Policy
and Private Enterprise
University of Maryland*

William J. Lynn
*Vice President
DFI International*
Jim Newman
*Director of E-Supply
Chain
Raytheon Company*

Major General Everett G.
Odgers
*Comptroller
Air Force Materiel
Command
U.S. Air Force*

Ronald Orr
*Principal Deputy Assistant
Secretary of the Air Force
(Installations,
Environment and
Logistics)*

William R. Phillips
*Partner
PricewaterhouseCoopers*

Kimberly M. Ross
*Executive Director
Center for Public Policy
and Private Enterprise
University of Maryland*

Sandra Swab
*Senior Policy Analyst
Department of Health &
Human Services*

Research/Coordination
Amitabh Brar
*Graduate Research
Assistant
School of Public Affairs
University of Maryland*

Dzintars Dzilna
*Graduate Research
Assistant
Robert H. Smith School of
Business
University of Maryland*

Brandon Griesel
*Graduate Research
Assistant
Robert H. Smith School of
Business
University of Maryland*

C. Dawn Pulliam
*Program Coordinator
Center for Public Policy
and Private Enterprise
School of Public Affairs
University of Maryland*

Pelin Turunc
*Graduate Research
Assistant
Robert H. Smith School of
Business
University of Maryland*

Sandra Young
*Graduate Research
Assistant
School of Public Affairs
University of Maryland*

E-Logistics Forum Participants
Affiliations current at the time of the forum: October 27–29, 2002

Speakers

David J. Falvey
Program Executive Officer
Business Systems
Modernization Program
Defense Logistics Agency

Jacques S. Gansler
Professor and Roger C.
Lipitz Chair
Center for Public Policy
and Private Enterprise
University of Maryland

Luke Gill
Vice President
Joint Strike Fighter
Integrated Customer
Support
Lockheed Martin
Aeronautics Company

Paul Joseph
Vice President
Client Services Division
Caterpillar Logistics
Services, Inc.

Major General John F.
Phillips (US Air Force,
Ret.)
Vice President
Government Services
Honeywell International,
Inc.

Anil Varma
Senior Professional
Service Algorithms
Laboratory
General Electric Global
Research Center

Participants

Mark Abramson
Executive Director
IBM Endowment for the
Business of Government

Dan Anglim
Director and General
Manager
Aerospace Support
Integrated Defense
System
The Boeing Company

Cecilia M. Coates
Director
Program Management
and Policy
U.S. Department of State

Thomas M. Corsi
Professor and Co-Director
Supply Chain
Management Center
Robert H. Smith School of
Business
University of Maryland

Stephen M. DeBlasio, Sr.
Director
Region II Administration &
Resource Planning
Division
Federal Emergency
Management Agency

James T. Eccleston
President
Advanced Software
Design Inc.

Bonnie A. Kornberg
Consultant

Deidre A. Lee
Director
Defense Procurement
Office of the Under
Secretary of Defense
(Acquisition, Technology,
and Logistics)

Robert E. Luby, Jr.
Partner
IBM Business Consulting
Services

William Lucyshyn
Research Scholar
Center for Public Policy
and Private Enterprise
University of Maryland

Michael D. Mahoney
*Chief of Logistics
Operations Center
Central Intelligence
Agency*

Mary Beth Marino
*Principal Consultant
IBM Business Consulting
Services*

Jim L. Newman
*Director
eSupply Chain
Raytheon Company*

David R. Oliver, Jr.
*Consultant
David R. Oliver, Jr.
Associates, Inc.*

Kimberly M. Ross
*Executive Director
Center for Public Policy
and Private Enterprise
University of Maryland*

Bruce W. Schoolfield
Consultant

Robert L. Sullivan
*Product Integration and
Assessment PFRMS
Champion
Precision Fires Rocket and
Missile Systems
U.S. Army*

General William G.T.
Tuttle, Jr. (US Army, Ret.)
Consultant

Research/Coordination

Dzintars Dzilna
*Graduate Research
Assistant
R. H. Smith School of
Business
University of Maryland*

Brandon Griesel
*Graduate Research
Assistant
R. H. Smith School of
Business
University of Maryland*

Jennifer Moughalian
*Graduate Research
Assistant
School of Public Affairs
University of Maryland*

Dawn Pulliam
*Program Coordinator
Center for Public Policy
and Private Enterprise
University of Maryland*

Sandra Young
*Graduate Research
Assistant
School of Public Affairs
University of Maryland*

Bibliography

Adams, Larry. "Diagnostics from Afar." *Quality*, November 2001, Vol. 40, Issue 11, 26.

Aldridge, E. C., Jr. Under Secretary of Defense for Acquisition, Technology, and Logistics, to staff, interoffice memo, *Evolutionary Acquisition and Spiral Development*, April 12, 2002.

American Institute of Certified Public Accountants. "About SAS 70." Viewed at http://www.sas70.com/about.htm, September 2002.

April, Carolyn. "BAM to Speed App Reports—Industry Heavyweights Target Business Process Performance." *InfoWorld*, November 4, 2002, Vol. 24, No. 44, 27.

Austin, Robert D., et al. "Enterprise Resource Planning." A Technology Note, 9-699-020, The Harvard Business School, March 14, 2003.

Bingi, Prasad, et al. "Critical Issues Affecting an ERP Implementation." *Information and Systems Management*, Summer 1999, Vol. 16, Issue 3, 7.

Boyson, Sandor and Thomas Corsi. "The Real-Time Supply Chain." *Supply Chain Management Review,* January/February 2001.

Byrne, John A., and Ben Elgin. "Cisco Behind the Hype: CEO John Chambers still thinks his company can grow 30% a year. But critics question its aggressive accounting." *Business Week*, January 21, 2002, 54.

Carter, Larry. "Cisco's Virtual Close." *Harvard Business Review*, Reprint F104A, April 2001, 2-3.

Carter, Larry. "Larry Carter: Finance Takes the Lead in the Internet Economy." *Cisco IQ*, February 15, 2001. Viewed at http://business.cisco.com/prod/tree.taf%3Fasset_id=48793&ID=48295&ListID=85932&SubListID=44694&public_view=true&kbns=1.html, February 2002.

Caterinicchia, Dan. "DLA begins rollout of Modernization System." *Federal Computer Week*, August 6, 2002. Viewed at http://www.fcw.com/fcw/articles/2002/0812/news-dla-08-12-02.asp, August 19, 2002.

Caterinicchia, Dan. "DoD Builds High-Tech Supply Chain." *Federal Computer Week*, February 24, 2003.

Center for Public Policy and Private Enterprise, University of Maryland. *Moving Toward an Effective Public-Private Partnership for the DoD Supply Chain*, June 2002.

Christopher, Martin. *Logistics and Supply Chain Management—Strategies for Reducing Cost and Improving Service*. London: Financial Times, Prentice Hall, 1998.

Cisco Systems, Inc. "Cisco Internet Business Roadmap: Financial Management." *Solution Guide*, 2001, 1.

Cisco Systems, Inc. "2Q03 Earnings Release." Viewed at http://newsroom.cisco.com/dlls/fin_020602.html, February, 6 2002.

Cisco Systems, Inc. "EIS to eExec Evolution." *Cisco Presentation Executive Information System*, February 2002, 3.

Cisco Systems, Inc. http://www.cisco.com.

Cooke, James A. "Is XML the Next Big Thing." *Logistics Management*, May 1, 2002, 53.

Covisint, Inc. http://www.covisint.com.

Defense Electronic Business Program Office. https://emall.prod.dodonline.net/scripts/EMLearn.asp.

Defense Logistics Agency. Business Systems Modernization Program Office. http://www.dla.mil/j-6/bsm/default.asp?page=COM.

Defense Medical Logistics Standard Support Program. http://www.tricare.osd.mil/dmlss/org.cfm.

Department of Defense. Defense Finance and Accounting Service. *DFAS Financial Systems Strategic Plan,* Washington, D.C.: GPO, January 2001.

Department of Defense. "Defense Reform Initiative Directive 43." *Defensewide Electronic Commerce*, May, 20 1998.

Department of Defense Dictionary of Military and Associated Terms, April 12, 2001 (as amended through August 14, 2002).

Department of Defense. *Joint Vision 2010*.

"Detroit-Area Internet Auto-Part Venture Hits Turbulence as Business Falls Flat." Tribune Business News, *Detroit Free Press,* December 9, 2002.

Edwards, Morris. "An EDI Whose Time Has Come." *Communications News*, Sept. 1999, Vol. 36, Issue 9, 104.

Ewalt, David M. "Pinpoint Control: Tiny Chips May Revolutionize All Areas of Supply Chain Management." *InformationWeek,* September 30, 2002. Viewed at http://www.informationweek.com/story/showArticle.jhtml?articleID=6503191, October 2002.

Federal Express. http://www.fedex.com.

Fliender, Gene. "CPRF: An Emerging Supply Chain Tool." *Industrial and Management Data Systems*, Vol. 103, Issue 1, 14-21.

Frontline Solutions. "Caterpillar Turns to Rival Logistics ASP." *Frontline Solutions*, March 2002.

Furness, Victoria. "Preparing for the Unexpected." *Computer Business Review*, July 2002, Vol. 10, Issue 7, 10.

Gansler, Jacques. "A Vision of the Government as a World-Class Buyer: Major Procurement Issues for the Coming Decade." IBM Center for The Business of Government, January 2002.

Gansler, Jacques. "Diffusing Netcentricity in DoD: The Supply Chain (An Example Case)." Presentation given on April 23, 2002.

Gansler, Jacques, William Lucyshyn, and Kimberly Ross. "Digitally Integrating the Government Supply Chain: E-Procurement, E-Finance, and E-Logistics." IBM Center for The Business of Government, February 2003.

GAO Report, "Challenges to Effective Adoption of Extensible Markup Language." GAO-02-327, April 2002.

GAO/AIMD Report. *Financial Management: Federal Aviation Administration Lacks Accountability for Major Assets*. AIMD-98-62, February 18, 1998.

General Accounting Office. *FFMIA Implementation Critical for Federal Accountability*, GAO-02-29, October 1, 2001, 34.

General Electric Company. http://www.ge.com.

Gonsalves, Antone. "Value of EAI Grows as Integration Needs Expand." *InformationWeek*, May 28, 2001, 60.

Gonsalves, Antone and Steve Konicki. "CEO Quits as Covisint Restructures." *InformationWeek*, June 28, 2002. Viewed at http://www.informationweek.com/story/IWK20020628S0005, April 10, 2003.

Grandy, Carlos. "Ford Recoups Its Investment in Covisint." *Financial Times*, July 2, 2001, 23.

Green, Mike. *Starting a Supply Chain Revolution*. New York: Cap Gemini Ernst & Young, February 2001. Viewed at http://www.infoworld.com/article/02/11/01/021104ctcpg_1.html.

Greengard, Samuel. "Portals Shape the Promise of the Internet." *Internet World*, April 2003, Vol. 9, Issue 4, 26.

Herman, George, and Stephanie L. Woerner. "Networked at Cisco." *Massachusetts Institute of Technology Teaching Case #1*, July 20, 2001, 2.

Horn, Steve. *The Department of Defense: What Must Be Done to Resolve DoD's Longstanding Financial Management Problems?* Oversight hearing before Subcommittee on Government Efficiency, Financial Management, and Intergovernmental Relations. 107th Congress, May 8, 2001.

Katzaman, Jim. "Knowing Customers Better Than They Know Themselves." Viewed at http://www.dla.mil/j-6/bsm/html/core_messages/customer_serv.htm, August 19, 2002.

Katzaman, Jim. "Process Reengineering: Jump the 'Fence,' Enjoy the Ride." Viewed at http://www.dla.mil/j-6/bsm/html/core_messages/process_reeng.htm, August 19, 2002.

Koch, Christopher. "The ABCs of ERP." *CIO.com*. Viewed at http://www.cio.com/research/erp/edit/erpbasics.html, April 16, 2003.

Konicki, Steve. "GM Buys $96 Billion in Materials via Covisint." *Information Week*, August 16, 2001. Viewed at http://www.informationweek.com/story/IWK20010816S0001, September 2001.

Kutz, Gregory. *The Department of Defense: What Must Be Done to Resolve DoD's Longstanding Financial Management Problems?* Oversight hearing before Subcommittee on Government Efficiency, Financial Management, and Intergovernmental Relations. 107th Congress, May 8, 2001.

Lambert, Douglas M., James R. Stock, and Lisa M. Ellram. *Fundamentals of Logistics Management*, Boston: Irwin McGraw-Hill, 1998, 10.

Lee, Jinyoul, et al. "Enterprise Integration with ERP and EAI." *Communications of the ACM*, February 2003, Vol. 46, No. 2, 54.

Lewandowski, Linda, and Jeffrey Cares, Department of Defense Office of Force Transformation. *Sense and Respond Logistics: Turning Supply Chains into Demand Networks*, December 20, 2002. (unpublished).

Lin, Grace. "Sense and Respond Value Chain Optimization." Presentation at 3rd Annual NetCentricity Conference, R.H. Smith Business School, University of Maryland, April 4, 2003. Viewed at http://www.rhsmith.umd.edu/netconference/presentations.html, April 2003.

Lin, Grace, et al. "The Sense and Respond Enterprise." *Operations Research and Management Science*, April 2002. Viewed at http://www.lionhrt-pub.com/orms/orms-4-02/valuechain.html, April 2003.

"Making the ERP Commitment: What Controllers Say about Implementation Time and Cost." *The Controller's Report*, May 2001.

Maswady, Maqzen and Craig Tonner. "Six Sigma." Viewed at http://isixsigma.com/dictionary/Six_Sigma-85.htm, September 2002.

McCrea, Bridget. "CPFR Comes of Age." *Supply Chain Management Review*, March/April 2003, Vol. 7, Issue 2, 65.

Millman, Howard. "A Brief History of EDI." *InfoWorld*, April 6, 1998, Vol. 20, Issue 14, 83.

National Science Foundation. *FY2001 Management and Performance Highlights*, February 2002. Viewed at www.nsf.gov/pubs/2002/nsf02099/nsf_return.pdf, February 2002.

Neef, Dale. *e-Procurement*. Upper Saddle River, N.J.: Prentice-Hall, Inc., 2001, 102.

Noe, Kathleen. "DoD's Future Integrated Financial Systems Architecture." *Armed Forces Comptroller*, Winter 1999, Vol. 44, Issue 6, 18.

Nolan, Richard L. "Cisco System Architecture: ERP and Web-enabled IT." *Harvard Business School Case Study 9-301-099*, October 15, 2001, 8-14.

Office of Management and Budget. *Performance and Management Assessments for FY 2004*. Viewed at www.whitehouse.gov/omb/budget/fy2004/pma.html, March 2003.

Pawling, G. Patrick. "Virtual Finance: Moving Toward the One-Day Close." *Cisco IQ*, May/June 2001. Viewed at http://business.cisco.com/prod/tree.taf%3Fasset_id=47909&MagID=48175&public_view=true&kbns=1.html, February 2002.

Phillips, Jeff, et al. "Portal Products vs. Vendors." *Transform Magazine*, October 1, 2002, 35.

Phinney, David. "Technology Helps DoD Better Track Equipment for Troops." *Federal Times Online*, March 31, 2003. Viewed at http://federaltimes.com/index.php?S=1718107, April 4, 2003.

Pool, Robert. "If It Ain't Broke, FIX IT." *Technology Review*, September 2001, 66-69.

Portals Community. *Fundamentals of Portals*. Viewed at http://www.portalscommunity.com/library/fundamentals.cfm, April 18, 2003.

Quiett, William Frank. "Embracing Supply Chain Management." *Supply Chain Management Review*, September 1, 2002.

Radjou, Navi. "Adaptive Supply Networks." *TechStrategy Brief*, Forrester Research, February 22, 2002.

Reason, Tim. "Federal Offenses: A dozen years after passage of the CFO Act, the U.S. Government still struggles to close its books." *CFO Magazine*, March 6, 2002. Viewed at http://www.cfo.com/article/1,5309,6768,00.html, March 2002.

Robb, Karen, "Navy Buys Into DoD's E-Mall," *Federal Times*, February 4, 2002.

Sandsmark, Fred. "Culture Shift: Is the Internet a part of your company's culture? Here's how to tell if it is—what to do if it is not." *Cisco IQ*, March/April 2001. Viewed at http://business.cisco.com/prod/tree.taf%3Fasset_id=49804&ID=85947&ListID=85932&SubListID=44756&public_view=true&kbns=1.html, February 2002.

Sarkar, Dibya. "People Key to Portal Process." *Federal Computer Week*, April 23, 2003. Viewed at http://www.fcw.com/fcw/articles/2003/0421/web-afcea-04-23-03.asp, April 2003.

Scheier, Robert L. "Internet EDI Grows Up." *Computerworld*, January 20, 2003, Vol. 37 Issue 3, 38.

Schenck, Jean. "CPRF: A Glimpse into Retail's Future?" *Automatic I.D.*, Nov. 1998, Vol. 14, Issue 12, 51.

"SCOR Model Is Key Link to Stronger Supply Chain." *Automatic I.D. News*, Sept. 1998, Vol. 14, Issue 10.

Simchi-Levi, David, Philip Kaminsky, and Edith Simchi-Levi. *Designing and Managing the Supply Chain*. Boston: Irwin McGraw-Hill, 2000.

Sonigini, Marc L. "Ford, Caterpillar Team with SAP on Supply Chain Project." *Computerworld*, August 5, 2002. Viewed at http://www.computerworld.com/softwaretopics/erp/story/0,10801,73207,00.html, August 2002.

Stonich, Mark. "GE Brings E-Procurement to Life." *PRTM Insight*, Summer/Fall 2001, Vol. 13, No. 2, 37.

Strom Thurmond National Defense Authorization Act for Fiscal Year 1999, Public Law 105–261, 17 Oct. 1998. Viewed at http://frwebgate.access.gpo.gov/cgi-bin/getdoc.cgi?dbname=105_cong_public_laws&docid=f:publ261.105, November 2001.

"Survey of Progress and Trend of Development and Use of Automatic Data Processing in Business and Management Control Systems of the Federal Government, as of December 1957—III." *Communications of the ACM*, September 1959, Vol. 2, Issue 9, 34.

Symonds, M. "The Next Revolution." *The Economist,* June 24, 2000.

Tapscott, Don, David Ticoll, and Alex Lowy. *Digital Capital,* Boston: Harvard Business School Press, 2000, 93-118.

Teradata, "The 2002 Teradata Report on Enterprise Decision-Making," NCR Corporation, Dayton, Ohio, 2002.

Thomas, Gerald W. "DoD's Critical Feeder Systems: Achieving Compliance With the Federal Financial Management Improvement Act of 1996." *Armed Forces Comptroller*, Winter 1999, Vol. 44, Issue 1.

Trebilcock, B. "Planning for Supply Chain Success." *Modern Materials Handling*, May 1, 2001.

U.S. Senate. Senator Robert Byrd speaking on the nomination of Donald Rumsfeld to be Secretary of Defense to the Senate Armed Services Committee, January, 11 2001.

Vitasek, Kate. "Logistics Terms and Glossary." *The Council of Logistics Management*, August 1, 2002. Viewed at http://www.clm1.org/resource/downloads/glossary.pdf, 18 April 18, 2003.

About the Contributors

Editors

The Honorable Jacques S. Gansler is a Professor at the University of Maryland School of Public Affairs, where he holds the Roger C. Lipitz Chair in Public Policy and Private Enterprise. He teaches graduate school courses, and leads the School's Center for Public Policy and Private Enterprise, which fosters collaboration among the public, private, and nonprofit sectors in order to promote mutually beneficial public and private interests. He is a Member of the National Academy of Engineering and a Fellow of the National Academy of Public Administration. He is also an Affiliate Faculty member of the A. James Clarke School of Engineering and a Senior Fellow at the James MacGregor Burns Academy of Leadership (both at the University of Maryland).

Previously, Dr. Gansler served as the Under Secretary of Defense for Acquisition, Technology and Logistics from November 1997 until January 2001. In this position, he was responsible for all matters relating to Department of Defense acquisition; research and development; logistics; acquisition reform; advanced technology; international programs; environmental security; nuclear, chemical, and biological programs; and the defense technology and industrial base. (He had an annual budget of over $180 billion and a workforce of over 300,000.)

Prior to this appointment, Dr. Gansler was executive vice president and corporate director for TASC, Incorporated, an applied information technology company, in Arlington, Virginia (from 1977 to 1997), during which time he played a major role in building the company from a small operation into a large, widely recognized and greatly respected corporation, serving both the government and the private sector.

From 1972 to 1977, he served in the government as Deputy Assistant Secretary of Defense (materiel acquisition), responsible for all defense procurements and the defense industry; and as Assistant Director of Defense Research and Engineering (electronics) responsible for all defense electronics research and development.

His prior industrial experience included vice president (business development), ITT (1970–1972); program manager, director of advanced programs, and director of international marketing, Singer Corporation (1962–1970); and engineering manager, Raytheon Corporation (1956–1962).

From 1984 to 1997, Dr. Gansler was a Visiting Scholar at the Kennedy School of Government, Harvard University (a frequent guest lecturer in Executive Management courses). He is the author of three books, a contributing author of 25 other books, author of over 100 papers, and a frequent speaker and congressional witness.

Dr. Gansler holds a B.E. (electrical engineering) from Yale University, an M.S. (electrical engineering) from Northeastern University, an M.A. (political economy) from the New School for Social Research, and a Ph.D. (economics) from American University.

Robert E. Luby, Jr., is a Partner in IBM Business Consulting Services (BCS). He leads the Supply Chain and Operations Solutions (SCOS) practice for the entire public sector. This practice includes over 400 supply chain and operations professionals. Mr. Luby has over 29 years of logistics experience. He is also a partner on the IBM BCS Defense Industry Team. His clients include the Defense Logistics Agency (DLA), various Defense Supply Centers, several major defense depots, public and private shipyards, aviation depots, and defense suppliers. Mr. Luby has been in the forefront of the development of supply change strategy for many of our defense clients and the major Defense original equipment manufacturers (OEMs).

Mr. Luby is also a leader in the IBM BCS project management practice. During his career, he has been involved in several complex projects, both as a project manager himself and as an advisor to many project leaders. He is a recognized leader in logistics, supply chain management, and complex project management. He was a key leader in the successful effort to completely redesign the logistics processes and support infrastructure for the U.S. Navy's approach to the overhaul and modernization of nuclear submarines. He is frequently called upon to advise key clients on complex project management challenges and critical supply chain management problems.

Mr. Luby is a graduate of the U.S. Naval Academy and also holds masters degrees from Northwestern University in engineering management and the Naval Postgraduate School in mechanical engineering.

Other Contributors

Amit Brar is Co-Team Leader of the Microfinance Impact Assessment Team for EDA Rural Systems Pvt. Ltd. in New Delhi, India. Previously, he served as a researcher for the World Bank on microfinance projects. Mr. Brar was also a project engineer at the Trane Company. He was a graduate assistant and research assistant for case studies with the Center for Public Policy and Private Enterprise at the University of Maryland. He holds a Bachelor of Technology from Banaras Hindu University, India, a Master of Science in mechanical engineering from the University of Cincinnati, and received his Master of Public Policy in international development from the University of Maryland's School of Public Affairs in 2003.

Douglas Chin was a Research Assistant for case studies with the Center for Public Policy and Private Enterprise at the University of Maryland. Previously, he held a position as a consultant at Independent Project Analysis, Inc. Prior to that, he was an engineer at United Technologies Research Center and the National Institute of Standards and Technology. He holds a Bachelor of Science in chemical engineering from the Massachusetts Institute of Technology, and a Master of Science in chemical engineering from Johns Hopkins University. He received a Master of Business Administration from the Robert H. Smith School of Business, University of Maryland, in 2002.

Dzintars Dzilna was a Research Assistant for case studies with the Center for Public Policy and Private Enterprise at the University of Maryland. Previously, he worked as research and business analyst for IBM and as a strategist for Worldwide Xceed Group. He holds a B.A. in English literature and a B.S. in mechanical engineering from Rutgers University. He received his M.B.A. with a concentration in information systems and finance from the University of Maryland's Robert H. Smith School of Business in 2003.

Brandon Griesel is Senior Revenue Management Analyst for Delta Airlines. Previously, he served as a Research Assistant for case studies with the Center for Public Policy and Private Enterprise at the University of Maryland. He conducted Performance Metric Analysis as an intern for the Specialty Materials Division of Honeywell International, Inc. Mr. Griesel also worked for Southwest Airlines as a business analyst and as a revenue management analyst. He holds a B.S. in aviation management from Central Missouri State University. He received his M.B.A. from the University of Maryland's Robert H. Smith School of Business in 2003.

Wesley Johnson is a Management Analyst at the National Business Center of the U.S. Department of the Interior in Washington D.C. Previously, he worked in the Office of Biological and Physical Research at NASA Headquarters and as a consultant for an e-commerce firm in Rochester, New York. Mr. Johnson was a research assistant for case studies with the Center for Public Policy and Private Enterprise at the University of Maryland. He received his Master of Public Management in international security and economic policy from the University of Maryland's School of Public Affairs in 2002.

Bonnie Kornberg is a consultant on operational and organizational effectiveness, business planning, and business investment analysis living in New York City. She has worked with government, nonprofit, and business clients that include the U.S. Navy, a venture capitalist, an immigrant coalition, an international student association, and a new foundation. Ms. Kornberg consulted as a writer and researcher with the Center for Public Policy and Private Enterprise at the University of Maryland on the book *Transforming Government Supply Chain Management*. Prior to pursuing her M.B.A., she managed an Anteon Inc. contract for U.S. Navy program management services and consulted to the Navy on foreign military sales programs. She holds a B.A. in international relations from Tufts University and received her M.B.A. from the University of Maryland's Robert H. Smith School of Business 2003.

William Lucyshyn is a Research Director at the Defense Advanced Research Projects Agency (DARPA) and a Visiting Senior Research Scholar at the Center for Public Policy and Private Enterprise in the School of Public Affairs at the University of Maryland. In this position, he conducts research into the public policy challenges posed by the increasing role information technologies play in improving government operations and their relationship with the private sector.

Previously, Mr. Lucyshyn served as the principal technical advisor to the director of DARPA on the identification, selection, research, development, and prototype production of advanced technology projects. Prior to this appointment, Mr. Lucyshyn completed a distinguished 25-year career in the U.S. Air Force, serving various operations, staff, and acquisition positions.

Mr. Lucyshyn received his bachelor's degree in engineering science from the City University of New York in 1971. In 1985 he earned his master's in nuclear engineering from the Air Force Institute of Technology. He was certified Level III as an acquisition professional in program management in 1994.

Sandra Young is a Graduate Assistant with the Center for Public Policy and Private Enterprise at the University of Maryland, and was a Research Assistant for case studies with the Center. Previously, Ms. Young was a consultant with Governmentum Solutions (fall 2002). She also served as program coordinator for park funding and management for the National Parks Conservation Association. Ms. Young holds a B.A. in international economics and environmental policy from American University. She is pursuing a joint degree with a Master in Public Management in public sector financial management anticipated in 2004 from the University of Maryland's School of Public Affairs and a J.D. with Environmental Certificate anticipated in 2005 from the University of Maryland's Law School.

About the IBM Center for
The Business of Government

Through research stipends and events, the IBM Center for The Business of Government stimulates research and facilitates discussion of new approaches to improving the effectiveness of government at the federal, state, local, and international levels.

The Center is one of the ways that IBM Business Consulting Services seeks to advance knowledge on how to improve public sector effectiveness. The IBM Center focuses on the future of the operation and management of the public sector.

Research stipends of $15,000 are awarded competitively to outstanding scholars in academic and nonprofit institutions across the United States. Each award winner is expected to produce a 30- to 40-page research report in one of the areas presented on pages 262-265. Reports will be published and disseminated by the Center.

Research Stipend Guidelines

Who is Eligible?
Individuals working in:
- Universities
- Nonprofit organizations
- Journalism

Description of Research Stipends

Individuals receiving research stipends will be responsible for producing 30- to 40-page research report in one of the areas presented on this page. The report will be published and disseminated by the IBM Center for The Business of Government. The manuscript must be submitted no later than six months after the start of the project. Recipients will select the start and end dates of their research project. The reports should be written for government leaders and should provide practical knowledge and insights.

Size of Research Stipends

$15,000 for each research paper

Who Receives the Research Stipends?

Unless otherwise requested, individuals will receive the research stipends.

Application Process

Interested individuals should submit:

- A three-page description of the proposed research (please include a 100-word executive summary describing the proposed project's: (a) purpose, (b) methodology, and (c) results)
- A résumé (no more than three pages)

Application Deadlines

There will be two funding cycles annually, with deadlines of:

- November 1
- March 1

  Applicants will be informed of a decision regarding their proposal no later than eight weeks after the deadlines. Applications must be received online or postmarked by the above dates.

Submitting Applications

Online:

businessofgovernment.org/apply

Hard Copy:

Mark A. Abramson

Executive Director

IBM Center for The Business of Government

1616 North Fort Myer Drive

Arlington, VA 22209

Research Areas

E-Government

Specific areas of interest:
- Government to Business (G2B)
- Government to Citizen (G2C)
- Government to Employees (G2E)
- Government to Government (G2G)
- Capital investment strategies
- Customer relationship management (CRM)
- Enterprise architecture
- Supply chain management
- E-Government On Demand

Examples of previous reports:
Digitally Integrating the Government Supply Chain: E-Procurement, E-Finance, and E-Logistics by Jacques S. Gansler, William Lucyshyn, and Kimberly M. Ross (February 2003)
State Web Portals: Delivering and Financing E-Service by Diana Burley Gant, Jon P. Gant and Craig L. Johnson (January 2002)
Federal Intranet Work Sites: An Interim Assessment by Julianne G. Mahler and Priscilla M. Regan (June 2002)
Leveraging Technology in the Service of Diplomacy: Innovation in the Department of State by Barry Fulton (March 2002)

Financial Management

Specific areas of interest:
- Asset management
- Auditing
- Cost accounting
- Erroneous payment
- Financial and resource analysis
- Internal controls
- Risk management and modeling
- Systems modernization
- Financial Management On Demand

Examples of previous reports:
Understanding Federal Asset Management: An Agenda for Reform by Thomas H. Stanton (July 2003)
Audited Financial Statements: Getting and Sustaining "Clean" Opinions by Douglas A. Brook (July 2001)
Using Activity-Based Costing to Manage More Effectively by Michael H. Granof, David E. Platt and Igor Vaysman (January 2000)
Credit Scoring and Loan Scoring: Tools for Improved Management of Federal Credit Programs by Thomas H. Stanton (July 1999)

Human Capital Management

Specific areas of interest:
- Aligning human capital with organizational objectives
- Workforce planning and deployment
- Talent: recruitment, retraining, and retention
- Pay for performance
- Leadership and knowledge management
- E-learning
- Human Capital Management On Demand

Examples of previous reports:
Modernizing Human Resource Management in the Federal Government: The IRS Model by James R. Thompson and Hal G. Rainey (April 2003)
A Weapon in the War for Talent: Using Special Authorities to Recruit Crucial Personnel by Hal G. Rainey (December 2001)
Life after Civil Service Reform: The Texas, Georgia, and Florida Experiences by Jonathan Walters (October 2002)
Organizations Growing Leaders: Best Practices and Principles in the Public Service by Ray Blunt (December 2001)

Managing for Performance and Results

Specific areas of interest:
- Strategic planning
- Performance measurement and evaluation
- Balanced scorecards and performance reporting
- Performance budgeting
- Program delivery

Examples of previous reports:
Using Performance Data for Accountability: The New York City Police Department's CompStat Model of Police Management by Paul E. O'Connell (August 2001)
Performance Management: A "Start Where You Are, Use What You Have" Guide by Chris Wye (October 2002)
How Federal Programs Use Outcome Information: Opportunities for Federal Managers by Harry P. Hatry, Elaine Morley, Shelli B. Rossman, and Joseph S. Wholey (April 2003)
The Baltimore CitiStat Program: Performance and Accountability by Lenneal J. Henderson (May 2003)

Market-Based Government

Specific areas of interest:
* Contracting out
* Competitive sourcing
* Outsourcing
* Privatization
* Public-private partnerships
* Government franchising
* Contract management

Examples of previous reports:
Moving Toward Market-Based Government: The Changing Role of Government as the Provider by Jacques S. Gansler (June 2003)
IT Outsourcing: A Primer for Public Managers by Yu-Che Chen and James Perry (February 2003)
Moving to Public-Private Partnerships: Learning from Experience around the World by Trefor P. Williams (February 2003)
Making Performance-Based Contracting Perform: What the Federal Government Can Learn from State and Local Governments by Lawrence L. Martin (November 2002, 2nd ed.)

Innovation, Collaboration, and Transformation

Specific areas of interest:
- Enhancing public sector performance
- Improving service delivery
- Profiles of outstanding public sector leaders
- Collaboration between organizations
- Change management
- Providing managerial flexibility

Examples of previous reports:
Managing "Big Science": A Case Study of the Human Genome Project by W. Henry Lambright (March 2002)
Understanding Innovation: What Inspires It? What Makes It Successful? by Jonathan Walters (December 2001)
Extraordinary Results on National Goals: Networks and Partnerships in the Bureau of Primary Health Care's 100%/0 Campaign by John Scanlon (March 2003)
The Power of Frontline Workers in Transforming Government: The Upstate New York Veterans Healthcare Network by Timothy J. Hoff (April 2003)

For more information about the Center

Visit our website at: www.businessofgovernment.org
Send an e-mail to: businessofgovernment@us.ibm.com
Call: (703) 741-1077